What Your Colleagues Are S

"This book brings together the best of Visible Learning and the teachi[...] learning intentions, success criteria, misconceptions, formative evaluation, and knowing my impact are stunning. Rich in exemplars, grounded in research about practice, and with the right balance about the surface and deep learning in math, it's a great go-to book for all who teach mathematics."

—John Hattie, **Laureate Professor,**
Deputy Dean of MGSE, Director of the Melbourne Education Research Institute,
Melbourne Graduate School of Education

"This handbook supports teachers in moving from pacing to planning instruction by providing the tools needed to ensure that mathematics lessons work for every student. More important, it will engage teachers in the critical process of continual improvement. It is a must-have for teachers, leaders, and mathematics educators alike!"

—Matt Larson, **Past President,**
National Council of Teachers of Mathematics

"Often teachers entering the classroom have had little opportunity for extensive lesson planning in their preparation programs. Throughout the book, definitions and explanations are clear so that readers share a common understanding of the language. As a teacher reads, the vignettes encourage the reader to reflect on similar situations in their own classrooms. The well-written questions included in the text will help guide teachers to personal insights that ultimately lead to increased student learning."

—Connie S. Schrock, **Emporia State University,**
National Council of Supervisors of Mathematics President, 2017–2019

"We all know that good instruction is well-planned instruction. We also know that effective lesson planning is a complicated decision-making process. This incredibly practical book—filled with delightful vignettes and clarifying examples—provides powerful ideas and structures for simplifying the complexities of planning great 3–5 mathematics lessons. This book is a wonderful resource for teachers, coaches, administrators, and teacher educators."

—Steve Leinwand,
American Institutes for Research

"Finally! *The Mathematics Lesson-Planning Handbook* provides that necessary blueprint for serious analysis of the planning process. Planning to teach mathematics is serious business, and this book goes way beyond thinking about the mathematics standard/objective for the next day's lesson, or jotting notes for a planning book. The handbook will truly engage teachers and communities of learning in a carefully choreographed grade-level designated thread of mathematics tasks, which will serve as anchors for developing understanding and use of each aspect of the planning process. This book is a treasure, and will be read, reread, and referenced daily!"

—Francis (Skip) Fennell, **Professor of Education,**
McDaniel College and Past-President of the National Council of
Teachers of Mathematics (NCTM) and the Association of Mathematics Teacher Educators (AMTE)

"The Mathematics Lesson-Planning Handbook is a comprehensive and practical guide for coaches and teachers of mathematics in Grades 3–5. It provides the background that teachers need before they even begin to write a lesson plan! It then incorporates the research on what teachers need to think about as they begin to lay out a plan for instruction that will meet the needs of all 3–5 students and moves on to effective facilitation. This guide provides a roadmap to planning effective lessons that will provide the essential foundation to ensure that all primary-level students begin their mathematics journey with high-quality teaching and learning. This book is a must for every 3–5 teacher, coach, or school's professional library!"

— Linda M. Gojak, **Past President,**
National Council of Teachers of Mathematics

"One of the hallmarks of accomplished elementary teachers of mathematics is the guidance they provide to help students own how to learn. In *The Mathematics Lesson-Planning Handbook: Your Blueprint for Building Cohesive Lessons,* authors Kobett, Harbin Miles, and Williams provide a clear, engaging, and masterful roadmap for helping each and every teacher own the lessons they design and use each and every day. The authors reveal the purposes, the success criteria, and the nature of the mathematical tasks and materials to be chosen. They describe in detail the student engagement necessary to design daily mathematics lessons that will significantly impact student learning. Reading, listening to, and using their wisdom and advice will result in an empowering impact on each and every teacher and teacher leader of elementary mathematics."

— Timothy Kanold, **Educator and Author**

"This is what we've been waiting for: a go-to resource for planning and facilitating mathematics lessons in elementary school! Teachers must consider the needs of their students, relevant mathematical content, and appropriate pedagogy when designing and implementing effective learning opportunities. Through authentic vignettes and examples, connections to relevant research, and guiding reflection questions, this *Handbook* guides readers through the process from beginning to end."

— Susie Katt, **Mathematics Coordinator, Lincoln Public Schools**

"Planning is so much more than identifying materials, making copies, or filling out a form. Many of us were not trained to identify purpose, think about our students, look for quality instructional tasks, consider representations, or anticipate what our students will do. Finally, this handbook is here! We have our blueprint. This tool is a must-have for anyone new to teaching mathematics or anyone else who supports those who teach mathematics."

— John SanGiovanni, **Coordinator, Elementary Mathematics,**
Howard County Public School System, MD

"This book is a must-read for anyone who wants to challenge themselves to reexamine their math instruction. The interesting examples and challenging reflection questions make this book perfect for individual or group reading."

— Janel Frazier, **Classroom Teacher,**
Montgomery County Public School System, Upper Marlboro, MD

"This must-have book has well-thought-out lesson plans that combine rich tasks with high-quality questions. I am confident that every teacher, administrator, specialist, and math supervisor needs to have a copy of this book."

—Kathleen Williams Londeree, **Math Specialist/Coach,**
Caroline County Schools, VA

"At a time when open educational resources are flooding our classrooms, *The Mathematics Lesson-Planning Handbook* helps bring focus and intentionality as to why we should choose one task over another. It thoughtfully lays out the smaller nuances that are most commonly overlooked and it helps bring clarity to the art of building coherence."

—Graham Fletcher, **Math Specialist, Atlanta, GA**

The Mathematics Lesson-Planning Handbook, Grades 3–5
at a Glance

A step-by-step guide to walk you through every facet of planning cohesive, standards-based mathematics lessons, including

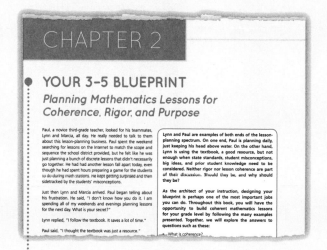

Using your curriculum to think about all of your lessons as a cohesive progression across units, throughout the year

Asking yourself essential questions about your standards-based learning intentions, lesson purpose, tasks, materials, lesson format, and how to anticipate and assess student thinking

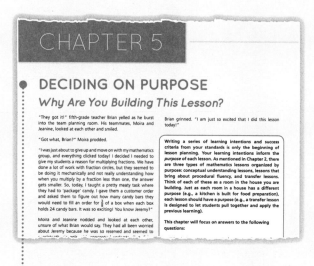

Determining whether you're designing a lesson to focus on conceptual understanding, procedural fluency, or transfer of knowledge

Choosing how to launch, facilitate, and close your lesson

CHAPTER 11

PLANNING TO
LAUNCH THE LESSON

Sally, a third-grade teacher, began her lesson by displaying the first picture in a series of three pictures (Figure 11.1).

She told her students that she would give them one minute to See, Think, and Wonder (Ritchhart, Church, & Morrison, 2011) about the picture. After a minute of silence, she told the students to find their Turn and Talk Buddies to discuss what they see, think, and wonder about the picture. The classroom buzzed with productive mathematics talk. Sally noticed some of the students pointing and counting as they looked at the picture. She then revealed two more pictures (Figure 11.2).

Once again, she gave the students a minute of silence to observe the pictures and then asked them to turn and talk with each other. As she surveyed the room, she noted that every single student appeared to be engaged.

Sally asked, "What do you notice about the pictures? Please raise your hands and let me know about something your Turn and Talk Buddy noticed."

Hands waved wildly in the air as students strained to share their partners' observations. Sally wrote quickly to include what they saw. Then she asked her students to share their think and wonders (Figure 11.3).

Figure 11.1

Figure 11.2

CHAPTER 12

PLANNING TO
FACILITATE THE LESSON

Barbara, a third-grade teacher, had always imagined herself as an educator. As a child, she collected worksheets from her teachers and stored them in her basement, which she set up as a school. She cajoled neighborhood friends into playing school with her for hours on end.

By the time that Barbara actually started teaching, she knew that the approach to education had shifted from her own days as a student. She recognized the need to encourage her students to construct meaning through carefully planned activities and to allow her students to talk to each other, explain their thinking, and even productively struggle, but she still felt conflicted with how to best support her students' communication skills. She hated to watch them struggle, even a little bit. She frequently found herself falling right into the trap of saving a student way too early instead of asking a question or providing a suggestion. Just the other day, one of her students, Justin, had asked for help, and she had picked up a pencil and started showing him what to do. She hadn't even realized it until she glanced at him and caught him grinning from ear to ear!

Barbara shared her concerns with her co-teacher, Dominic, a

Mrs. Petry has been given permission to design a reading nook that has area that equals 400 square feet. Prepare a proposal for Mrs. Petry. Include the design, measurements, and prepare a mathematical argument why you think this is the best design.

Both Barbara and Dominic had been amazed at how well the fourth graders had worked on the project, particularly as they had negotiated decisions about the best design for the reading nook. Barbara and Dominic had spent all of their time supporting the students and questioning them as they worked.

As the teachers discussed this lesson with their math coach, Dominic asked, "So how can we capture that kind of energy and student-centered learning every day?"

Capturing those moments when students are engaged productively in mathematical thinking, reasoning, and communication is so exciting to see. Sometimes they just happen, but most likely, they happen when all of

CHAPTER 13

PLANNING TO
CLOSE THE LESSON

The fifth-grade team members at Hollins Elementary School were discussing some of their closure experiences.

"Closure?" questioned Abe, a third-year teacher. "I hardly ever get a chance for closure. My lessons always go to the last minute and sometimes even run over into recess."

"I have that problem sometimes," chimed in Jane, the veteran teacher in the group. "I am getting better, but last week my class had to remind me to stop because it was time for lunch! My goal for this year is to improve my closure. I'm working on it."

Cilia, a second-year teacher, spoke up. "I went to a workshop this summer and they talked about how important closure is to determine how students are grasping a lesson. I have been trying some of the suggestions. I like using exit slips, and my kids seem to like them. I let them write me notes at the end of the lesson to tell me if there was anything they didn't understand. I have been using those notes to help me launch

Jane said, "It's funny that you mentioned a workshop. I went to a workshop about closure two years ago. We discussed how closure is about reflection. And we used exit slips too, but we learned that there are other things you can do, like pair sharing. Another option is to do a more in-depth exit task, like we learned in the formative assessment workshop."

"Stop keeping all these ideas a secret!" Abe said. Then he smiled and added, "You two need to do a closure workshop for me!"

If you have ever looked at the clock and realized that you not only lack time for closure but also have run overtime, you are not alone. Abe, Jane, and Cilia have been working on closure for a few years and continue to struggle to fit it all in. Planning for closure is the first step in using it in your classroom. This chapter will discuss closure and several different closure formats while examining the following guiding ques-

Illustrative vignettes at the start of each chapter focus on a specific part of the lesson-planning process

In every chapter you will find

Connects to the Process Standards and Standards for Mathematical Practice

The tasks you select should be designed to encourage students to exhibit process standards. Sometimes, teachers believe the way to challenge learners is by presenting them with higher-level content. However, this act alone does not necessarily support all students to reason, communicate mathematically, use and apply representations, see and use patterns, and recognize the underlying structure of the mathematics they are learning. By ensuring that a task incorporates opportunities for students to demonstrate the process standards, you support their learning.

To determine if a task is worthwhile for you to use in a lesson, use the rubric shown in Figure 6.2. The first column identifies the characteristic, and the next three columns allow you to rate the degree to which you feel the task has met that characteristic by checking the box, with 3 being not acceptable and 1 being a good example of that characteristic. The final column is for any comments you would like to discuss with your colleagues. Note: You may deem a task worthwhile even if you do not rate all of the characteristics as a 1. Not all worthwhile tasks will have all of the characteristics.

Figure 6.2

Determining a Worthwhile Task Rubric

Characteristic	1	2	3	Notes
Uses significant mathematics for the grade level				
Rich				
Problem solving in nature				
Authentic/interesting				
Equitable				
Active				
Connects to Standards for Mathematical Practice or Process Standards				

This Determining a Worthwhile Task Rubric can be downloaded for your use at resources.corwin.com/mathlessonplanning/3-5

Thinking about Jennifer and Carlos and their tasks, rate the tasks using the checklist in Figure 6.2. Discuss your results with a colleague. Whose example is a worthwhile task and why? Note your thoughts below.

Opportunities to stop and reflect on your own instruction

Examples of each lesson feature from classrooms in Grades 3–5

WHAT IS THE ROLE OF REPRESENTATIONS IN MATHEMATICS LESSONS?

The Annenberg Learner Foundation (2003) offers this definition:

"Mathematical representation" refers to the wide variety of ways to capture an abstract mathematical concept or relationship. A mathematical representation may be visible, such as a number sentence, a display of manipulative materials, or a graph, but it may also be an internal way of seeing and thinking about a mathematical idea. Regardless of their form, representations can enhance students' communication, reasoning, and problem-solving abilities; help them make connections among ideas; and aid them in learning new concepts and procedures. (paragraph 2)

Since mathematical concepts are abstract, when we teach, we represent the concepts in a variety of ways. Representations can be thought of as a broad category of models. According to Van de Walle, Karp, and Bay-Williams (2016), there are seven ways to represent or model mathematical concepts:

1. Manipulatives
2. Pictures or drawings
3. Symbols
4. Language (written or spoken)
5. Real-world situations
6. Graphs
7. Tables

Selecting a representation is a vital part of your decision making while lesson planning. You must decide, "What representations will help me achieve the learning intentions of today's lesson?" Here is an example of a teacher using a representation to help students make sense of rounding.

Example: Al

When planning a lesson that involves placing fractions on a number line, Al, a third-grade teacher, told his students to place $\frac{1}{3}$ on the number line and asked, "Is $\frac{1}{3}$ closer to 0 or 1?"

Al used a number line as a representation to model the relationship of unit fractions between 0 and 1. By using this representation, students can see that $\frac{1}{3}$ is closer to 0 than 1, working toward a conceptual understanding of fractions.

The charts in Figures 7.1, 7.2, and 7.3 show examples of representations that can be used with selected standards.

Building Unit Coherence

Connecting lesson purposes across a unit develops coherence because you are strategically linking conceptual understanding, procedural fluency, and transfer lessons to build comprehensive understanding of the unit standards. As you develop a lesson, consider the purposes of the lessons that come before and after the lesson you are constructing. Over the course of one unit, you should develop and facilitate lessons with all three purposes, bearing in mind how and when the lesson purposes should be positioned within the unit based on the learning intentions and how they relate to each other. Some teachers map out their unit with lesson purposes in mind to ensure that they are developing coherence within lesson purpose (Figure 5.8).

Figure 5.8

Unit:

Day 1	Day 2	Day 3	Day 4	Day 5
Conceptual	Conceptual	Conceptual	Procedural Fluency	Procedural Fluency

Day 6	Day 7	Day 8	Day 9	Day 10
Conceptual	Conceptual	Conceptual	Procedural Fluency	Transfer

Now that you have been introduced to the three lesson purposes, reflect on the lessons in your curriculum guide, textbook, or supplemental materials. Can you categorize the lessons into these three categories? Do you notice one type being more prevalent than the others? Note any thoughts or concerns here.

_____
_____
_____
_____
_____
_____
_____
_____
_____
_____
_____

How features of a lesson are interrelated to build cohesiveness across a unit

Bolded key terms that are defined in a glossary in Appendix D

Appendix D

Glossary

academic language. The vocabulary used in schools, textbooks, and other school resources.

access to high-quality mathematics instruction. Phrase refers to the National Council of Teachers of Mathematics (NCTM) position statement on equal opportunity to a quality K–12 education for all students. Related to the NCTM position on equitable learning opportunities.

agency. The power to act. Students exercise agency in mathematics when they initiate discussions and actively engage in high-level thinking tasks. When students exercise agency, they reason, critique the reasoning of others, and engage in productive struggle.

algorithm. In mathematics, it is a series of steps or procedures that, when followed accurately, will produce a correct answer.

big ideas. Statements that encompass main concepts in mathematics that cross grade levels, such as place value.

classroom discourse. Conversation that occurs in a classroom. Can be teacher to student(s), student(s) to teacher, or student(s) to student(s).

close-ended questions. Questions with only one correct answer.

closure. The final activity in a lesson with two purposes: (1) helps the teacher determine what students have learned and gives direction to next steps; (2) provides students the opportunity to reorganize and summarize the information from a lesson in a meaningful way.

coherence. Logical sequencing of mathematical ideas. Can be vertical, as in across the grades (e.g., K–2), or horizontal, as in across a grade level (e.g., first-grade lessons from September through December).

common errors. Mistakes made by students that occur frequently; usually these mistakes are anticipated by the teacher due to their frequency.

computation. Using an operation such as addition, subtraction, multiplication, or division to find an answer.

conceptual understanding. Comprehension of mathematical concepts, operations, and relationships.

content standards. See *standards.*

decompose. To break a number down into addends. A number may be decomposed in more than one way (e.g., 12 can be decomposed as 10 + 2, 9 + 3, and 5 + 5 + 2).

discourse. See *classroom discourse.*

district-wide curriculum. A K–12 document outlining the curriculum for a school system.

drill. Repetitive exercises on a specific math skill or procedure.

English Language Learner (ELL). A person whose first language is not English but who is learning to speak English.

essential question. A question that unifies all of the lessons on a given topic to bring the coherence and purpose to a unit. Essential questions are purposefully linked to the big idea to frame student inquiry, promote critical thinking, and assist in ... learning transfer.

... the end of a lesson or group of lessons that provides a sampling of student performance. An exit task is ... *exit slip.*

... form of lesson closure where students answer a question related to the main idea of the lesson on a slip of ... these slips of paper.

HOW DO IDENTITY AND AGENCY INFLUENCE LESSON PLANNING?

Identity and **agency** are two concepts that help teachers understand the dynamics that take place in a classroom, which, in turn, helps teachers better understand their students and how best to meet their needs. Identity is how individuals know and see themselves (i.e., student, teacher, good at sports, like math, etc.) and how others know and see us (i.e., short, smart, African American, etc.). When defined broadly, identity is a concept that brings together all the interrelated elements that teachers and students bring to the classroom, including beliefs, attitudes, emotions, and cognitive capacity (Grootenboer, 2000).

Agency is the power to act. Students develop their agency when they actively engage in the learning process (Wenmoth, 2014). Since student learning is greatest in classrooms where students are engaged in high-level thinking and reasoning (Boaler & Staples, 2008), teachers need to ensure that tasks they choose promote this engagement on a regular basis.

The types of lessons teachers design, the approach they take to teaching, the tasks they select, the types of questions they ask, the classroom climate, and social norms of the classroom all affect student engagement and are influenced by the teachers' identity. For example, in a classroom where the teacher sees his or her identity as the giver of knowledge, students are passive recipients of knowledge, working individually at their desks on assignments designed by the teacher. In this approach, there is no opportunity for students to exercise agency. In addition, student identities are lost as they are treated as a group with all the same learning needs rather than as individuals with unique learning needs.

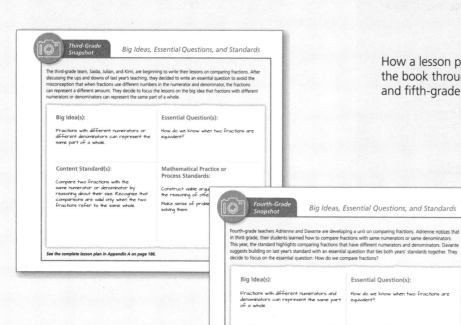

Third-Grade Snapshot — Big Ideas, Essential Questions, and Standards

The third-grade team, Saida, Julian, and Kimi, are beginning to write their lessons on comparing fractions. After discussing the ups and downs of last year's teaching, they decided to write an essential question to avoid the misconception that when fractions use different numbers in the numerator and denominator, the fractions can represent a different amount. They decide to focus the lessons on the big idea that fractions with different numerators or denominators can represent the same part of a whole.

Big Idea(s):
Fractions with different numerators or different denominators can represent the same part of a whole.

Essential Question(s):
How do we know when two fractions are equivalent?

Content Standard(s):
Compare two fractions with the same numerator or same denominator by reasoning about their size. Recognize that comparisons are valid only when the two fractions refer to the same whole.

Mathematical Practice or Process Standards:
Construct viable arguments and critique the reasoning of others.
Make sense of problems and persevere in solving them.

See the complete lesson plan in Appendix A on page 186.

How a lesson plan builds across the course of the book through snapshots of third-, fourth-, and fifth-grade classrooms

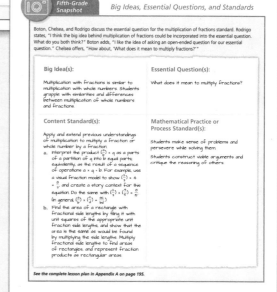

Fourth-Grade Snapshot — Big Ideas, Essential Questions, and Standards

Fourth-grade teachers Adrienne and Davante are developing a unit on comparing fractions. Adrienne notices that in third grade, their students learned how to compare fractions with same numerators or same denominators. This year, the standard highlights comparing fractions that have different numerators and denominators. Davante suggests building on last year's standard with an essential question that ties both years' standards together. They decide to focus on the essential question: How do we compare fractions?

Big Idea(s):
Fractions with different numerators and denominators can represent the same part of a whole.

Essential Question(s):
How do we know when two fractions are equivalent?

Content Standard(s):
Explain why a fraction $\frac{a}{b}$ is equivalent to a fraction $\frac{(n \times a)}{(n \times b)}$ by using visual fraction models, with attention to how the number and size of the parts differ even though the two fractions themselves are the same size. Use this principle to recognize and generate equivalent fractions.

Mathematical Practice or Process Standards:
Model with mathematics.
Look and make use of structure.

See the complete lesson plan in Appendix A on page 191.

Fifth-Grade Snapshot — Big Ideas, Essential Questions, and Standards

Boton, Chelsea, and Rodrigo discuss the essential question for the multiplication of fractions standard. Rodrigo states, "I think the big idea behind multiplication of fractions could be incorporated into the essential question. What do you both think?" Boton adds, "I like the idea of asking an open-ended question for our essential question." Chelsea offers, "How about, 'What does it mean to multiply fractions?'"

Big Idea(s):
Multiplication with fractions is similar to multiplication with whole numbers. Students grapple with similarities and differences between multiplication of whole numbers and fractions.

Essential Question(s):
What does it mean to multiply fractions?

Content Standard(s):
Apply and extend previous understandings of multiplication to multiply a fraction or whole number by a fraction.
a. Interpret the product $\left(\frac{a}{b}\right) \times q$ as a parts of a partition of q into b equal parts; equivalently, as the result of a sequence of operations $a \times q \div b$. For example, use a visual fraction model to show $\left(\frac{2}{3}\right) \times 4 = \frac{8}{3}$, and create a story context for this equation. Do the same with $\left(\frac{2}{3}\right) \times \left(\frac{4}{5}\right) = \frac{8}{15}$ (In general, $\left(\frac{a}{b}\right) \times \left(\frac{c}{d}\right) = \frac{ac}{bd}$.)
b. Find the area of a rectangle with fractional side lengths by tiling it with unit squares of the appropriate unit fraction side lengths, and show that the area is the same as would be found by multiplying the side lengths. Multiply fractional side lengths to find areas of rectangles, and represent fraction products as rectangular areas.

Mathematical Practice or Process Standard(s):
Students make sense of problems and persevere while solving them.
Students construct viable arguments and critique the reasoning of others.

See the complete lesson plan in Appendix A on page 195.

A place to consider each facet of a lesson in your own classroom, building your own complete lesson across the course of the book

Under Construction

Now it is your turn! You need to decide what big idea, essential question, and standards you want to build a lesson around. Start with your big idea and then identify the remaining elements.

Big Idea(s):

Essential Question(s):

Content Standard(s):

Mathematical Practice or Process Standards:

online resources — Download the full Lesson-Planning Template from resources.corwin.com/mathlessonplanning/3-5. Remember that you can use the online version of the lesson plan template to begin compiling each section into the full template as your lesson plan grows.

Appendix A shows how the complete lesson plan has come together for each grade

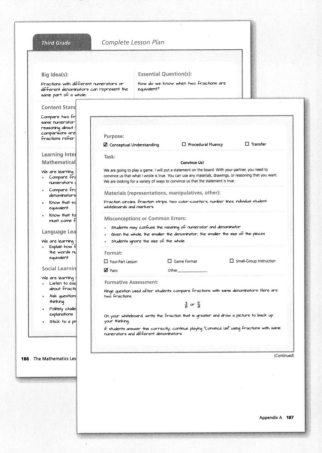

Appendix B includes a blank lesson-planning template for your ongoing use (also available for download at resources.corwin.com/mathlessonplanning/3-5)

Appendix C includes additional key reading and online resources

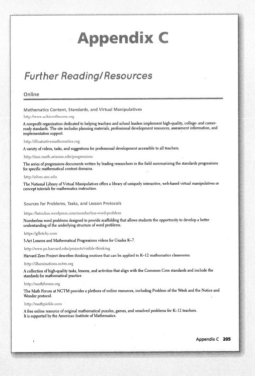

The Mathematics Lesson-Planning Handbook

Grades 3–5

Your Blueprint for Building Cohesive Lessons

Ruth Harbin Miles

Beth McCord Kobett

Lois A. Williams

Name: _____

Department: _____

Learning Team: _____

A JOINT PUBLICATION

 CORWIN MATHEMATICS

 NCTM | NATIONAL COUNCIL OF TEACHERS OF MATHEMATICS

FOR INFORMATION:

Corwin

A SAGE Company

2455 Teller Road

Thousand Oaks, California 91320

(800) 233–9936

www.corwin.com

SAGE Publications Ltd.

1 Oliver's Yard

55 City Road

London EC1Y 1SP

United Kingdom

SAGE Publications India Pvt. Ltd.

B 1/I 1 Mohan Cooperative Industrial Area

Mathura Road, New Delhi 110 044

India

SAGE Publications Asia-Pacific Pte. Ltd.

3 Church Street

#10–04 Samsung Hub

Singapore 049483

Program Manager, Mathematics: Erin Null

Editorial Development Manager: Julie Nemer

Editorial Assistant: Jessica Vidal

Production Editor: Melanie Birdsall

Copy Editor: Gillian Dickens

Typesetter: Integra

Proofreader: Susan Schon

Indexer: Sheila Bodell

Cover Designer: Rose Storey

Interior Designer: Scott Van Atta

Marketing Manager: Margaret O'Connor

Copyright © 2019 by Corwin

See, Think, Wonder Task in Chapter 11 submitted by Sally Dawson. Used with permission.

Library of Congress Cataloging-in-Publication Data

Names: Miles, Ruth Harbin, author. | Kobett, Beth McCord, author. | Williams, Lois A., author.

Title: The mathematics lesson-planning handbook, grades 3–5 : your blueprint for building cohesive lessons / Ruth Harbin Miles, Beth McCord Kobett, Lois A. Williams.

Other titles: Mathematics lesson planning handbook, grades 3–5

Description: Thousand Oaks, California : Corwin, [2018] | Includes bibliographical references and index.

Identifiers: LCCN 2018007533 | ISBN 9781506387864 (spiral: alk. paper)

Subjects: LCSH: Mathematics—Study and teaching (Elementary) | Curriculum planning.

Classification: LCC QA11.2 .M55 2018 | DDC 372.7/044—dc23 LC record available at https://lccn.loc.gov/2018007533

Printed in the United States of America

This book is printed on acid-free paper.

18 19 20 21 22 10 9 8 7 6 5 4 3 2 1

Contents

Visit the companion website at
resources.corwin.com/mathlessonplanning/3-5
for downloadable resources.

Acknowledgments

Special thanks is due to the very best teacher I have ever known, my incredible father, Dr. Calvin E. Harbin, who taught me to value my education and at the age of 101 is still modeling lifelong learning. Acknowledgment and thanks must also be given to my extraordinary mentors, Dr. Ramona Anshutz and Dr. Shirley A. Hill, who both inspired me to become a mathematics education leader. Their influence and guidance completely changed my life's work. Words could never express the thanks and credit I owe to my incredible writing partners, Dr. Ted H. Hull, Dr. Don S. Balka, Linda Gojak, Dr. Lois A. Williams, Dr. Beth E. Kobett, Dr. Jean Morrow, and Dr. Sandi Cooper, who over the years helped me coauthor 36 published books. Most important, I thank my loving husband, Sam Miles, for *always* supporting me.

—Ruth Harbin Miles

To Tim, Hannah, and Jenna for their continuing love, support, and patience. Thank you, Kitty, for always listening. Thank you to Skip and Jon for your warm friendship and our productive collaboration. I am also grateful to my Stevenson University family, David and Debby, for supporting my ideas and to my students (past and present) for inspiring me with your passion and commitment to teaching.

—Beth McCord Kobett

Thank you to all my teaching colleagues in Albemarle County, Virginia, who, over the years, have generously shared their wisdom about teaching and planning mathematics lessons. Some of that wisdom resulted directly from questions for which I had no answers. Additional wisdom resulted from coincidental meetings in the halls between classes when I needed a friendly comment or math joke. I am grateful for what you have taught me.

And to Mike, my husband, for always standing by me.

—Lois A. Williams

We would also like to thank Erin Null for her enduring support for our work on this book, incredible creativity, and commitment to this project. Her insightful perspective, vision for the project, and ability to ask just the right question at just the right time are appreciated and valued.

—Beth, Ruth, and Lois

Publisher's Acknowledgments

Corwin gratefully acknowledges the contributions of the following reviewers:

Graham Fletcher
Math Specialist
McDonough, GA

Steve Leinwand
Researcher/Change Agent
American Institutes for Research
Washington, DC

Kathleen Williams Londeree
Math Specialist
Caroline County Schools
Caroline County, VA

Letter to 3–5 Teachers

Dear Grades 3–5 Teachers,

As a teacher, you make hundreds of decisions every day! Many of these decisions fall into the categories of classroom management or paperwork, such as selecting which student gets to be line leader or determining if you need to call that parent tonight or tomorrow. Some decisions are crucial to the classroom climate and environment and set the stage for how students learn. Among the hundreds of decisions you make, the most important are those that influence student learning. Designing, planning, and facilitating lessons reflect critical teacher decision-making opportunities that affect student learning. Oftentimes, these decisions get relegated to a few moments of planning time.

In this book, *The Mathematics Lesson-Planning Handbook: Your Blueprint for Building Cohesive Lessons*, you will experience the decision-making processes that are involved in planning lessons, and you will get to build a lesson of your own using a specially designed format just for you. Your decisions will revolve around creating mathematics lessons with purpose, rigor, and coherence. In addition, we will help you address the decisions involved in selecting your resources (e.g., "How do I make the best use of my textbook or state/district instructional materials?"), your classroom structure (e.g., "Do I use a small group or a large group?"), your worthwhile tasks (e.g., "How do I know one when I see it?"), your learning intentions (e.g., "What are my objectives?"), and your success criteria (e.g., "How will I know my students have learned?"). We will show you the importance of identifying big ideas, anticipating student misconceptions, implementing formative assessment, facilitating a lesson with questioning, and closing a lesson with reflection techniques.

Each chapter includes a vignette, examples for each grade level (3–5), an opportunity to reflect on the ideas presented, suggestions for building a unit from your lesson, and an Under Construction section to help you build a lesson on the content of your choice. A glossary in Appendix D provides definitions for words highlighted in each chapter.

Keep in mind that the goal of teaching is student learning. The best lessons that students can experience always begin with a prepared teacher.

Sincerely,

Ruth Harbin Miles
Beth McCord Kobett
Lois A. Williams

Letter to Elementary Principals

Dear Elementary Principals,

Some teachers *implement lesson plans* written by textbook publishers or by other professional curriculum writers. We argue that this is not enough. To positively affect the learning of their students, teachers need professional decision-making opportunities.

In this book, *The Mathematics Lesson-Planning Handbook: Your Blueprint for Building Cohesive Lessons,* your teachers will experience the decision-making processes that are involved in planning lessons for purpose, rigor, and coherence, and they will build a lesson of their own using a format created for them. In addition, we will help them address the decisions involved in selecting resources (e.g., "How can teachers make the best use of their textbook or state/district instructional materials?"), classroom structure (e.g., "Should there be small-group or large-group instruction?"), worthwhile tasks (e.g., "How do they recognize them?"), lesson intentions (e.g., "What are the objectives?"), and success criteria (e.g., "How will the teachers know their students have learned?"). We will help them examine the importance of identifying big ideas, anticipating student misconceptions, implementing formative assessment, facilitating a lesson with questioning, and closing a lesson with reflection techniques.

Your faculty of individual classroom and special education teachers all bring different knowledge, unique skills, and distinct ideas to the lesson-planning process. As a leader, you may wish to supply every teacher with a personal copy of the book for use as a schoolwide initiative or book study. Providing the opportunity for teachers to engage and use the book in grade-level planning with colleagues will allow teachers to dig deeply into their standards and collaborate to leverage each other's knowledge and experience. Be sure to invite teachers to bring this resource to all planning and professional development sessions. You may even want teachers to start or end a meeting by sharing a lesson they have planned based on the suggestions and strategies found in this book. As part of a faculty book study, this book will influence professional practice in lesson planning that promotes student achievement. After all, your best-prepared teachers are the most effective players on your team!

Sincerely,

Ruth Harbin Miles
Beth McCord Kobett
Lois A. Williams

Letter to Mathematics Coaches

Dear Mathematics Coaches,

Your work with teachers must, undoubtedly, encompass a great deal of time and effort planning mathematics lessons. This guide is designed to unpack the lesson-planning process to help teachers understand the importance of teacher decision making as they plan effective mathematics lessons to support student growth. Currently, some teachers simply *implement lesson plans* written by textbook publishers or by other professional curriculum writers. We argue that this is not enough. To positively affect the learning of their students, teachers need professional decision-making opportunities.

As you know, collaborative planning can be particularly powerful for teams of teachers. You may find that a three-step process, incorporating a planning, trying, and reflective cycle, will be most helpful for your teachers. Consider beginning small, tackling the content by chapter, to increase successful implementation.

In this book, *The Mathematics Lesson-Planning Handbook: Your Blueprint for Building Cohesive Lessons*, your teachers will experience the decision-making processes that are involved in planning lessons for purpose, rigor, and coherence, and they will build a lesson of their own using our format. In addition, we will help them address the decisions involved in selecting resources (e.g., "How can teachers make the best use of their textbook or state/district instructional materials?"), classroom structure (e.g., "Should there be small-group or large-group instruction?"), worthwhile tasks (e.g., "How do they recognize them?"), lesson intentions (e.g., "What are the objectives?"), and success criteria (e.g., "How will the teachers know their students have learned?"). We look at the importance of identifying big ideas, anticipating student misconceptions, implementing formative assessment, facilitating a lesson with questioning, and closing a lesson with reflection techniques.

Your faculty of individual classroom and special education teachers all bring different knowledge, skills, and distinct ideas to the lesson-planning process. Providing the opportunity for teachers to engage and use the book in grade-level planning with colleagues will allow teachers to dig deeply into their standards and collaborate to leverage each other's knowledge and experience. Be sure to invite teachers to bring this resource to all planning and professional development sessions. You may even want teachers to start or end a meeting by sharing a lesson they have planned based on the suggestions and strategies found in this book. As part of a faculty book study, this book will influence professional practice in lesson planning that promotes student achievement. After all, your best-prepared teachers are the most effective players on your team!

Sincerely,

Ruth Harbin Miles
Beth McCord Kobett
Lois A. Williams

Letter to Preservice College and University Instructors

Dear Preservice College and University Instructors,

Preservice teachers for Grades 3 to 5 must learn how to develop lesson plans to professionally prepare for teaching their students. One of the critical goals of a methods class is to guide preservice teachers and help them learn to create effective, well-crafted, and engaging mathematics lesson plans.

A recent study published in the *American Educational Research Journal* states that elementary preservice teachers remember and use what they learned in teacher-prep programs about writing lesson plans for mathematics (Morris & Hiebert, 2017). You have a major role to play, and this book can help you unpack the lesson-planning process.

The Mathematics Lesson-Planning Handbook: Your Blueprint for Building Cohesive Lessons helps your preservice teachers experience the decision-making processes involved in planning lessons for purpose, rigor, and coherence, and it guides them through the steps of building a lesson of their own using a format created for them. In addition, we help them address the decisions involved in selecting resources (e.g., "How can teachers make the best use of their textbook or state/district instructional materials?"), classroom structure (e.g., "Should there be small-group or large-group instruction?"), worthwhile tasks (e.g., "How do they recognize them?"), lesson intentions (e.g., "What are the objectives?"), and success criteria (e.g., "How will the teachers know their students have learned?"). We look at the importance of identifying big ideas, anticipating student misconceptions, implementing formative assessment, facilitating a lesson with questioning, and closing a lesson with reflection techniques.

The handbook includes 14 chapters that may easily be incorporated into a 14-, 15-, or 16-week methods course. The resource provides the opportunity for preservice teachers to engage and study the content chapter by chapter. As a result of their learning, this book will influence professional practice in lesson planning. After all, the preservice teachers' knowledge influences how they plan for instruction throughout their career.

Sincerely,

Ruth Harbin Miles
Beth McCord Kobett
Lois A. Williams

How to Use This Book

In the words of Benjamin Franklin, "Failing to plan is planning to fail." The best lessons students can experience always begin with a prepared teacher who considers student learning the primary goal of instruction.

Searching the Internet for lessons plans to use or adapt may seem to be an efficient way to plan. However, you will likely spend hours searching for the perfect lesson only to find that what you needed/wanted was not quite what you found. In contrast, planning your own lessons is a special skill that has invaluable rewards both for you and for your students. This guide will help you plan lessons that are strategically designed with YOUR students in mind.

When you are able to build your own mathematics lessons, you have the power to make decisions about all aspects of your students' learning, including how to make the content meet your students' individual needs. This approach may seem overwhelming in the beginning, because creating an effective lesson plan requires thinking and practice to consider all the factors you need. The good news is that after a bit of practice, it will become second nature.

Start slowly and take each chapter one at a time. We find that teachers who follow this process gain new insight into the mathematics they are teaching, which, in turn, helps them to better facilitate their students' learning.

Part I of this book begins with the premise that good instruction should be planned with purpose, coherence, and rigor in mind. It includes a chapter emphasizing that children all have different needs and that, as a teacher, you need to plan lessons in accordance with those needs. At the end of Part I, you will find the lesson-planning template that reflects all of the decisions a teacher makes when planning and facilitating a lesson. It may seem overwhelming at first glance. However, with practice, you will find that these decisions become second nature to your planning process.

Part II comprises a series of chapters for each component of the template. Each chapter includes the following:

- A real-world scenario of Grades 3–5 teachers wrestling with the decision-making part of the component
- Ideas and information to help with your decision-making process
- Snapshots that model the gradual construction of a third-, fourth-, and fifth-grade lesson plan chapter by chapter
- A section highlighting the importance of coherence for future lessons in a unit
- Questions for reflection
- An Under Construction section for you to begin planning your own lesson

Part III helps you put it all together with suggestions for planning to launch, facilitate, and close your lesson. Appendix A will show you the complete lesson plan for each grade so that you can see how it has come together in the end. A blank template can also be found in Appendix B and is available to download online at resources .corwin.com/mathlessonplanning/3-5.

Appendix C also offers suggestions of further reading and resources, and throughout the book, you will find words that appear in bold type. You can find their meanings in the glossary in Appendix D.

You may wish to begin the planning process by tackling one chapter at a time. You can read about an approach, try it out, and then, after completing the next chapter, integrate additional new concepts into your planning process. Take it slow, reflect along the way, and, before you know it, you will be planning robust mathematics lessons! Let's begin!

PART I

YOU ARE THE ARCHITECT OF YOUR CLASSROOM

CHAPTER 1

SURVEYING YOUR SITE
Knowing Your Students

Hannah took a deep breath as her fourth graders charged into the room waving their brown paper "Me Bags" bulging with special items. Most of the students ran right up to her excitedly, while others hung back shyly. She ushered them in and showed them their desks, decorated with brightly covered nametags that the students had picked out during the Back to School Open House. For two days, Hannah called each student to the hallway and conducted a brief "get to know you" activity. During this activity, Hannah shared a "Me Bag" containing special artifacts that revealed information about her life. She began by sharing her fourth-grade picture. The students giggled at the picture and asked to see more. She also showed them her favorite book from fourth grade and a macramé potholder she made when she was in fourth grade. The students had asked so many questions! They wanted to know if she liked school when she was in fourth grade and if she ever got in trouble. She gave each student a brown Me Bag and asked them to find three things to put in the bag for the first week of class. She spent the rest of the time asking the students to pick colors and decorations for their desk nametags. Hannah followed up the student meeting with a phone call to each family to introduce herself and let them know about the Me Bag activity.

She smiled as Miguel, a new English Language Learner (ELL) student whose family had just moved here from Colombia, walked into the room. He grinned broadly at her and held up his Me Bag for her to see. She had sent a note home in Spanish about the Me Bag with him last week and had received a handwritten reply written in Spanish. Miguel had told her that his friend, Tomas, was his best friend and helped him with English so she had placed their desks together. She didn't think it was possible, but Miguel's smile grew even larger when he saw Tomas sitting in the desk next to his.

She turned to see Rachel arrive with her para educator. Rachel was confined to a wheelchair and in her prior classroom had been placed at the back of the room at a table. During the "get to know you" activity, Rachel revealed that she longed to sit with the other students in a group of desks. Hannah spent several hours hunting the school looking for a small table that could be matched up to the desks. Rachel screamed with joy when she saw her new desk nestled in desk grouping.

"Miss Leonardo, I forgot my Me Bag," sniffed Bailey. Hannah looked down to see Bailey's eyes pool with tears. She knew that Bailey had been diagnosed with severe anxiety and often became paralyzed with fear when unexpected events occurred. She crouched down to make sure she was eye level with Bailey and calmly said, "I understand that this is stressful for you, but only five or six students are going to share their Me Bags today. We are going to stretch this out all week! You have plenty of time to bring it in." Bailey sighed with relief and hugged her.

As the last group of students finally entered the classroom and settled into their desks, Hannah greeted each one with a smile. She was so very glad she had planned special activities that would allow the students to collaborate and learn about each other. She knew that the "getting to know you" time was just as important to her as it was to them.

How would you describe your students? Every classroom is distinctive. The students you teach are uniquely yours, and they enter your classroom with a vast array of learning needs, interests, hopes, and even dreams about how they will spend their time with you. The focus of this chapter is to encourage you to think about the many needs of your learners and connect it to your preparation for planning. We will explore the following questions:

- Why is it so important to know your students?
- What do access and equity really mean?
- How do identity and agency influence lesson planning?
- What is prior knowledge in mathematics?
- What do culturally and linguistically diverse students need?
- What do students living in poverty need?
- What are learning needs?
- What are the common themes?

WHY IS IT SO IMPORTANT TO KNOW YOUR STUDENTS?

As a teacher, you surely appreciate the value of knowing the children in your classroom because you recognize how this intricately connects your teaching to your students' learning. Consider a time when you looked at a lesson plan constructed by someone else and thought, "This will never work with my kids." You know your students, and you were able to imagine how they would respond to the particular activities, content, or facilitation in the lesson plan.

As Bransford, Brown, and Cocking (1999) note, your knowledge of students is critical because students "come to formal education with a range of prior knowledge, skills, beliefs, and concepts that significantly influence what they notice about the environment and how they organize and interpret it. This, in turn, affects their abilities to remember, reason, solve problems, and acquire new knowledge" (p. 10). While it is vitally important to understand the mathematics content you teach, it is equally important to know and understand everything you can about the students you teach.

The children in your classroom have unique backgrounds that influence the ways in which they respond to you. At the same time, the ways you respond to your students may be influenced by your own cultural and language preferences and beliefs. All this information can help you plan lessons and design learning activities that both capitalize on students' cognitive, behavioral, and social-emotional strengths and **scaffold** their learning challenges.

As you work your way through this book, you will be constructing a mathematics lesson on the topic of your choice for your grade level. While this book is about lesson planning, it is essential for you to begin the lesson-planning process with a focus on your own learners' needs. As you read the brief discussion about different learning needs, consider how the descriptions apply to your own group of students.

> **Think about a situation when knowing about a student's needs in your class helped you plan an instructional activity that supported mathematical learning. Briefly describe the details here.**
>
> _____
> _____
> _____
> _____
> _____

WHAT IS PRIOR KNOWLEDGE IN MATHEMATICS?

As a teacher of elementary students, you know firsthand that students walk into your classroom with a wide array of backgrounds and experiences. **Prior knowledge** refers to the mathematics knowledge or content that students know as they enter your classroom. If you do not help students engage their prior knowledge, they may not be able to integrate new knowledge meaningfully. Accessing and connecting prior knowledge to new learning can affect students' motivation to learn and how much they will learn (Dolezal, Welsh, Pressley, & Vincent, 2003).

How students experience mathematics at home is one influence on their mathematics learning in the classroom. For example, if your students count regularly at home or shop with their parents at the grocery store, you can connect these experiences to your instructional activities. If students do not regularly have access to these kinds of opportunities, you will need to create instructional activities that help your students construct foundational knowledge for standards you will be teaching in the future. One way you can do this is by integrating number sense routines into your overall instructional plan.

Example: Amanda

Amanda, a third-grade teacher, conducts a **number sense routine** three times a week. These number sense routines help students think about numbers and computation in flexible ways, provide an entry point for every student, and offer Amanda opportunities to use students' ideas to facilitate mathematical discussions. At the beginning of the year, she asks students to represent numbers in multiple ways (Figure 1.1).

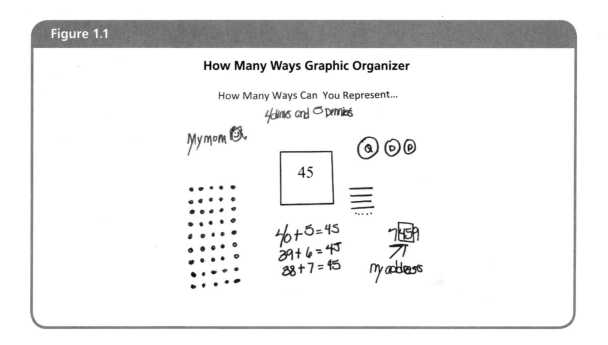

Figure 1.1

How Many Ways Graphic Organizer

Amanda supplies students with counting cubes, empty ten frames, base ten materials, and hundreds charts to stimulate discussion and investigation. Students draw their representations and then post them on a special bulletin board lined with plastic sleeves for each student. This number sense routine prompts students to demonstrate their understanding of numbers and provides Amanda with information about how students make connections and apply the mathematics they have already learned. While all students may not need more opportunities to develop foundational knowledge before moving to grade-level lessons, Amanda knows that all students will benefit from the exploration and conversation that this number sense routine elicits.

Amanda uses the bulletin board display to ensure that every student has work represented in the classroom and to highlight student strategies for particular lessons that she is going to teach. For example, when she introduced place value, she took pictures of the students' place value representations and asked the students to discuss what all the representations had in common.

What do you know about your students' prior knowledge? Make a list and share it with another teacher who knows your students.

_____

_____

_____

_____

_____

WHAT DO ACCESS AND EQUITY REALLY MEAN?

Knowing your students is the first step in providing equitable learning opportunities and **access** to **high-quality mathematics instruction**. The National Council of Teachers of Mathematics' (2014a) Access and Equity Position Statement states the following:

> Creating, supporting, and sustaining a culture of access and equity require being responsive to students' backgrounds, experiences, cultural perspectives, traditions, and knowledge when designing and implementing a mathematics program and assessing its effectiveness. Acknowledging and addressing factors that contribute to differential outcomes among groups of students are critical to ensuring that all students routinely have opportunities to experience high-quality mathematics instruction, learn challenging mathematics content, and receive the support necessary to be successful. Addressing equity and access includes both ensuring that all students attain mathematics proficiency and increasing the numbers of students from all racial, ethnic, linguistic, gender, and socioeconomic groups who attain the highest levels of mathematics achievement. (www.nctm.org/Standards-and-Positions/Position-Statements/Access-and-Equity-in-Mathematics-Education/)

Without equal access, students' opportunities to learn are reduced. Students' knowledge gaps are often the result of instructional gaps, which happen when students are not appropriately challenged because beliefs about what they learn and how they can learn are reflected in the types of instruction they receive. Equitable instruction is a key factor in supporting students' opportunities for access to high-quality mathematics instruction. Knowledge of your students should inform and support high expectations and beliefs about what your students can learn and do in your mathematics classroom. Later in this book, you will have an opportunity to apply what you know about your students to your own lesson-planning process.

> **How do you ensure that *all* your students have access to high-quality mathematics instruction? Record your response here.**
>
> _____
>
> _____
>
> _____
>
> _____

HOW DO IDENTITY AND AGENCY INFLUENCE LESSON PLANNING?

Identity and **agency** are two concepts that help teachers understand the dynamics that take place in a classroom, which, in turn, helps teachers better understand their students and how best to meet their needs. Identity is how individuals know and see themselves (i.e., student, teacher, good at sports, like math, etc.) and how others know and see us (i.e., short, smart, African American, etc.). When defined broadly, identity is a concept that brings together all the interrelated elements that teachers and students bring to the classroom, including beliefs, attitudes, emotions, and cognitive capacity (Grootenboer, 2000).

Agency is the power to act. Students develop their agency when they actively engage in the learning process (Wenmoth, 2014). Since student learning is greatest in classrooms where students are engaged in high-level thinking and reasoning (Boaler & Staples, 2008), teachers need to ensure that tasks they choose promote this engagement on a regular basis.

The types of lessons teachers design, the approach they take to teaching, the tasks they select, the types of questions they ask, the classroom climate, and social norms of the classroom all affect student engagement and are influenced by the teachers' identity. For example, in a classroom where the teacher sees his or her identity as the giver of knowledge, students are passive recipients of knowledge, working individually at their desks on assignments designed by the teacher. In this approach, there is no opportunity for students to exercise agency. In addition, student identities are lost as they are treated as a group with all the same learning needs rather than as individuals with unique learning needs.

If teachers think about teaching and learning as social activities (Vygotsky, 1964, 1978), then they must take the initiative to put structures into place in the classroom that support the social nature of learning. These include creating a classroom climate in which students feel safe to test hypotheses and ask questions. In this environment, teachers present tasks that afford students the opportunity to act, to explore, to move, and to exercise some choice. They set social norms in the classroom that encourage students to work together on challenging tasks and engage in productive struggle. They not only encourage student-to-student discourse but also intentionally plan for it. Students hypothesize, listen to one another, critique ideas, and formulate questions. They exercise their agency. In this student-centered approach, students become "authors" of mathematical ideas and texts and not "overhearers" (Larson, 2002).

Let's look at an example in which students from racial groups often challenged to find voice and agency in classrooms were engaged in a task that allowed them to exercise their agency. Arthur Powell (2004), a researcher from Rutgers University, captured African American and Latinx students exercising their agency during a study under a grant from the National Science Foundation (REC-0309062). In this study, Powell describes how students who had never before used Cuisenaire Rods were given a set to help them investigate fractions. Cuisenaire Rods are proportional rods of ten different colors, with each color corresponding to a different length as pictured in Figure 1.2.

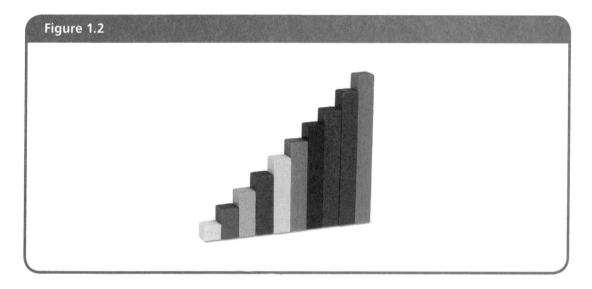

Figure 1.2

Powell (2004) describes,

> Students were invited to work on the question, "If the blue rod is 1, what is yellow?" Many students manipulated the rods to observe how many white rods they needed to place end-to-end to construct a length equivalent to the blue rod. Malika lists how many white rods make up each of the other rods. She calls the yellow rod 5, and later she and Lorrin say that yellow is five-ninths. Building a model of a blue rod alongside a train of one yellow and four white rods, with a purple rod beneath the white rods, Lorrin and Malika show that the purple rod is four ninths. The students at their table determine number names for all the rods, except that they are uncertain about what to call the orange rod. Eventually, this group of students resolves what number name to give to the orange rod. One student remarks that ten-ninths is an improper fraction. A male colleague [student] … says assertively, "It's still ten-ninths. That ain't gonna change it because it's an improper fraction. That makes it even more right." (p. 46)

In this example, the teacher did not overtly give students a set procedure to follow to work out the name for the yellow rod. The teacher did, however, establish the social norms of the classroom so that students knew what was expected of them. Malika manipulated the materials to name all of the rods. Student-to-student discussion provided the opportunity to use reasoning to name the orange rod, a question that was not asked by the investigator. Students were posing their own questions at this point in the investigation. Powell reports that the students held a misconception about fractions when the investigation began—the numerator cannot be larger than the denominator—but, through their own exploration, had convinced themselves by the end of the session that the belief was incorrect. The students had agency in this example because of the task they engaged in and the social norms in place to help them. The teacher expected students to move around, manipulate objects, engage in the task by talking with one another, and challenge each other's ideas.

In this book, you will read more about tasks, misconceptions, and discourse to support students in exercising their agency.

WHAT DO CULTURALLY AND LINGUISTICALLY DIVERSE STUDENTS NEED?

If you are lucky enough to teach culturally and linguistically diverse students, then you know of the rich experiences these students bring to your classroom. An **English Language Learner (ELL)** is defined as "an active learner of the English language who may benefit from various types of language support programs" (National Council of Teachers of English, 2008, p. 2). While these students may share some common needs because they are learning English and mathematics as well as other subjects, they also can, and often do, have very different learning needs. You can gather information about these students by asking them to show you what they know, observing them as they interact with other students, speaking to them often, using visual cues to communicate, and encouraging them to draw pictures. The National Council of Supervisors of Mathematics' (2009) position paper, titled "Improving Student Achievement in Mathematics by Addressing the Needs of English Language Learners," recommends that mathematics educators do the following:

- Realize that mathematics is neither value free nor culture free but instead is a product of human activity. Thus, race, class, culture, and language play key roles in its teaching and learning.

- Understand that language is not only a tool for communicating but also a tool for thinking. Every mathematics teacher is a language teacher—particularly the **academic language** used to formulate and communicate mathematics learning (Lager, 2006).

- Realize that regular and active classroom participation—in the form of discussing, explaining, writing, and presenting—is crucial to ELLs' success in mathematics and that ELLs can produce explanations, participate in presentations, and engage in discussions as they are learning English.

- Recognize that ELLs, like English-speaking students, require consistent access to high-cognitive-demand tasks in mathematics.

- Learn to see the evidence of ELLs' mathematical thinking, hear how ELLs use language to communicate about mathematics, understand the competence that ELLs bring, build on this competence, and provide access to opportunities for advancing their learning.

- Value the home language of each ELL student and find ways to promote its use whenever possible.

- Provide and participate in ongoing professional development to help mathematics teachers shape instructional practices to foster success of ELLs in mathematics, including the development of language-rich classrooms for the benefit of all students.

- Establish district- and school-wide structures that promote collaboration among teachers of mathematics, specialists in English as a second language, bilingual teachers, and language arts teachers, in order to meld skills and knowledge in the service of ELLs' learning of mathematics.

Culturally and linguistically diverse students also benefit from particular strategies that invite them to regularly engage in mathematical discourse (Banse, Palacios, Merritt, & Rimm-Kaufman, 2016). This discourse is critical because the ELL students need to have opportunities to talk as well as to listen. Banse et al. (2016) recommend that ELL teachers should proceed as follows:

1. Ask **open-ended questions** that invite student thinking and explanation and support students' development of conceptual understanding (Figure 1.3).

Figure 1.3

Example	Nonexample
What do you notice about these fractions: $\frac{1}{2}, \frac{3}{4}, \frac{1}{4}, \frac{4}{8}$?	Write an equivalent fraction for $\frac{1}{4}$.

2. As needed, follow open-ended questions with **close-ended questions** that are scaffolded to help the ELLs focus on one or two options (Figure 1.4).

Figure 1.4

Example	Nonexample
Which one of these shapes has a perimeter of six [pointing to a square and hexagon]?	Count the sides of the hexagon to find the perimeter.

3. Scaffold students' responses by repeating, extending, and rephrasing so ELLs can benefit from having additional conversations about their explanations and solutions, which can be extended by peers and/or the teacher (Figure 1.5).

Figure 1.5

Example	Nonexample
You made $\frac{4}{8}$ with the fraction strips next to the $\frac{1}{2}$. You said that the two fractions are the same amount. When we see that the fractional amounts are the same, we call them equivalent fractions. Can you use the fraction strips to find another equivalent fraction?	Let me show you how the fractional amounts are the same (places $\frac{4}{8}$ fraction pieces next to $\frac{1}{2}$).

4. Model mathematical vocabulary in context, always using correct vocabulary and applying it in context so that ELLs can make connections about meaning (Figure 1.6).

Figure 1.6

Example	Nonexample
An acute angle measures less than 90°.	An acute angle is just a "cute little angle"!

5. Strive to include ELLs in mathematical discourse each day; ideally, both teachers and students should engage in mathematical discourse with ELL students (Figure 1.7).

Figure 1.7

Example	Nonexample
ELL students and non-ELL students work in pairs and participate in flexible grouping.	ELL students are isolated in their own group.

Review the five recommendations for teachers of ELL students. Which ones do you already use in your planning? Which ones would you like to integrate more? How might you do that? Briefly list the details here.

_____

_____

_____

_____

WHAT DO STUDENTS LIVING IN POVERTY NEED?

About 21% of the children living in the United States live below the poverty threshold. Another 22% live in low-income homes, comprising 43%, or 30.6 million, of all the children in the United States (National Center for Children in Poverty, 2017). Given this statistic, it is quite likely that you are teaching at least one child living in poverty.

While it is important to not overgeneralize or make assumptions about children living in poverty, research suggests that some children in this situation may experience prolonged stress that may influence the ways in which they respond to the classroom environment and that may negatively affect school performance (Harvard Center for the Developing Child, 2007). Students may have difficulty concentrating or attending to tasks (Erickson, Drevets, & Schulkin, 2003), reduced ability to navigate in social situations (National Institute of Child Health and Human Development Early Child Care Research Network, 2005), and impaired memory, critical thinking, and creativity (Farah et al., 2006; Lupien, King, Meaney, & McEwen, 2001). While there are many strategies that can support your students who are living in poverty, the following three strategies may support your instructional decision making about lesson planning.

1. **Build upon the students' strengths.** Students in poverty need educators to recognize the strengths that they bring to school. Ensure that you are focusing on and building students' specific strengths by first determining those strengths and then highlighting them during lessons.

2. **Consistently work toward building relationships with your students.** Intentionally pursue relationships with your students. Ensure that you use their names in positive ways, and provide opportunities for students to build relationships with each other. Consider using the students' names and interests in **word problems** and contexts for lessons.

3. **Seek to understand your students' responses to stressful situations.** Consider why students might be responding to classroom situations in particular ways by observing and noting potential triggers. As you plan your lessons, partner students to increase access to problems. Think about how your problem contexts might engage or alienate students who are living in poverty. For example, problems that focus on acquisition or buying items may create unintentional consequences.

Example: Marty

Lance, a fourth-grade teacher, used all three of these strategies to attend to one of his fourth grader's needs. He had noticed that Marty usually entered the classroom in the morning very agitated and had trouble settling into the routine. The student had developed a pattern of entering the room, slamming his books down, and then engaging in conflict with another student. To counteract this pattern, Lance decided to greet Marty at the classroom door to have a positive conversation about how he was doing. Lance enlisted Marty's help by asking him to help take photographs for a lesson launch. After about a week of making this effort, Lance noticed that Marty was much calmer, focused, and ready to learn at the start of each day. He seemed to look forward to their daily chats and was often ready to tell him a story.

How do you use students' strengths to design instructional activities? Briefly note the details here.

_____

_____

_____

_____

_____

_____

_____

_____

_____

WHAT ARE LEARNING NEEDS?

Every student you teach is distinct, possessing specific learning strengths and learning challenges. Students with explicit learning disabilities typically possess a significant learning challenge in one or more of the following areas: memory, self-regulation, visual processing, language processing (separate from ELL), academic skills, and motor skills. The Individuals With Disabilities Education Act (IDEA) requires public schools to provide the least restrictive environment to children with identified disabilities. Students' **Individualized Education Plan (IEP)** must reflect the individual needs of the students.

As you consider the learning needs of your students, you will need to study their IEPs carefully to determine how you can meet their needs in your instructional planning. You may want to develop learning profiles of your students' mathematics strengths and needs to inform your instructional decision making. You might complete a learning profile for each student with the IEP accommodations at the beginning of the year and then add to it as you learn new information throughout the year.

Example: Rachel

Figure 1.8 shows a completed learning profile that Hannah, the teacher in our vignette, created after getting to know Rachel. In the form, she noted Rachel's strengths in self-regulating her behavior and her advanced critical thinking skills. After just one day, Hannah was beginning to gather some excellent evidence about Rachel's strengths.

Learner Profile for Mathematics Teaching and Learning

Name: Rachel

Memory and Retention	Self-Regulation	Visual Processing	Language Processing	Academic Skills	Motor Skills
Strengths	Strengths Monitors behavior and expresses her needs with maturity	Strengths	Strengths	Strengths Demonstrates advanced critical thinking skills	Strengths
Challenges	Challenges	Challenges	Challenges	Challenges	Challenges Fine motor, particularly for writing Physical mobility

IEP Accommodations:

Provide extra time to move from classroom to special areas.

Extra time to complete assignments. Recorder for some assignments.

 This tool can be downloaded from resources.corwin.com/mathlessonplanning/3-5

By providing students with opportunities to see and use multiple representations in learning activities, from concrete to abstract, you can support their mathematical understanding. This concrete-to-abstract sequence is described in two ways—Concrete-Representation-Abstract (CRA) and Concrete-Semiconcrete-Abstract (CSA)—and it supports students with disabilities' conceptual understanding (Sealander, Johnson, Lockwood, & Medina, 2012). This teaching sequence is very familiar to elementary educators because it begins with concrete experiences using manipulatives, moves to a representational stage where students draw pictures and use visuals to show their thinking, and then provides opportunities for students to apply their learning using abstract symbols. As you make instructional decisions for your students with learning needs, you will want to consider giving ample time for students to use manipulatives before moving to the representation stage. They may also need opportunities to move back and forth between the stages of the CRA/CSA sequence to continue to build fluency (Van de Walle, Karp, & Bay-Williams, 2016). For instance, Figure 1.9 shows the concrete to abstract continuum for multiplication.

Figure 1.9

Concrete	Representation/ Semiabstract	Abstract
	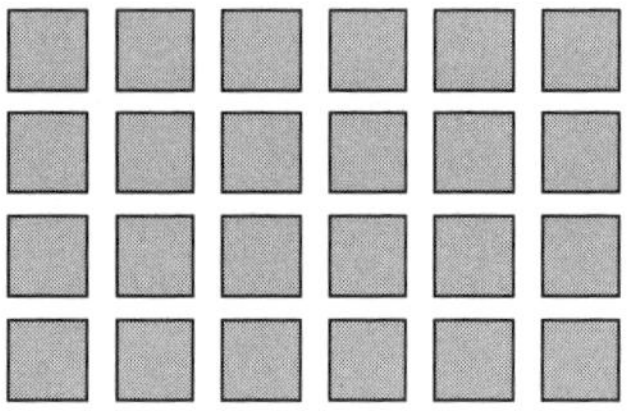	$4 \times 6 = 24$

> **How do you integrate your students' learning needs into your instructional planning? Briefly note the details here.**
>
> _____
>
> _____
>
> _____
>
> _____
>
> _____
>
> _____
>
> _____
>
> _____
>
> _____
>
> _____
>
> _____
>
> _____

WHAT ARE THE COMMON THEMES?

As you were reading this chapter, you may have thought that many of the suggested strategies could be applied to all of your learners. Instructional decision making begins with building relationships with students by getting to know them. This newfound knowledge helps you to create positive connections and build a learning community that fosters a rich learning environment. When you know your students, you can make the very best instructional decisions that will best meet their academic and social-emotional needs. Knowledge and awareness of each student's learning needs makes for purposeful lesson planning.

Consider all of the learning needs discussed in this chapter. Make a list of your own students' learning needs using the categories listed in this chapter. What do you notice? What will you need to keep in mind as you plan your lessons? Record your thoughts and concerns below.

Notes

CHAPTER 2

YOUR 3–5 BLUEPRINT

Planning Mathematics Lessons for Coherence, Rigor, and Purpose

Paul, a novice third-grade teacher, looked for his teammates, Lynn and Marcia, all day. He really needed to talk to them about this lesson-planning business. Paul spent the weekend searching for lessons on the Internet to match the scope and sequence the school district provided, but he felt like he was just planning a bunch of discrete lessons that didn't necessarily go together. He had had another lesson fall apart today, even though he had spent hours preparing a game for the students to do during math stations. He kept getting surprised and then sidetracked by the students' misconceptions.

Just then Lynn and Marcia arrived. Paul began telling about his frustration. He said, "I don't know how you do it. I am spending all of my weekends and evenings planning lessons for the next day. What is your secret?"

Lynn replied, "I follow the textbook. It saves a lot of time."

Paul said, "I thought the textbook was just a resource."

Marcia, a 20-year veteran, said, "Paul, you are absolutely right. The textbook is just a resource. But just picking lessons off the Internet, no matter how cute or enticing they are, can really mess with the coherence we are trying to create for students. I feel badly that you have been struggling. I think it is time that we sit down as a team and start planning together."

Paul smiled, relieved at last.

Lynn and Paul are examples of both ends of the lesson-planning spectrum. On one end, Paul is planning daily, just keeping his head above water. On the other hand, Lynn is using the textbook, a good resource, but not enough when state standards, student misconceptions, big ideas, and prior student knowledge need to be considered. Neither rigor nor lesson coherence are part of their discussion. Should they be, and why should they be?

As the architect of your instruction, designing your blueprint is perhaps one of the most important jobs you can do. Throughout this book, you will have the opportunity to build coherent mathematics lessons for your grade level by following the many examples presented. Together, we will explore the answers to questions such as these:

- What is coherence?
- What is rigor?
- What is the purpose of a lesson?
- How can you ensure that you plan lessons for coherence, rigor, and purpose?

Let's begin by looking at foundational planning principles of coherence and rigor, which Paul and Lynn need to know. As you read, reflect upon how you currently think about your own lesson planning.

WHAT IS COHERENCE?

Coherence is probably the most crucial step in providing a quality mathematics education to students (Schmidt, Wang, & McKnight, 2005). Coherence is a logical sequencing of mathematical ideas. When lessons are coherent, they have a logical flow and are well organized to promote sense making. Lesson coherence should be both vertical and horizontal. For **vertical coherence,** you can look at the standards at the grade level before and after yours. How does your content fit in with what your students have already been taught, and how can you bridge that knowledge to what they will be learning next year? You need to consider what prior knowledge students are likely to have and where they'll be going next so that you can ensure a vertical coherence—planning lessons logically, allowing students to make sense of the mathematics across the grades. For example, Figure 2.1 shows a vertical articulation of selected 3–5 standards.

Figure 2.1

Third Grade	Fourth Grade	Fifth Grade
Explain equivalence of fractions in special cases, and compare fractions by reasoning about their size.	Explain why a fraction $\frac{a}{b}$ is equivalent to a fraction $\frac{(n \times a)}{(n \times b)}$ by using visual fraction models, with attention to how the number and size of the parts differ even though the two fractions themselves are the same size. Use this principle to recognize and generate equivalent fractions.	Add and subtract fractions with unlike denominators (including mixed numbers) by replacing given fractions with equivalent fractions in such a way as to produce an equivalent sum or difference of fractions with like denominators. *For example,* $\frac{2}{3} + \frac{5}{4} = \frac{8}{12} + \frac{15}{12} = \frac{23}{12}$. *(In general,* $\frac{a}{b} + \frac{c}{d} = \frac{(ad + bc)}{bd}$.*)*

Horizontal coherence refers to daily lesson planning. Do your daily lessons follow a logical order, a gradual building up of a concept and/or skill over time? For example, in third grade, students need to understand a fraction as a quantity before you introduce equivalent fractions. Daily lesson plans that allow children to practice recognizing and counting fractions make sense. Teaching place value on Mondays, subtraction on Tuesdays, and fractions recognition on Wednesdays is not a logical, coherent sequence.

Why do you think coherence is considered such a crucial part of planning in mathematics? Briefly discuss your answer below.

_____

_____

_____

_____

Some teachers believe planning for **rigor** means providing more difficult material or asking students to complete more problems. This is not correct. Some even say that rigor means mathematical content is accelerated. However, as Hull, Harbin Miles, and Balka (2014) explain, mathematical rigor within a classroom is actually

> a direct result of active participation in deep mathematical thinking and intensive reasoning. There are dual meanings for rigor when planning great lessons. First, *content rigor* is the depth of interconnection concepts and the breadth of supporting skills students are expected to know and understand. Next, *instructional rigor* is the ongoing interaction between teacher instruction and students reasoning and thinking about concepts, skills, and challenging tasks that result in a conscious, connected, and transferable body of valuable knowledge for every student. (p. 22)

Since rigor results from active student participation and deep mathematical thinking and reasoning, let's compare two third-grade examples of what it is and what it is not.

Alicia and Anna are teaching place value, which is embedded in their standards.

Example: **Alicia**

Alicia gives the following task (Figure 2.2) to her students and explains, "Place the numbers at the bottom of your worksheet into the chart."

Figure 2.2

Fill in the chart with the missing numbers.

Thousands	Hundreds	Tens	Ones
	5		
		6	3
3			5
5	6		
	0		0

562

1,263

3,295

5,607

7,000

Example: Anna

Like Alicia, Anna is teaching place value. She passes out the task in Figure 2.3 to students and asks, "Which boxes have an amount equal to 2,645?" Students then pair up and work together, trying different strategies to answer the question. Some students write down the amounts as numbers and add. Others use mental arithmetic. After the students arrive at their answers, Anna brings the class together for a discussion where students share their results and strategies. After the class discussion of the task, Anna asks a follow-up question to see if the students can transfer the knowledge. She asks, "Everyone, please write the number 243 in a box and **decompose** it any way you want using place value words so it looks like the examples we checked on our worksheet."

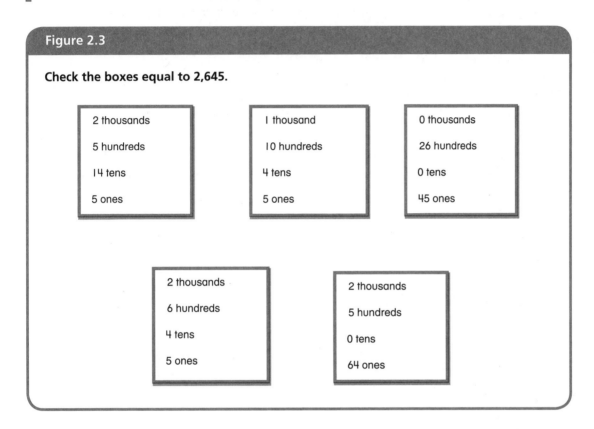

Figure 2.3

Check the boxes equal to 2,645.

2 thousands	1 thousand	0 thousands
5 hundreds	10 hundreds	26 hundreds
14 tens	4 tens	0 tens
5 ones	5 ones	45 ones

2 thousands	2 thousands
6 hundreds	5 hundreds
4 tens	0 tens
5 ones	64 ones

Both of these teachers are working with place value. However, Anna's lesson is more rigorous. Students in Anna's class are encouraged to think and use reasoning as they develop conceptual place value. Through the task, they have the opportunity to actively delve into the concept and have discourse that results from a shared experience. The follow-up task encourages students to extend the current task and be creative. Anna may take the students' work from the follow-up task and use some of the student examples to begin the next days' lesson.

On the other hand, Alicia's task does not require any reasoning. Students are simply filling in a chart with numbers, in the order they appear, a lower-level skill that will not extend beyond the task as written. Obviously, students need the skill of place naming, but is that all we expect? Or do we want students to go beyond place naming to understanding the values of the places in a number? Alicia's task does not encourage students to reason. Her task is not rigorous.

Think about a rigorous lesson you have taught, observed, or read recently. Identify the parts of the lesson that make it rigorous. Briefly discuss your findings here.

_____

_____

_____

_____

WHAT IS THE PURPOSE OF A LESSON?

We can trace the purposes of mathematics lessons back to the National Research Council's (2001) conclusions in *Adding It Up: Helping Children Learn Mathematics*. The authors cite **conceptual understanding** and procedural fluency as two major strands that must be integrated into the teaching and learning of mathematics. It is important to note that not all mathematics lessons have the same purpose.

What Is Conceptual Understanding?

Conceptual understanding means comprehension of mathematical concepts, operations, and relations. It involves knowing that mathematics is more than a set of rules or procedures; it is about really understanding what is happening in different mathematical concepts. For example, students can recognize, interpret, and generate examples of concepts and identify and apply principles, facts, definitions, and so forth. The different approaches of two more teachers, Jorge and Randy, show what a conceptual lesson looks like and what it does not.

Example: Jorge

Jorge introduces the "Cookie Stacks" task (Figure 2.4) to his class.

Figure 2.4

Cookie Stacks

This is an example of 7 × 9. How can you change this to show 8 × 6? How are your new stacks of cookies the same and how are they different from the 7 × 9 stacks?

Source: iStock.com/zoomstudio

Jorge's students work in pairs and use round counters to develop the meanings of seven groups of 9 and eight groups of 6. Student pairs then share how they thought about the groupings and how they changed them to show 8 × 6. They discussed the differences and similarities between the two sets of stacks.

Example: Randy

Randy asks his students to complete the timed facts practice in Figure 2.5.

Figure 2.5

Answer all the facts in 30 seconds.

7 × 9 =	7 × 1 =	7 × 3 =	7 × 7 =	7 × 8 =	7 × 4 =	7 × 2 =	7 × 6 =
7 × 5 =	7 × 2 =	8 × 9 =	8 × 2 =	8 × 8 =	8 × 5 =	8 × 7 =	8 × 3 =
8 × 0 =	8 × 5 =	8 × 4 =	8 × 1 =	9 × 9 =	9 × 1 =	9 × 7 =	9 × 3 =
9 × 5 =	9 × 2 =	9 × 8 =	9 × 2 =	9 × 1 =	9 × 0 =	9 × 4 =	9 × 9 =

Both teachers have a beginning fourth-grade lesson working with the multiplication facts for 6s, 7s, 8s, and 9s. However, when you compare the lessons to the criteria of conceptual understanding—which involves students recognizing, interpreting, and generating examples of concepts, as well as identifying and applying principles, facts, and definitions—you see that only Jorge's lesson fits the criteria. His lesson requires students to interpret a model of multiplication and then generate another example by modifying the first. Students need opportunities to apply what they know about multiplication as groupings.

On the other hand, Randy's worksheet can be completed by students using only memorization. While basic facts fluency is a skill we want students to master, such a worksheet does not build a conceptual understanding foundation. Students can arrive at the correct answers without understanding what multiplication means.

A more in-depth discussion of conceptual understanding lessons appears in Chapter 5.

What Is Procedural Fluency?

Procedural fluency describes the ability to use procedures accurately, efficiently, and flexibly. Students demonstrate procedural fluency when they refer to knowledge of procedures and have skill in performing them. They transfer procedures to different problems and contexts, and they know when a **strategy** or procedure is more appropriate to apply to a particular situation.

A lesson that develops procedural fluency is one in which students leverage their conceptual understanding and flexibly use various strategies that they find work best for the types of problems they are solving. **Distributed practice** over time helps students become proficient with the procedures so that they are more able to understand and manipulate more complex concepts in future learning.

When you start with lessons for conceptual understanding, you use representations to help students see the meaning behind the mathematical concept. Because children do not think abstractly, they support their thinking through the use of representations. A representation that helps students understand a concept can be a reliable tool that helps them understand procedures and thus develop procedural fluency.

Example: Katie

Katie, a fourth-grade teacher, wants her students to practice factoring. She knows that one of the best ways to develop procedural fluency is to play games. She decides to play the Factor Game. She displays a hundreds chart on the wall. See Figure 2.6.

Figure 2.6

Hundreds Chart

1	2	3	4	5	6	7	8	9	10
11	12	13	14	15	16	17	18	19	20
21	22	23	24	25	26	27	28	29	30
31	32	33	34	35	36	37	38	39	40
41	42	43	44	45	46	47	48	49	50
51	52	53	54	55	56	57	58	59	60
61	62	63	64	65	66	67	68	69	70
71	72	73	74	75	76	77	78	79	80
81	82	83	84	85	86	87	88	89	90
91	92	93	94	95	96	97	98	99	100

> The class works as two teams and take turns selecting a number from the hundreds chart. They will receive 1 point for each factor they find for their number. For example, Team A selected the number 24. Katie puts an X on 24. Team A finds the factors of 24: 1, 24, 2, 12, 3, 8, 4, 6. So Team A gets 8 points. Team B strategizes that they want more than 8 points. If they select a perfect square, they get an odd number of factors that could work in their favor. They know to stay away from prime numbers because they have only two factors. They know 36 appears often as a product in their multiplication facts, so they pick 36. They find the factors of 36: 1, 36, 2, 18, 3, 12, 4, 9, 6. So Team B gets 9 points. Understanding that the multiplication facts are tied to factors of a number (fact families) is the conceptual understanding linked to the procedures for finding factors.

In this game, Katie had her students practice factoring numbers in a manner that had them rely on previous conceptual understandings rather than using a drill worksheet of numbers that had to be factored. This game had students engaged and thinking strategically to win while factoring numbers 1 to 100.

Procedural fluency lessons are discussed in more detail in Chapter 5.

What Is Transfer?

A third purpose of a lesson in mathematics is **transfer.** A transfer lesson is a lesson in which students demonstrate transfer of learning; that is, they show that they are able to effectively use content knowledge and skill in a problem situation. According to Hattie and colleagues (2016), a transfer task should encourage connections. It is a task that can be open-ended with multiple entry points. Hattie and colleagues (2016) also point out that transfer, as a goal, "means that teachers want students to begin to take the reins of their own learning, think metacognitively, and apply what they know to a variety of real-world contexts" (p. 175).

In a lesson designed for transfer, students make sense of a problematic situation, think about how they can apply their skills and foundational understandings to solve the problem, and reflect on their own **problem-solving** process.

> Example: Stuart
>
> To create a transfer lesson, Stuart begins with the following fifth-grade **computation** standard.
>
> > Solve word problems involving addition and subtraction of fractions referring to the same whole, including cases of unlike denominators, e.g., by using visual fraction models or equations to represent the problem. Use benchmark fractions and number sense of fractions to estimate mentally and assess the reasonableness of answers. *For example, recognize an incorrect result $\frac{2}{5}+\frac{1}{2}=\frac{3}{7}$ by observing that $\frac{3}{7}<\frac{1}{2}$.*
>
> From this standard, he decides to create a transfer lesson that asks students to demonstrate their understanding of word problems and addition of fractions by posing the following task:
>
> > Jimmy solved a word problem by using the equation $\frac{2}{5}+\frac{1}{2}=\frac{3}{7}$. After school, his dog ate part of the paper, and Jimmy lost the word problem that went with the equation. Write a new word problem that works with Jimmy's equation.

For this transfer lesson, students are creating new and original content. There are **multiple entry points** for this task as well as an endless number of correct responses. Students need to relate their content knowledge about the addition equation to their conceptual understanding of addition in order to create a word problem. This is a **metacognitive** thought process because the students must reflect on everything they have learned and pull it all together to create a word problem.

Tasks in a transfer lesson may be similar to or even the same as those in a conceptual understanding lesson. The difference is in the learning intention of the lesson. When you use a task to develop conceptual understanding, students do not already have a set of efficient strategies to solve the problem. They explore, use their background knowledge, and try to figure out how to solve the problem. They may unearth new ideas and test them. When you use the task to determine if students have mastered a concept and skill at the end of a unit, students bring the conceptual understandings and skills learned in the unit and use them efficiently and effectively to solve the problem.

We discuss transfer lessons in more detail in Chapter 5.

HOW CAN YOU ENSURE THAT YOU PLAN LESSONS FOR COHERENCE, RIGOR, AND PURPOSE?

Faced with so many decisions, teachers may feel forced to make daily planning decisions that individually work but, when examined together, do not promote coherence, rigor, and an overall purpose.

Lessons on a given mathematics topic need to be connected to enhance learning. They must involve a mix of conceptual understanding, procedural fluency, and transfer. When several coherent lessons on a topic come together as a whole, it is called a **unit plan.**

Fifth-grade teacher Marilyn was planning a measurement unit. She was short on time and gathered resources from several sources to cover the 15 lessons she would need for the unit, as directed by the district's pacing guide. She found two fun activities from last year that involved volume. Then she found on Pinterest three conversion lessons where students convert like measurement units within a system that she knew her students would love doing and two more lessons in her textbook that asked children to measure items in the classroom. Her teaching partners gave her six more lessons on using a balance for mass, so she assembled a total of 13 lessons. She left two lessons open for review.

After teaching the unit, Marilyn reviewed the collection of lessons and reflected on the instruction. She asked herself these questions:

- Did these lessons bring rigor to the study of measurement?
- Did the lessons meet/match grade-level standards?
- Did the lessons sequentially build students' mathematical understanding?
- Did the lessons connect the big ideas of measurement concepts?

While Marilyn felt that she did teach some successful lessons, she found that when she reviewed them as a unit, her lessons did not connect to enhance the students' learning. There was no coherence. Lessons did not build on one another but jumped from topic to topic. She decided that for next year, she will ensure that her teaching of measurement is rigorous, coherent, and purposeful by redesigning the entire unit with those goals in mind.

It is important to note that an individual lesson is not necessarily completed in one class period. Sometimes a lesson may take two sessions to complete. The lesson template in this book was designed to help you plan individual lessons. As you use this template to create successive lessons, be sure to keep big ideas and standards in mind. These steps will help ensure that you create a coherent unit plan. Each chapter in Part II of this book will have a discussion on unit coherence.

Big Idea(s):

Essential Question(s):

Content Standard(s):

Mathematical Practice or Process Standards:

Learning Intention(s) (mathematical/language/social):

Success Criteria (written in student voice):

Purpose:

☐ Conceptual Understanding   ☐ Procedural Fluency   ☐ Transfer

Task:

Materials (representations, manipulatives, other):

Misconceptions or Common Errors:

Format:

☐ Four-Part Lesson   ☐ Game Format   ☐ Small-Group Instruction

☐ Pairs   ☐ Other_____

Formative Assessment:

Launch:

Facilitate:

Closure:

PART II

DRAFTING YOUR 3-5 BLUEPRINT

CHAPTER 3

LAYING YOUR FOUNDATION

It Starts With Big Ideas, Essential Questions, and Standards

As required by a new district policy, two veteran third-grade teachers, Rosemarie and Mike, sat down with their school administrative leader to review their students' benchmark assessments. Rosemarie, who had not yet seen the results, had been nervous all day about this meeting. She knew that Linda, the school principal, supported their work.

Linda pulled up the screen with the results and displayed them. "Let's just take a few minutes to look at the data before we discuss. Let's start with the successes. I am noticing that the students performed beautifully on geometry concepts. These scores are way up from last year."

Rosemarie commented, "We really hit geometry hard this year. In fact, I was truly amazed with their understanding."

Linda said, "I am so glad that all this effort paid off! Now, let's look at what we need to work on."

Rosemarie said, "My students were completely confused about the representations used for fractions."

Mike exclaimed, "Mine were, too! Do you think it has anything to do with the new standards? We always taught fractions, but we never used those representations that were on the test."

Linda replied, "I think you are on to something, Mike. How could we strategically plan for the new standards so that we can create the same kind of success you had with geometry?"

Rosemarie and Mike's surprise about the assessment results may mirror the feelings of many teachers after states and districts implement new standards. In this chapter, we will focus on big ideas, essential questions, and standards as the building blocks of a lesson taught at the 3–5 grade levels. We will also address the following questions:

- What are state standards for mathematics?
- What are essential questions?
- What are process standards?

WHAT ARE STATE STANDARDS FOR MATHEMATICS?

Grade-level standards describe what students should know and be able to do at the end of the grade level. For many years, research studies of mathematics education concluded that in order to improve mathematics achievement in the United States, standards needed to become more focused and coherent. The development of common mathematics **standards** began with research-affirmed **learning progressions** highlighting what is known about how students develop mathematical knowledge, skills, and understanding. The resulting document became known as the *Common Core State Standards for Mathematics* (CCSS-M) (National Governors Association Center for Best Practices & Council of Chief State School Officers, 2010). The landmark document was intended to be a set of shared goals and expectations for the knowledge and skills students need in mathematics at each grade level. The overall goal was college and career readiness.

Currently, the majority of states have adopted the *Common Core State Standards for Mathematics* as their own state standards. However, it is important to note that while many states adopted the *CCSS-M*, others have updated, clarified, or otherwise modified them, adopting the updated set as their new state standards. A few states have written their own standards.

Most standards documents are composed of **content standards** and **process standards** of some kind. It is important to recognize that no state standards describe or recommend what works for all students. Classroom teachers, not the standards, are the key to improving student learning in mathematics. The success of standards depends on teachers knowing how to expertly implement them. It is important as a teacher to be very knowledgeable about your own state standards and what they mean—not only at your grade level but also at the one above and below the one you teach. They are at the heart of planning lessons that are engaging, purposeful, coherent, and rigorous.

Regardless of whether your state has adopted CCSS-M, has modified the standards, or has written its own, the **big ideas** of 3–5 mathematics are universal. Big ideas are statements that describe concepts that transcend grade levels. Big ideas provide focus on specific content. Here are the big ideas for Grades 3 through 5 on fractions.

Third Grade

In third grade, students use visual models, including area models, fraction strips, and the number line to develop conceptual understanding of the meaning of a fraction as a number in relationship to a defined whole. They work with unit fractions to understand the meaning of the numerator and denominator. Students build equivalent fractions and use a variety of strategies to compare fractions. In Grade 3, fractions are limited to halves, thirds, fourths, sixths, and eighths.

Fourth Grade

Fourth graders extend understanding from the third-grade experiences, composing fractions from unit fractions and decomposing fractions into unit fractions. They then apply this understanding to addition and subtraction with like denominators. Students begin with visual models and progress to making generalizations for addition and subtraction of fractions with like denominators. They compare fractions from the same whole using a variety of strategies. Students build equivalent fractions with denominators of 10 and 100 and connect that work to decimal notation for tenths and hundredths. Students add and subtract fractions with like denominators.

Fifth Grade

Fifth-grade students build on previous experiences with fractions and use a variety of visual representations and strategies to add and subtract fractions with unlike denominators. Problem solving provides contexts for students to use mathematical reasoning to determine whether answers make sense. They extend their interpretation of a fraction as part of a whole to fractions as a division representation of the numerator divided by the denominator. Students continue to build conceptual understanding of multiplication of fractions using visual models and problem-solving contexts. Once conceptual understanding is established, students generalize efficient procedures for multiplying and dividing fractions.

While the major topics in third- through fifth-grade mathematics are the same, states may vary in their focus at each grade level. Compare your state standards for your grade level with the summary above. Are there any differences? If so, what are they? Briefly describe them here.

_____

_____

_____

_____

WHAT ARE ESSENTIAL QUESTIONS?

It is estimated that over the course of a career, a teacher can ask more than two million questions (Vogler, 2008). If teachers are already asking so many questions, why do we need to consider essential questions? An **essential question** is a building block for designing a good lesson. It is the thread that unifies all of the lessons on a given topic to bring the coherence and purpose discussed previously. Essential questions are purposefully linked to the big idea to frame student inquiry, promote critical thinking, and assist in transferring learning. (See Chapter 5 for more information on essential questions in transfer lessons.) As a teacher, you will revisit your essential question(s) throughout your unit.

Essential questions include some of these characteristics:

- *Open-ended.* These questions usually have multiple acceptable responses.

- *Engaging.* These questions ignite lively discussion and debate and may raise additional questions.

- *High cognitive demand.* These questions require students to infer, evaluate, defend, justify, and/or predict.

- *Recurring.* These questions are revisited throughout the unit, school year, other disciplines, and/or a person's lifetime.

- *Foundational.* These questions can serve as the heart of the content. Students need to understand foundational questions in order to understand the content that follows.

Not all essential questions need to have all of the characteristics. Here are some examples of essential questions that follow from big ideas for 3–5.

- When and why do people estimate?

- How are fractions used in real life?

- How do we know that fractions are numbers?

- How are common and decimal fractions alike and different?

- How do I identify the whole when working with fractions?

- How does changing the size of a whole affect the size or amount of a fractional part?

- What patterns do you see when we look at place value?

- What would life be like if there were no numbers?

- What do mathematicians do when they get stuck on a problem?

> **Look at the list of sample essential questions. Decide which characteristics describe which question. Note any thoughts or comments below.**
>
> _____
>
> _____
>
> _____
>
> _____

WHAT ARE PROCESS STANDARDS?

Up to this point, we have been discussing content standards. However, every state also has a set of standards that define the **habits of mind** students should develop through mathematics. In 1989, the National Council of Teachers of Mathematics (NCTM) introduced these standards as process standards, stating that "what we teach [in mathematics] is as important as how we teach it" (NCTM, 1991), encouraging us to teach mathematics though these processes. Those standards are the following:

1. **Problem solving:** Students use a repertoire of skills and strategies for solving a variety of problems. They recognize and create problems from real-world situations within and outside mathematics to find solutions.

2. **Communication:** Students use mathematical language, including terminology and symbols, to express ideas precisely. Students represent, discuss, read, write, and listen to mathematics.

3. **Reasoning and proof:** Students apply inductive and deductive reasoning skills to make, test, and evaluate statements to justify steps in mathematical procedures. Students use logical reasoning to analyze and determine valid conclusions.

4. **Connections:** Students relate concepts and procedures from different topics in mathematics to one another and make connections between topics in mathematics and other disciplines.

5. **Representations:** Students use a variety of representations, including graphical, numerical, algebraic, verbal, and physical, to represent, describe, and generalize. They recognize representation as both a process and a product.

The Common Core State Standards have eight **Standards for Mathematical Practice** (SMPs), which also describe the habits of mind students should develop as they do mathematics (National Governors Association Center for Best Practices & Council of Chief State School Officers, 2010). The SMPs listed below are the same across all grade levels.

1. **Make sense of problems and persevere in solving them.** Students work to understand the information given in a problem and the question that is asked. They use a strategy to find a solution and check to make sure their answer makes sense. As third-, fourth-, and fifth-grade students work to make sense of multiplication and division, problem solving helps them develop conceptual understanding. This is also true with the focus on fractions in these grades.

2. **Reason abstractly and quantitatively.** Students make sense of quantities and their relationships in problem situations. They develop operation sense by associating context to numbers. Reasoning in problem situations using concrete materials helps students understand the meaning of multiplication and division and build a foundation for work with fractions.

3. **Construct viable arguments and critique the reasoning of others.** Students in Grades 3 through 5 explain their thinking, justify, and communicate their conclusions both orally and in writing. Mathematical discussions should be a common expectation in mathematics lessons. Explaining thinking and listening to each other's thinking helps develop deeper conceptual understanding.

4. **Model with mathematics.** Students use representations, models, and symbols to connect conceptual understanding to skills and applications. They may also represent or connect what they are learning to real-world problems.

5. **Use appropriate tools strategically.** Students in Grades 3 through 5 use a variety of concrete materials and tools, such as counters, tiles, cubes, rubber bands, and physical number lines, to represent their

LI and SC

Purpose

Tasks

Materials

Student Thinking

Lesson Structures

Form. Assess.

Lesson Launch

Lesson Facilitation

Closure

thinking when solving problems. Representations such as making equal groups, arrays, and area models help students make connections between multiplication and division as well as the importance of place value in understanding these operations. Bar models, area models, and the number line help students understand fraction concepts.

6. **Attend to precision.** Students learn to communicate precisely with each other and explain their thinking using appropriate mathematical vocabulary. Students in Grades 3 through 5 expand their knowledge of mathematical symbols, which should explicitly connect to vocabulary development.

7. **Look for and make use of structure.** Students discover patterns and structure in their mathematics work. For example, students begin their work using unit fractions, which helps them learn the meaning of numerator and denominator. They extend understanding of unit fractions to other common fractions as they develop a sense of equivalence, addition, and subtraction of all fractions, including mixed numbers. The relationship between multiplication and division of whole numbers extends to work with fractions.

8. **Look for and express regularity in repeated reasoning.** Learners notice repeated calculations and begin to make generalizations. By recognizing what happens when multiplying tens or hundreds, students extend that understanding to more difficult problems. This standard mentions shortcuts. However, shortcuts are only appropriate when students discover them by making generalizations on their own and understand why they work.

The SMPs are not intended to be taught in isolation. Instead, you should integrate them into daily lessons because they are fundamental to thinking and developing mathematical understanding. As you plan lessons, determine how students use the practices in learning and doing mathematics.

Both sets of standards overlap in the habits of mind that mathematics educators need to develop in their students. These processes describe practices that are important in mathematics. Not every practice is evident in every lesson. Some lessons/topics lend themselves to certain practices better than others. For instance, you might use **classroom discourse** to teach geometry.

> Example: Manny
>
> Manny, a fourth-grade teacher, engages his students in geometry to construct viable arguments and critique the reasoning of others.
>
> Manny: What is this shape?
>
>
>
> Billy: It is a box.
>
> Manny: Why do you call it a box?
>
> Billy: Because you can put things in it.
>
> Mario: Yes, but we learned that box is not a math word. It is a square.
>
> Manny: Why do you think it is a square?
>
> Mario: Because it has four angles *(as Mario points to the four angles on the front face of the shape).*
>
> Manny: Does everyone agree with Mario's reasoning?
>
> Rosa: I don't. I think it is a cube. Mario said it has four angles but that is just the front flat square. *(Rosa places her hand over the front face to make her point.)* This has other faces. It is three-dimensional and squares are only two dimensions.

Through classroom discourse, Manny asked carefully selected questions to have his students engage in constructing viable arguments and critiquing the reasoning of the others. He did not point out his students' misconceptions. He let them critique each other's reasoning. This is an example of how content can be taught through important mathematical practices.

> **Think about the process standards/mathematical practices included in your state standards. Select one and reflect on how you weave it into your lessons.**
>
> _____
> _____
> _____
> _____
> _____
> _____
> _____
> _____
> _____
> _____
> _____
> _____
> _____
> _____
> _____
> _____
> _____
> _____
> _____
> _____
> _____
> _____

It is important to note that the decision to start with a big idea, essential question, or standard is up to you. Some districts have **pacing guides,** which dictate the order in which the standards must be taught. In that case, you need to do the following:

- Look at your standards and decide which big ideas it covers.
- Identify the common thread or essential question you want to weave through your lessons on this big idea.

If your district does not have a pacing guide, you may first want to select a big idea to teach and then select the state standards you will cover in the lessons.

Standards

LI and SC

Purpose

Tasks

Materials

Student Thinking

Lesson Structures

Form. Assess.

Lesson Launch

Lesson Facilitation

Closure

Building Unit Coherence

One of the best ways to build coherence between and among lessons within your unit is through the big ideas, essential questions, and standards. Keep in mind that connecting individual lessons through these three main elements promotes in-depth conceptual understanding, supports coherence, and unifies individual lessons. A big part of creating a coherent unit is strategically deciding how these three elements will be connected. Consider mapping the three components for the entire unit as you develop the lesson plan (Figure 3.1).

Figure 3.1

Unit-Planning Template

Unit Topic:

Unit Standards	Unit Big Ideas	Unit Essential Questions

 Download the Unit-Planning Template from resources.corwin.com/mathlessonplanning/3-5

LI and SC

Purpose

Tasks

Materials

Student Thinking

Lesson Structures

Form. Assess.

Lesson Launch

Lesson Facilitation

Closure

Third-Grade Snapshot

Big Ideas, Essential Questions, and Standards

The third-grade team, Saida, Julian, and Kimi, are beginning to write their lessons on comparing fractions. After discussing the ups and downs of last year's teaching, they decided to write an essential question to avoid the misconception that when fractions use different numbers in the numerator and denominator, the fractions can represent a different amount. They decide to focus the lessons on the big idea that fractions with different numerators or denominators can represent the same part of a whole.

Big Idea(s):

Fractions with different numerators or different denominators can represent the same part of a whole.

Essential Question(s):

How do we know when two fractions are equivalent?

Content Standard(s):

Compare two fractions with the same numerator or denominator by reasoning about their size. Recognize that comparisons are valid only when the two fractions refer to the same whole.

Mathematical Practice or Process Standards:

Construct viable arguments and critique the reasoning of others.

Make sense of problems and persevere in solving them.

See the complete lesson plan in Appendix A on page 186.

What kinds of essential questions can you ask that encompass big ideas in your class? Record some of your responses below.

Fourth-grade teachers Adrienne and Davante are developing a unit on comparing fractions. Adrienne notices that in third grade, their students learned how to compare fractions with same numerators or same denominators. This year, the standard highlights comparing fractions that have different numerators and denominators. Davante suggests building on last year's standard with an essential question that ties both years' standards together. They decide to focus on the essential question: How do we compare fractions?

Big Idea(s):

Fractions with different numerators and denominators can represent the same part of a whole.

Essential Question(s):

How do we know when two fractions are equivalent?

Content Standard(s):

Explain why a fraction $\frac{a}{b}$ is equivalent to a fraction $\frac{(n \times a)}{(n \times b)}$ by using visual fraction models, with attention to how the number and size of the parts differ even though the two fractions themselves are the same size. Use this principle to recognize and generate equivalent fractions.

Mathematical Practice or Process Standards:

Model with mathematics.

Look and make use of structure.

See the complete lesson plan in Appendix A on page 191.

What kinds of essential questions can you ask that encompass big ideas in your class? Record some of your responses below.

_____

_____

_____

_____

_____

_____

_____

_____

_____

Big Ideas, Essential Questions, and Standards

Boton, Chelsea, and Rodrigo discuss the essential question for the multiplication of fractions standard. Rodrigo states, "I think the big idea behind multiplication of fractions could be incorporated into the essential question. What do you both think?" Boton adds, "I like the idea of asking an open-ended question for our essential question." Chelsea offers, "How about, 'What does it mean to multiply fractions?'"

Big Idea(s):

Multiplication with fractions is similar to multiplication with whole numbers. Students grapple with similarities and differences between multiplication of whole numbers and fractions.

Essential Question(s):

What does it mean to multiply fractions?

Content Standard(s):

Apply and extend previous understandings of multiplication to multiply a fraction or whole number by a fraction.

a. Interpret the product $\left(\frac{a}{b}\right) \times q$ as a parts of a partition of q into b equal parts; equivalently, as the result of a sequence of operations $a \times q \div b$. For example, use a visual fraction model to show $\left(\frac{2}{3}\right) \times 4 = \frac{8}{3}$, and create a story context for this equation. Do the same with $\left(\frac{2}{3}\right) \times \left(\frac{4}{5}\right) = \frac{8}{15}$. (In general, $\left(\frac{a}{b}\right) \times \left(\frac{c}{d}\right) = \frac{ac}{bd}$.)

b. Find the area of a rectangle with fractional side lengths by tiling it with unit squares of the appropriate unit fraction side lengths, and show that the area is the same as would be found by multiplying the side lengths. Multiply fractional side lengths to find areas of rectangles, and represent fraction products as rectangular areas.

Mathematical Practice or Process Standard(s):

Students make sense of problems and persevere while solving them.

Students construct viable arguments and critique the reasoning of others.

See the complete lesson plan in Appendix A on page 195.

 Are there other topics in your grade level that could be guided by an essential question? Give some examples below.

_____

_____

_____

_____

Now it is your turn! You need to decide what big idea, essential question, and standards you want to build a lesson around. Start with your big idea and then identify the remaining elements.

Big Idea(s):

Essential Question(s):

Content Standard(s):

Mathematical Practice or Process Standards:

Download the full Lesson-Planning Template from resources.corwin.com/mathlessonplanning/3-5
Remember that you can use the online version of the lesson plan template to begin compiling each section into the full template as your lesson plan grows.

CHAPTER 4

REINFORCING YOUR PLAN
Learning Intentions and Success Criteria

Johanna, a fifth-grade teacher, felt her throat clench as she stood up to share her opinion. The entire staff at Roosevelt Elementary had gathered together to brainstorm and decide upon goals for the following school year. Teachers had worked all morning deciding upon the language arts goals, and they were starting to get tired. She had been thinking about her idea for a school-wide mathematics focus since a very awkward moment occurred in her classroom over two months ago. She just didn't know if she had the guts to tell the entire school. She looked at the expectant faces, took a deep breath, and began.

> I know that we have been posting objectives for years. I know that most of us also have the kids repeat or read the objective, too. Two months ago, I posted an operations and algebraic standard and read it to the students at the beginning of the lesson. Usually, they just stare at me and we move on. The standard said something like "use brackets or braces in numerical expressions, and evaluate these expressions with symbols."
>
> On this day, Rita raised her hand and said, "What does that mean?" At first I said, "Well, you will find out when we do the lesson." But you know Rita; she wasn't satisfied with that answer. I ended up launching into this whole explanation about how they would evaluate expressions with and without parentheses and they would discover what happens to the value of the expressions when parentheses or brackets are used.
>
> Rita raised her hand again and said, "Why can't you just say that?"

The teachers erupted in laughter, agreeing that elementary students have a special way of making an obvious point for adults. Rita continued,

> About a week later, I ran across a blog about John Hattie's work, specifically regarding the importance of developing learning intentions and success criteria that students can understand. I think this is something

we should explore. It just doesn't make sense to me that we are using learning objectives that our kiddos don't understand. Hattie's point is that students need to know what they are going to do and what success looks like. I was thinking about it with our staff meeting today. Right at the start, Julia [the principal] told us what she wanted us to do and what we needed to accomplish before we left. Imagine if we didn't know the purpose of the meeting or what she needed from us before we left. We would be all over the place!

Again, the teachers laughed. One of Leah's colleagues, Jason, said,

> This seems so obvious! Let's think about how we can rewrite our objectives in kid-friendly language, and let's be sure to share them more deliberately in every lesson.

Just as builders decide on the impact of structural changes, upgrades, and the timeline for completion, they must also envision how each of these decisions will affect the completed house. Just as builders need short- and long-term goals, teachers and students need specific learning intentions, or learning goals, that describe what you want the students to know, understand, and be able to do as a result of the learning experiences (Hattie et al., 2016). This chapter will explore the following questions:

- What are learning intentions?
- What are mathematics learning intentions?
- What are language and social learning intentions?
- How do you communicate learning intentions with students?
- What are success criteria?
- How do learning intentions connect to the success criteria?
- When should learning intentions and success criteria be shared with students?

WHAT ARE LEARNING INTENTIONS?

You begin the lesson-planning process by identifying the **learning intention.** The learning intention is "a statement of what students are expected to learn from the lesson" (Hattie et al., 2016). The learning intention serves two purposes. First, it informs your design of the learning experience by focusing you and students on deep learning rather than on completing activities. Second, it provides clarity to your students about their goal for the lesson. When students know the learning intention, they are more likely to focus on the lesson and take ownership for learning (Hattie et al., 2016). To ensure that the learning is rich and purposeful, students need to be active participants in discussing and understanding how the mathematics task or activity connects to the learning intention. Teachers design mathematics, language, and social learning intentions.

WHAT ARE MATHEMATICS LEARNING INTENTIONS?

Mathematics learning intentions are aligned to the content standards. They focus on mathematics knowledge, skills, and/or concepts. The National Council of Teachers of Mathematics' (NCTM's) (2014b) *Principles to Action: Ensuring Mathematical Success for All* identifies the importance of mathematics learning intentions in the first Exemplary Teaching Practice:

> Establish mathematics goals to focus learning. Effective teaching of mathematics establishes clear goals for the mathematics that students are learning, situates goals within learning progressions, and uses the goals to guide instructional decisions. (p. 10)

The mathematics learning intention is not a restatement of the standard. Rather, it is a scaffolded, student-friendly statement that reflects the part of the standard you are currently teaching. To design a mathematics learning intention, first begin with the standard and then construct one or more learning intentions using student-friendly language written from the students' point of view (see Figure 4.1).

Figure 4.1

Standard	Mathematics Learning Intention
Explain patterns in the number of zeros of the product when multiplying a number by powers of 10, and explain patterns in the placement of the decimal point when a decimal is multiplied or divided by a power of 10. Use whole-number exponents to denote powers of 10.	I can explain a power of ten. I can explain the pattern of zeros when I multiply a number by a power of ten. I can explain the decimal point patterns when I multiply or divide a decimal by a power of ten. I can use exponents to represent powers of ten.

You can also connect prior knowledge to mathematics learning intentions as you prompt students to share and talk about what they have already learned and how this connects to what they will be learning next. Some elementary teachers prompt students to ask questions and pose "wonders" about what they will be learning on a Mathematics Wonder Wall (Figure 4.2), activating students' prior knowledge and creating curiosity about new learning.

Standards

LI and SC

Purpose

Tasks

Materials

Student Thinking

Lesson Structures

Form. Assess.

Lesson Launch

Lesson Facilitation

Closure

Figure 4.2

I Wonder …

How small is a decimal?

Is there a pattern in decimals?

How can $\frac{1}{2} = \frac{2}{4}$ when the numbers are different?

How many hundreds are in a billion?

WHAT ARE LANGUAGE AND SOCIAL LEARNING INTENTIONS?

Language Learning Intentions

Language learning intentions connect to the Standards for Mathematical Practice (National Governors Association Center for Best Practices & Council of Chief State School Officers, 2010), state process standards, and mathematical vocabulary. Students are expected to develop and defend mathematical arguments, understand and explain their reasoning, and critique each other's reasoning.

When you create language learning intentions in addition to the mathematics content learning intentions, you help your students develop and use rich mathematics vocabulary (Hattie et al., 2016). Elementary students need to use new mathematics vocabulary often so it can be learned, integrated, and applied. Furthermore, English Language Learners are better supported with additional opportunities to speak about mathematics.

One way you can prompt language opportunities is to encourage your students to explain and justify their thinking. By providing specific language intentions, you create expectations for all of your students for using mathematical language in your classroom. You can develop the language learning intentions for the unit and then revisit them daily as they align to the mathematics learning intentions (Figure 4.3).

Figure 4.3

Standard	Mathematics Learning Intentions	Language Learning Intentions
Draw a scaled picture graph and a scaled bar graph to represent a data set with several categories.	We are learning that • Data can be represented by drawing picture graphs on a scale • Data can be represented by drawing a bar graph on a scale	We are learning to • Describe, compare, and explain data on picture and bar graphs • Use mathematical words like *picture graph*, *bar graph*, and *scale*

Social Learning Intentions

Social learning intentions also connect to the Standards for Mathematical Practice (National Governors Association Center for Best Practices & Council of Chief State School Officers, 2010) and state process standards. Social learning intentions focus on particular social skills that students need to exhibit as they work together to collaboratively solve problems and communicate their thinking. Elementary students naturally construct learning through play, collaboration, and problem solving in formal and informal settings. Since learning is socially constructed through communication and collaboration with others (Vygotsky, 1978), you can tailor these social learning intentions to reflect what your students need. For instance, you can construct your social learning intentions to highlight the social skills your students need so they can work together to solve problems (Hattie et al., 2016). As with the language learning intentions, you can develop social learning intentions for the unit and specify the particular intentions you want students to work toward.

Example: Anzetta

Anzetta, a fourth-grade teacher, has been steadily working on helping her fourth graders solve problems in cooperative problem-solving groups. She decides to include four social learning intentions (Hattie et al., 2016) to target her fourth graders' listening skills (see Figure 4.4).

Figure 4.4

Learning Intentions for Cooperative Group Problem Solving

We are learning to:

- Listen when others are speaking.
- Look at our group members when they are speaking.
- Ask a question about what our group members shared with us.
- Summarize what we heard our group members say.

Example: Barbara

Barbara is one of many teachers responsible for integrating the Standards for Mathematical Practice (National Governors Association Center for Best Practices & Council of Chief State School Officers, 2010) and other state process standards that ask students to "construct viable arguments and critique the reasoning of others" (paragraph 3). To address this, she regularly arranges her third graders in pairs to help solve a "debate" between two fictitious students who cannot agree on a mathematical solution (Figure 4.5).

Figure 4.5

Who wins the debate?

Teddy and Tyree both have $\frac{1}{2}$ of a candy bar. Teddy says that they both have one half of a candy bar so they must have the same amount. Tyree says that his one half is definitely bigger than Teddy's one half. Explain Teddy's and Tyree's reasoning. How can they each be right? How can Teddy or Tyree be wrong? Be prepared to present your thinking to another pair of students.

Barbara's students must work together to understand the reasoning presented by the students in the example, explain their own reasoning to each other, come to an agreed-upon decision, and present their solution to another pair of students. Without such clear social and language learning intentions, the students might become confused about Barbara's expectation for this learning activity and miss out on important learning.

HOW DO YOU COMMUNICATE LEARNING INTENTIONS WITH STUDENTS?

As you think about how to share learning intentions with your students, consider the way in which you communicate how the learning intentions reflect your beliefs about your students. By using positive and accessible language to frame what the students will learn, you can use learning intentions "as a means for building positive relationships with students" (Hattie et al., 2016, p. 48).

Consider two ways in which you might discuss the following place value standard and learning intentions.

Standard: Fluently add and subtract within 1000 using strategies and algorithms based on place value, properties of operations, and/or the relationship between addition and subtraction.

Learning Intentions: We are learning to:

- Use place value strategies to add and subtract.
- Use place value algorithms to add and subtract.
- Use properties of operations to add and subtract.
- Use what we know about relationship between addition and subtraction to add and subtract.

Now look at Figure 4.6. Which dialogue would you use to convey the intentions to students?

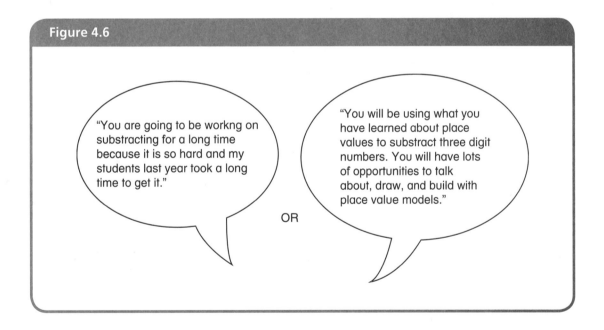

Figure 4.6

"You are going to be workng on substracting for a long time because it is so hard and my students last year took a long time to get it."

OR

"You will be using what you have learned about place values to substract three digit numbers. You will have lots of opportunities to talk about, draw, and build with place value models."

You can develop and post the language and social learning intentions for a series of lessons or the unit. Some teachers like to post the language and social learning intentions as they introduce the unit to the students. It can be particularly beneficial to focus on these learning intentions at the beginning of the year as you develop students' collaborative problem-solving and communication skills.

Standards

LI and SC

Purpose

Tasks

Materials

Student Thinking

Lesson Structures

Form. Assess.

Lesson Launch

Lesson Facilitation

Closure

How does the way in which you communicate learning intentions support a positive environment for learning mathematics? Are there particular topics in your grade level that invite more positive discussions with students? Record some of your thoughts on this topic below.

_____

_____

_____

_____

WHAT ARE SUCCESS CRITERIA?

Students also need to know how to tell when they have learned the mathematics. While learning intentions provide the purpose of the learning, the **success criteria** describe what the learning looks like when students understand and can do the mathematics they are learning. Clear success criteria can increase learner motivation because students know when they have learned and do not need to rely on a sticker, smiley face, or checkmark to tell them. Success criteria also prompt deeper, more meaningful learning because teachers can make sure that the success criteria mirror the learning intentions and their students' learning needs. While all students are guided by the same learning intentions, you can differentiate the success criteria to match your learners (Wiliam, 2011).

HOW DO LEARNING INTENTIONS CONNECT TO THE SUCCESS CRITERIA?

It is also critical for you to include the students in understanding, monitoring, and celebrating achievement of the success criteria. Hattie and Yates (2013) identify five learning components that are valuable to determining learning intentions and success criteria. These include the following:

1. *Challenge.* Teachers must construct learning experiences that appropriately mix what students know with what they do not know.

2. *Commitment.* Teachers should also develop lessons that engage students' commitment to the learning.

3. *Confidence.* Students and teachers need to have confidence that the students will be able to learn the material. Confidence can be generated from the students' prior learning experiences, the teacher's skill in listening and providing targeted feedback, the selection of appropriate lesson tasks, and appropriate peer feedback.

4. *High expectations.* Teachers need to have high expectations for all students and believe that they can and will learn.

5. *Conceptual understanding.* Students need to be able to develop rich understanding of mathematics content.

As with learning intentions, as you write success criteria, be sure to use student-friendly language that focuses specifically on indicators of success.

Example: Rodrigo

When Rodrigo writes success criteria for his fifth graders, he uses the same success criteria stem ("I know I am successful when I can ...") to purposely trigger students' ownership. He also revisits the same success criteria in individual progress conferences with students. During these conferences, he first focuses the students on the successes they have achieved. Then he identifies one or two criteria they have not *yet* achieved. Rodrigo emphasizes the word *yet* to help his students understand that they are on their way. Together, Rodrigo and his students determine strategies for improvement.

WHEN SHOULD LEARNING INTENTIONS AND SUCCESS CRITERIA BE SHARED WITH STUDENTS?

Your decisions about when to share the learning intentions and success criteria with your students should depend solely on the purpose of your lesson. If you are presenting a problem or task for students to investigate because you want them to explore mathematics concepts first, then you can withhold the mathematics learning intention until later in the lesson. Once the mathematics learning intention is revealed, you can and should refer to the learning intention throughout the lesson.

Example: Emily

Emily, a third-grade teacher, posts the mathematics learning intention for problem-solving lessons but keeps it covered up until the point in the lesson when students begin to develop conceptual understanding and make connections. When her students see that a new learning intention has been posted and covered up, they get very excited because they know they will be exploring and problem solving. In a very strategic way, Emily is communicating to the students that they are expected to solve the problem using multiple solutions, representations, and explanations. Once you have revealed the mathematics learning intention, you can and should refer to the learning intention throughout the lesson.

How can you communicate success criteria with your students? Record a few of your ideas below.

Purpose

Tasks

Materials

Student Thinking

Lesson Structures

Form. Assess.

Lesson Launch

Lesson Facilitation

Closure

The focus on learning intentions and success criteria provides another good way to construct coherence across your lesson plans. Many of your learning intentions, particularly the language and social learning intentions, will be reflected over a longer time period, making this an ideal way to support coherence across your unit plan. As you design your lesson, keep a running list of those learning intentions and success criteria that students accomplish throughout the unit. Many teachers post the success criteria for the entire unit to help students see and understand what they are working toward.

Example: Christina

Christina, a fourth-grade teacher, uses a system of stars to signal to the students what they have achieved and an arrow to indicate the current success criteria (Figure 4.7). This approach creates a coherent vision for both the teacher and her students.

Figure 4.7

Unit: Represent and interpret data

Success Criteria:

★   I can collect, organize, and sort objects into groups.

★   I can show what I have sorted on a graph.

★   I can put labels and title on my graph.

⟶   I can talk about the information on a graph using math words.

Notes

Learning Intentions and Success Criteria

Saida, Julian, and Kimi are talking about their lesson on comparing fractions and want their students to uncover the concepts. Julian says, "You know, having the students talk about the ideas will really help them figure out how fractions compare." Saida pipes in, "And if they are talking to one another we can encourage the use of the words *numerator* and *denominator!*" Kimi adds, "Sounds like we have some good learning intentions here. Let's write them down so we don't forget!"

Learning Intention(s):
Mathematical Learning Intentions

We are learning to:
- Compare fractions when the numerators are the same
- Compare fractions when the denominators are the same
- Know that sometimes fractions are equivalent
- Know that to compare fractions, they must come from the same whole

Language Learning Intentions

We are learning to:
- Explain how fractions compare using the words numerator, denominator, and equivalent

Social Learning Intentions

We are learning to:
- Listen to each other's explanations about fraction comparisons
- Ask questions about other students' thinking
- Politely challenge or disagree with explanations
- Stick to a problem to solve it

Success Criteria
(written in student voice):

I know that I am successful when I can:
- Determine which fraction is greater than another
- Determine if two fractions are equivalent
- Talk about fractions using the words numerator, denominator, and equivalent correctly
- Listen to my classmates' explanations about fractions
- Politely offer a different way of thinking about comparing fractions
- Stick to a problem to solve it

See the complete lesson plan in Appendix A on page 186.

How could you communicate learning intentions and success criteria with your students? Record some of your ideas below.

_____

_____

_____

_____

_____

Standards

LI and SC

Purpose

Tasks

Materials

Student Thinking

Lesson Structures

Form. Assess.

Lesson Launch

Lesson Facilitation

Closure

Adrienne and Davante are discussing their success criteria. They feel very strongly that students should know when they have achieved the objectives. Adrienne says, "Last year we wrote our success criteria and let the students know what they were but I don't feel like we really made use of them throughout our teaching." Davante responded, "I know what you mean. It is like we talked about them and then forgot we had them. How about we post them this year at the start of our unit? Since our social learning intentions are similar for several topics, it will help us stay focused and let students see some continuity." Adrienne agrees, "Let's try it!"

Learning Intention(s):

Mathematical Learning Intentions

We are learning to:

- Use a model to demonstrate how two fractions are equivalent
- Create fractions that are equivalent to another fraction

Language Learning Intentions

We are learning to:

- Explain why two fractions are equivalent using the words for the parts of the fraction (numerator, denominator)

Social Learning Intentions

We are learning to:

- Listen to each other's explanations about equivalence
- Ask questions about other students' thinking
- Politely challenge or disagree with explanations
- Apply my reasoning about equivalence to different kinds of fraction models

Success Criteria (written in student voice):

I know I am successful when I can:

- Show equivalent fractions with models
- Recognize that two fractions are equivalent
- Find a fraction that is equivalent to another fraction
- Use the correct words to describe why two fractions are equivalent
- Participate in a class discussion about equivalent fractions
- Use the rules I found for equivalent fractions with several different models

See the complete lesson plan in Appendix A on page 191.

How could you communicate learning intentions and success criteria with your families? Briefly write some ideas below.

_____

_____

_____

_____

_____

Fifth-Grade Snapshot

Learning Intentions and Success Criteria

LI and SC

Purpose

Tasks

Materials

Student Thinking

Lesson Structures

Form. Assess.

Lesson Launch

Lesson Facilitation

Closure

Fifth-grade teachers Boton, Chelsea, and Rodrigo have always posted mathematical learning intentions. Boton asks, "I think we should add some learning intentions and success criteria that include the Standards for Mathematical Practice (National Governors Association Center for Best Practices & Council of Chief State School Officers, 2010) that we want students to exhibit while learning mathematics." Chelsea responds, "Yes, let's do this! I think this will also help the students understand what we want to see them exhibit as they learn the mathematics." Rodrigo agrees, "I know that thinking about the success criteria for the Standards for Mathematical Practice will help us think about how we will frame our **instructional decisions** to align with these learning intentions and success criteria. This will also help the students think about how they can be successful!" Take a look at this team's work for this specific content standard.

Learning Intention(s):

Mathematical Learning Intentions

We are learning to:

- Multiply a fraction by a fraction
- Multiply fractional side lengths to find areas of rectangles

Language Learning Intentions

We are learning to:

- Explain what happens to the product when multiplying fractions

Social Learning Intentions

We are learning to:

- Listen to each other's explanations and provide feedback
- Ask questions about other students' thinking
- Politely challenge or disagree with explanations
- Apply my reasoning about multiplication of fractions to other situations

Success Criteria (written in student voice):

I know I am successful when I can:

- Use a model to show multiplication of fractions
- Use a model to multiply fractional side lengths to find the area
- Use mathematics vocabulary to explain my reasoning
- Convince others of my thinking
- Work with my classmates to solve mathematics problems
- Communicate with others to solve mathematics problems
- Create and use a representation to explain my thinking to others

See the complete lesson plan in Appendix A on page 195.

 Consider the process standards that you are required to use. How could you communicate the success criteria to your students? Write some of your ideas below.

_____

_____

_____

Your turn! Construct learning intentions and success criteria for the standard you previously identified.

Learning Intentions (mathematical/language/social):	Success Criteria (written in student voice):

Download the full Lesson-Planning Template from resources.corwin.com/mathlessonplanning/3-5
Remember that you can use the online version of the lesson plan template to begin compiling each section into the full template as your lesson plan grows.

CHAPTER 5

DECIDING ON PURPOSE
Why Are You Building This Lesson?

"They got it!" fifth-grade teacher Brian yelled as he burst into the team planning room. His teammates, Moira and Jeanine, looked at each other and smiled.

"Got what, Brian?" Moira prodded.

"I was just about to give up and move on with my mathematics group, and everything clicked today! I decided I needed to give my students a reason for multiplying fractions. We have done a lot of work with fraction circles, but they seemed to be doing it mechanically and not really understanding how when you multiply by a fraction less than one, the answer gets smaller. So, today, I taught a pretty meaty task where they had to 'package' candy. I gave them a customer order and asked them to figure out how many candy bars they would need to fill an order for $\frac{3}{8}$ of a box when each box holds 24 candy bars. It was so exciting! You know Jeremy?"

Moira and Jeanine nodded and looked at each other, unsure of what Brian would say. They had all been worried about Jeremy because he was so reserved and seemed to consistently struggle with conceptual understanding. Brian spent a fair amount of time working with him individually.

"Well, first, he was engaged the whole time! Then at the end of the lesson, Jeremy said, 'I just noticed that when I multiplied by $\frac{3}{8}$ to the boxes of candy, I had less candy bars! When you multiply by a small fraction, your answer is small. They could not be ordering more than 24 bars!'"

Brian grinned. "I am just so excited that I did this lesson today!"

Writing a series of learning intentions and success criteria from your standards is only the beginning of lesson planning. Your learning intentions inform the *purpose* of each lesson. As mentioned in Chapter 2, there are three types of mathematics lessons organized by purpose: conceptual understanding lessons, lessons that bring about procedural fluency, and transfer lessons. Think of each of these as a room in the house you are building. Just as each room in a house has a different purpose (e.g., a kitchen is built for food preparation), each lesson should have a purpose (e.g., a transfer lesson is designed to let students pull together and apply the previous learning).

This chapter will focus on answers to the following questions:

- What is the role of a conceptual understanding lesson?
- What is procedural fluency and how does it build from a conceptual understanding lesson?
- How do you know if you need a conceptual understanding or procedural fluency lesson?
- How do you create a transfer lesson?

The National Research Council (2001) recommends five strands of proficiency that should be integrated into the teaching and learning of mathematics. These include the following:

Conceptual understanding. Comprehension of mathematical concepts, operations, and relationships.

Procedural fluency. The skill in carrying out procedures flexibly, accurately, efficiently, and appropriately.

Strategic competence. The ability to formulate, represent, and solve mathematical problems.

Adaptive reasoning. The ability to think logically, reflect, explain, and provide justification.

Productive disposition. The inclination to see mathematics as sensible, useful, and worthwhile, coupled with a belief in diligence and one's own efficacy.

These five stands of proficiency underlie the three types of mathematics lessons: conceptual understanding, procedural fluency, and transfer.

WHAT IS THE ROLE OF A CONCEPTUAL UNDERSTANDING LESSON?

As described in Chapter 2, conceptual understanding involves comprehension of mathematical concepts, operations, and relations. In our scenario, Brian was very concerned that his students were not getting that depth of understanding about multiplying fractions. The National Assessment of Educational Progress's definition of conceptual understanding includes students demonstrating that they can recognize and generate examples of concepts using multiple representations (Braswell, Dion, Daane, & Jin, 2005). In addition, students compare and contrast concepts, operations, and relations.

Conceptual understanding lessons focus on providing opportunities for students to make sense of the mathematics they are learning. Students need an abundance of time and contexts to develop conceptual understanding. Therefore, your lessons need to provide time for students to build ideas through concrete experiences, engage in discourse about the mathematics they are learning, represent their thinking in multiple ways, and connect the concrete and pictorial **representations** to abstract ideas.

Your learning intentions, which come from your standards, help you decide if you need a conceptual lesson. For example, learning intentions that include verbs such as *understand, demonstrate, explain, relate, compose/decompose, represent,* and so forth imply that you want your students to show evidence that they can recognize, label, and generate examples of concepts. What follows are standards with their related learning intentions for Grades 3, 4, and 5 (Figures 5.1, 5.2, and 5.3) that call for a conceptual lesson along with a conceptual task.

Third-Grade Standard: Recognize area as an attribute of plane figures and understand concepts of area measurement.
- A square with side length 1 unit, called "a unit square," is said to have "one square unit" of area and can be used to measure area.
- A plane figure, which can be covered without gaps or overlaps by *n* unit squares, is said to have an area of *n* square units.

Figure 5.1

Learning Intention	Conceptual Task
We are learning that area means we measure in square units.	**How Many Ways?** 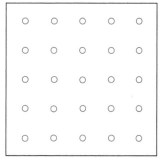 How many different shapes can you make on this geoboard with an area of 4 square units?
We are learning to estimate area using square units.	**How Many Do We Need?** Working in pairs, students receive a bucket of 1-inch square tiles. They are first asked to estimate how many square tiles will cover the top of their math book without overlaps. After they write down an agreed-upon estimate, students work to find the area of the top of their math book using the square tiles.

(Continued)

Standards

LI and SC

Purpose

Tasks

Materials

Student Thinking

Lesson Structures

Form. Assess.

Lesson Launch

Lesson Facilitation

Closure

Figure 5.1 (*Continued*)

Learning Intention

We are learning that the number of unit squares covering a plane figure is the area of the figure in square units.

Conceptual Task

What's the Area?

Working in small groups, students receive a set of pentominoes and 1-inch square graph paper. The task is to determine the area of all 12 pentomino pieces.

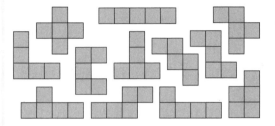

How Big Is My House?

Given a sheet of 1-inch square graph paper, draw a robot that has an area of 25 square units.

Fourth-Grade Standard: Classify two-dimensional figures based on the presence or absence of parallel or perpendicular lines, or the presence or absence of angles of a specified size. Recognize right triangles as a category.

Figure 5.2

Learning Intentions	Conceptual Tasks
We are learning to demonstrate the difference between parallel and perpendicular lines.	**Where Is It?** In the classroom, assign half the class to find parallel lines in the room. Assign the other half the task to find perpendicular lines. Once the groups share their findings, ask the groups how they know the lines are parallel and not perpendicular. **Magazine Scavenger Hunt** Using a variety of magazines, assign students the task of finding four examples of parallel and four examples of perpendicular lines. Have students cut them out of the magazine and mount on a large class-size poster divided in half—half for pictures of parallel lines and half for pictures of perpendicular lines. After completing the task, ask the class for words to add to the poster that tell how parallel is different from perpendicular.
We are learning to reason about parallel and perpendicular lines.	**What Is My Rule?** Provide each student with a geoboard. Ask them to create a four-sided figure. Walk around the room and collect the geoboards and display them in two groups. The first group should have only one set of parallel lines. The second set should have two sets of parallel lines. Ask students to work in pairs to discuss and find the rule that you used to sort the geoboard figures.

(Continued)

Standards

LI and SC

Purpose

Tasks

Materials

Student Thinking

Lesson Structures

Form. Assess.

Lesson Launch

Lesson Facilitation

Closure

Figure 5.2 (*Continued*)

Learning Intentions	Conceptual Tasks
We are learning to categorize triangles by their angles.	**Triangles Everywhere!** Create and distribute a template with 12 triangles. There should be three of each: obtuse, acute, and right. No two triangles should look alike. Ask students to cut out the triangles and sort them into categories of their choice. They can give the categories any names they wish, but students need to identify the attribute(s) they used for sorting. They should record their sort and sort again, another way. Have a final class discussion about what attributes they used to sort. Conclude that right triangles are a category of triangle.

Fifth-Grade Standard: Compare two decimals to thousandths based on meanings of the digits in each place, using >, =, and < symbols to record the results of comparisons.

Figure 5.3

Learning Intentions	Conceptual Tasks
We are learning to represent and explain the value of each digit in a decimal to thousandths.	**Make the Decimal!** Students work in pairs to roll three place value die. From the numbers they roll, they write the corresponding decimal. Then students use place value blocks to represent the decimal. Finally, students record the number and draw the blocks on a recording sheet.  Source: EAI® Education Place Value Dice. EAI Education/www.eaieducation.com

Figure 5.3 *(Continued)*

Learning Intentions	Conceptual Tasks
We are learning to compose decimals to the thousandths place.	**Who Am I?** Create one set of playing cards per three students. There should be ten cards with tenths, ten with hundredths, and ten with thousandths. Each card should follow the format: 16 hundredths, 25 tenths, 3 thousandths. Randomly select which numbers you want on the cards. Students group the cards by decimal place and put the three piles face down. Students take turns selecting one card from each pile and compose the number. For example, a student selects three cards: 3 tenths, 13 hundredths, and 14 thousandths. This represents the number 0.444.
We are learning to compare decimals to thousandths using place value.	**En Garde!** In this game, students challenge one another to find a decimal that is greater than, less than, or equal to a particular decimal value. Student A writes a decimal number in the thousandths on a sheet of paper and presents it to Student B and says "En garde! I challenge you to find a decimal greater than (or less than or equal to) this!" Student B must then write a decimal greater than the one presented and explain how he or she knows his or her number is greater. If Student B is correct, he or she wins the challenge and receives a point. If he or she is incorrect, Student A must meet his or her own challenge for a point. The students alternate roles until someone reaches 10 points.

(Continued)

Figure 5.3 *(Continued)*

Learning Intentions	Conceptual Tasks
	Whose Decimal Is Greater?
	Each pair of students needs the playing cards A to 9 (Ace represents 1) and a recording sheet.
	The first student selects a card from the pile that is face down. All students secretly enter that number on their recording sheet where they believe it should go to make the greatest decimal possible—in the tenths, hundredths, or thousandths place. Students may not change the placement of the digit once they write it on the recording sheet. The second student selects a second card, and the process of entering this digit on the recording sheet repeats. This happens one more time with the selection of a third card. Students compare their numbers to determine who made the greater decimal by explaining their reasoning for placing the digits.
	Example: Cards selected—5, 7, 2 Student A—0.725 Student B—0.752

Recording Sheet

0._ _ _   0._ _ _

0. _ _ _   0. _ _ _

WHAT IS PROCEDURAL FLUENCY, AND HOW DOES IT BUILD FROM A CONCEPTUAL UNDERSTANDING LESSON?

While conceptual knowledge is an essential foundation, procedural fluency has its own prominent place in the mathematics curriculum. For decades, there has been debate in the mathematics education community over which is more important, conceptual understanding or procedural fluency. When procedural fluency involves more than simply memorizing basic facts and performing steps to an algorithm, conceptual understanding and procedural fluency have a balanced role to play in a student's mathematics education. All students need to be flexible in their thinking and know more than one way to perform a procedure. In addition, they should be able to select the most appropriate procedure for the situation (National Research Council, 2001). Here is an example where Juan, a third grader, is able to select the most appropriate strategy for a given question.

Teacher: What is 49 plus 32?

Juan: 81.

Teacher: How did you do that so quickly?

Juan: I put 1 with 49 to make 50. Then I had 31 left. 50 and 31 is 81.

Standards

LI and SC

Purpose

Tasks

Materials

Student Thinking

Lesson Structures

Form. Assess.

Lesson Launch

Lesson Facilitation

Closure

Teacher: What is 36 + 36?

Juan: 72.

Teacher: And how did you do that?

Juan: I thought 40 plus 40 is 80. Then I subtract 8 because I put on 4 to each 36. So, the answer is 72.

Juan demonstrated that he knew two different ways to add. In each situation, he used the procedure that was more efficient. In the first example, he turned the 49 into the compatible number 50. In the second example, he added 4 to each 36 to work with numbers that ended in zeroes.

In its 2014 position statement on procedural fluency, the NCTM defined procedural fluency as "the ability to apply procedures accurately, efficiently, and flexibly; to transfer procedures to different problems and contexts; to build or modify procedures from other procedures; and to recognize when one strategy or procedure is more appropriate to apply than another" (NCTM, 2014a). This definition involves more than memorization and more than knowing when to apply a given algorithm in a particular situation. From our example, we can see that Juan was able to recognize when one strategy was more appropriate/efficient than another.

Let's consider another example. Cassidy, a fifth grader, knows that composing and decomposing numbers also applies in multiplication. Consider the following conversation between Cassidy and her fifth-grade teacher:

Teacher: What is 36 × 4?

Cassidy: 144.

Teacher: How did you know that so quickly?

Cassidy: Well, I know that four 30s are 120 and 4 × 6 is 24. So, 120 and 24 is 144.

Cassidy showed that she knew her basic facts, how to compose and decompose numbers, as well as multiply by 10. She was able to think flexibly. She demonstrated procedural fluency.

Just as your learning intentions help you decide if you should teach a conceptual understanding lesson, learning intentions also help you decide when procedural lessons are needed. In the previous example with Cassidy, the teacher's learning intention was this: *We will learn to multiply fluently.*

To develop procedural fluency, students need to experience integrating concepts and procedures. According to the mathematical teaching practices listed in *Principles to Actions: Ensuring Mathematical Success for All* (NCTM, 2014a), procedural fluency builds from conceptual understanding:

> Effective teaching of mathematics builds fluency with procedures on a foundation of conceptual understanding so that students, over time, become skillful in using procedures flexibly as they solve contextual and mathematical problems.

In Juan's example, he may not have been able to compose and decompose large numbers had he not had lessons that integrated addition and subtraction. Juan's learning experiences were rooted in conceptual understanding. He had already been introduced to the idea that numbers can be composed and decomposed. But then he had the experience integrating that understanding with addition and subtraction. Research backs up this sequencing of lessons, suggesting that once students memorize and practice a particular procedure or **algorithm,** they have little interest in learning how the procedure ties back to any concepts (Hiebert, 1999). Conceptual understanding lessons provide the foundation for flexible thinking with procedures, as in the examples with Juan and Cassidy. For this reason, conceptual understanding lessons precede procedural fluency lessons. However, it is possible that you will need to go back and forth between conceptual and procedural lessons to help students make the connections.

Effective procedural fluency lessons connect procedures with the related concepts. Representations and discourse are the mortar that binds the lessons together. For example, let's look at a procedure that students in Grade 4 would be familiar with: multiplication. One example of a procedural lesson for multiplication involves asking students to complete a worksheet of 20 two-digit by two-digit multiplication equations. A different lesson might center on the task shown in Figure 5.4.

Figure 5.4

Herbie completed a multiplication equation. Here is his work:

$$
\begin{array}{r}
27 \\
\times\ 19 \\
\hline
183 \\
270 \\
\hline
453
\end{array}
$$

Herbie made a mistake. Find the correct answer. Write Herbie a letter telling him what he did wrong and explain to him how to solve the equation correctly.

Student response:

Herbie,

You made a big mistake! What were you thinking? The answer cannot be 453. Look at the partial products. They just don't add up to what you have.

$$
\begin{array}{r}
27 \\
\times\ 19 \\
20 \times 10 = 200 \\
10 \times 7 = 70 \\
20 \times 9 = 180 \\
9 \times 7 = 63 \\
\hline
513
\end{array}
$$

The correct answer is 513. You can see that you got the 270 correct but your mistake is in the 183. It should be 243. I think you forgot to add the 60. Be careful!

In the Herbie task, the student used discourse to connect two different algorithms with what he understands about multiplication. He explained what he knows. At the same time, the teacher can be investigating any common errors/misconceptions about multiplication. Students have an opportunity to justify their procedures and practice at the same time. This practice is brief, engaging, and purposeful. **Discourse** (written or spoken) allows students to link their conceptual understanding to the procedure.

The other lesson, the worksheet of 20 equations, does not tie into students' conceptual understanding of multiplication. The lesson may be ineffective and lead to math anxiety as per the findings of Isaacs and Carroll (1999). Computational methods that are overpracticed without understanding are forgotten or remembered incorrectly. This leads to student **misconceptions** (see Chapter 8).

The 20-equation worksheet scenario is an example of a traditional drill. **Drill** and **practice** are assignments often given to students to develop their procedural fluency. Traditionally, the terms *drill* and *practice* have been used synonymously. However, there is a difference. Practice, as noted previously, should be brief, engaging, and purposeful. Practice involves spreading out tasks or experiences on the same basic idea over time. Practice allows students the opportunity to solidify the conceptual understanding as the foundation for the procedures. The Herbie problem is an example of practice; students are being asked to solidify their reasoning of the procedure for multiplication. There is only one problem as opposed to 10, 20, or more, which is characteristic of drill. Drill refers to repetitive exercises designed to improve skills or procedures already known. It is a myth that drill is a learning tool. Drill is intended to be repetitive practice of what a student already knows.

Traditional **timed tests** of basic facts are examples of anxiety-producing drills. Some people erroneously equate timed tests with fluency. However, fluency involves the flexible use and understanding of numbers and quantities. A timed test of basic facts is based on memorization. There is no flexibility in thinking required.

Research suggests that timed tests can cause **math anxiety** in children of all ability levels as early as five years old. This math anxiety can be seen in changes in the structure and workings of the child's brain (Young, Wu, & Menon, 2012), regardless of achievement levels. In fact, according to Boaler (2012), the highest achievers can have the *greatest* amount of anxiety.

Fluency is *not* something that happens all at once in a single grade. Instead, it requires teachers to pay attention to student understanding and help them develop fluency over time.

> Think of a computation lesson you have read in a textbook or other source. How does it fit (or not fit) this summary mathematical fluency? Note your answer here.
>
> _____
> _____
> _____
> _____

HOW DO YOU KNOW IF YOU NEED A CONCEPTUAL UNDERSTANDING OR PROCEDURAL FLUENCY LESSON?

Your standards and learning intentions give you direction as to whether a lesson should be for conceptual understanding or procedural fluency. Standards and learning intentions that focus on understanding mathematics call for a conceptual lesson. A few examples can be found in the table shown in Figure 5.5.

Figure 5.5

Standard	Conceptual Understanding	Procedural Fluency
Read and write decimals to thousandths.		✓
Explain patterns in the number of zeroes of a product when multiplying by powers of ten.	✓	
Understand addition and subtraction of fractions as joining and separating parts referring to the same whole.	✓	
Fluently add and subtract within 1000.		✓

Standards

LI and SC

Purpose

Tasks

Materials

Student Thinking

Lesson Structures

Form. Assess.

Lesson Launch

Lesson Facilitation

Closure

Notice that some standards easily point to a purpose because they use the words *understand* or *add*. However, other standards are not so obvious. Let's look at a standard that is not so clear:

Fluently add and subtract within 1000 using strategies and algorithms based on place value, properties of operations, and/or the relationship between addition and subtraction.

The reason this standard is not so clear is because it calls for conceptual and procedural understanding. We can unpack this standard into several learning intentions:

- We are learning to relate addition and subtraction.
- We are learning to use place value as a strategy for addition and subtraction.
- We are learning to demonstrate the properties of addition as strategies.
- We are learning to fluently add within 1000 using algorithms.
- We are learning to fluently subtract within 1000 using algorithms.

These mathematical learning intentions indicate that for students to master the standard, they must engage in conceptual understanding *and* procedural fluency lessons.

> **Look at the standards you are about to teach. Collaborate with a colleague and decide what the purpose of the lessons should be to meet those standards. Note the key points from your discussion here.**
>
> _____
> _____
> _____
> _____
> _____
> _____
> _____
> _____
> _____
> _____

How Do You Create a Transfer Lesson?

The ultimate goal of all instruction is to ensure that students are able to use what they have learned in the real world. This goal informs the third type of lesson in mathematics: transfer. While there are many different interpretations of transfer, we refer to a transfer lesson as one in which students demonstrate a transfer of learning (their ability to effectively use conceptual knowledge and procedural fluency skills in a problem situation). In Chapter 1, we discussed Hattie et al.'s (2016) definition of a transfer task as one that should encourage connections and be open-ended with multiple entry points.

So, the question you must ask yourself in planning for transfer is "What is the understanding that my students will need in the future when they are no longer in school?" This should remind you of the essential questions discussion in Chapter 3. While your conceptual understanding and procedural fluency lessons are based on your learning intentions, your transfer lessons are based on your essential questions. After all, if you don't design lessons for transfer, why design lessons at all? If people know how to use a hammer and nails, it does not mean they can build a house. Likewise, if students know how to add or subtract in school, it does not mean they can balance a checkbook as an adult.

To know if you have created a transfer lesson, use the checklist in Figure 5.6.

Standards

LI and SC

Purpose

Tasks

Materials

Student Thinking

Lesson Structures

Form. Assess.

Lesson Launch

Lesson Facilitation

Closure

Figure 5.6

Rubric for Creating a Transfer Lesson

Does the lesson allow students to	Yes or No
• Make sense of a real-world problem as opposed to a contrived word problem?	
• Persevere in solving the problem?	
• Apply mathematical reasoning?	
• Reason abstractly and quantitatively?	
• Use appropriate tools strategically?	
• Work with content of the big ideas or essential questions of the topic taught?	
• Construct viable arguments or critique the reasoning of others?	

online resources ➘ You can locate this Rubric for Creating a Transfer Lesson at resources.corwin.com/mathlessonplanning/3-5

Figure 5.7 shows examples of transfer tasks for Grades 3 to 5 based on essential questions.

Figure 5.7

Third-Grade Essential Question	Transfer Task
How does place value help you solve triple-digit addition and subtraction problems?	Joey and his study partner were working on adding 234 and 569. Joey's answer was 793. His partner's answer was 803. You are their math teacher! Using place value language, explain who has the correct answer and why.
Fourth-Grade Essential Question	**Transfer Task**
How do I use fractions in real life?	The equation is $2\frac{1}{2} \times \frac{2}{3}$. Create a real-life word problem that fits this equation.

(Continued)

Figure 5.7 *(Continued)*

Fifth-Grade Essential Question	Transfer Task
How does the type of data influence the choice of a graph?	The cafeteria manager needs your help. She needs to know what lunches your classmates prefer to eat. You plan to send her a graph of the information you collect. Here is what you discovered:

Pizza	25
Hot dogs	10
Hamburgers	20
Chicken tenders	13
Fish sticks	5
Salad	9
Grilled cheese	20
Spaghetti	15

What do you think is the best type of graph to use to send these data to your cafeteria manager? Justify your thinking.

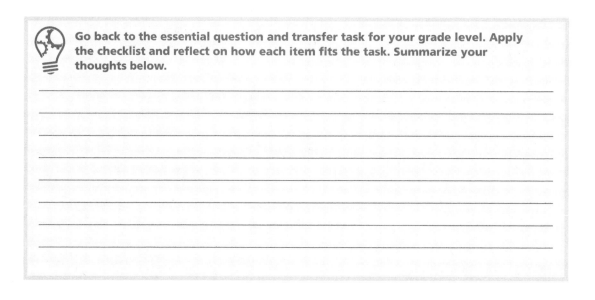

Go back to the essential question and transfer task for your grade level. Apply the checklist and reflect on how each item fits the task. Summarize your thoughts below.

_____

_____

_____

_____

_____

_____

_____

_____

Building Unit Coherence

Connecting lesson purposes across a unit develops coherence because you are strategically linking conceptual understanding, procedural fluency, and transfer lessons to build comprehensive understanding of the unit standards. As you develop a lesson, consider the purposes of the lessons that come before and after the lesson you are constructing. Over the course of one unit, you should develop and facilitate lessons with all three purposes, bearing in mind how and when the lesson purposes should be positioned within the unit based on the learning intentions and how they relate to each other. Some teachers map out their unit with lesson purposes in mind to ensure that they are developing coherence within lesson purpose (Figure 5.8).

Figure 5.8

Unit:

Day 1	Day 2	Day 3	Day 4	Day 5
Conceptual	Conceptual	Conceptual	Procedural Fluency	Procedural Fluency
Day 6	**Day 7**	**Day 8**	**Day 9**	**Day 10**
Conceptual	Conceptual	Conceptual	Procedural Fluency	Transfer

Now that you have been introduced to the three lesson purposes, reflect on the lessons in your curriculum guide, textbook, or supplemental materials. Can you categorize the lessons into these three categories? Do you notice one type being more prevalent than the others? Note any thoughts or concerns here.

_____

_____

_____

_____

_____

_____

_____

_____

_____

_____

_____

_____

Standards

LI and SC

Purpose

Tasks

Materials

Student Thinking

Lesson Structures

Form. Assess.

Lesson Launch

Lesson Facilitation

Closure

Third-grade teacher Saida begins the professional learning community meeting (PLC) by sharing the following:

"I know that we always focus on conceptual understanding with our students. I will be the first to admit that I can get sidetracked by cute ideas I see on Pinterest. Sometimes, I feel like we need to make sure that we are really, truly purposeful in our lesson planning. I just need to be reminded that the lesson purpose centers on these ideas about conceptual, procedural, and transfer learning instead of the activity."

Julian suggests that they should indicate the purpose of every lesson in their PLC planning. Kimi quickly agrees that this is a great idea. Using the suggested template, they check the conceptual understanding box after deciding in PLC that the first lesson will be one on concepts.

Purpose:

☑ Conceptual Understanding   ☐ Procedural Fluency   ☐ Transfer

---

See the complete lesson plan in Appendix A on page 186.

How do you decide on the purpose for your lessons? Write your thoughts below.

_____

_____

_____

_____

_____

_____

_____

_____

_____

_____

_____

_____

_____

_____

_____

_____

_____

_____

_____

_____

Standards

LI and SC

Purpose

Tasks

Materials

Student Thinking

Lesson Structures

Form. Assess.

Lesson Launch

Lesson Facilitation

Closure

Fourth-Grade Snapshot

Lesson Purpose

Fourth-grade teachers Adrienne and Davante look over their plans from the previous year. Davante shares, "I would like to include more transfer lessons in our planning. I think the students need more experiences applying what they learn to new situations."

Adrienne replies, "I love this idea. I think this will be really motivating for our students." They check the transfer box on their lesson-planning template and move on to discuss the lesson.

Purpose:

☐ Conceptual Understanding   ☐ Procedural Fluency   ☑ Transfer

See the complete lesson plan in Appendix A on page 191.

How do you decide on the purpose of your lessons? Write your thoughts below.

_____

_____

_____

_____

_____

_____

_____

_____

_____

_____

_____

_____

_____

_____

_____

_____

_____

_____

_____

_____

_____

Fifth-Grade Snapshot

Lesson Purpose

Boton, Chelsea, and Rodrigo are in a planning session for their fraction unit. Rodrigo says, "I want to make sure that we spend plenty of time developing conceptual understanding for this fraction unit. Although they had a lot of opportunity to develop conceptual understanding in fourth grade, it seems like whenever we introduce the procedure, the students' conceptual understanding falters a bit."

Chelsea agrees, "I want make sure we take our time with the conceptual understanding! They will learn the procedure really quickly!"

Boton says, "Yes, let's plan to teach these concepts conceptually for several days. I know that our school district pacing guide is limited, but I think we can maximize our instructional time."

Purpose:

☑ Conceptual Understanding   ☐ Procedural Fluency   ☐ Transfer

See the complete lesson plan in Appendix A on page 195.

This fifth-grade team begins with a conceptual lesson. Would there ever be a time when you might begin with a procedural fluency or transfer lesson? Why? Explain your thinking below.

_____

_____

_____

_____

_____

_____

_____

_____

_____

_____

_____

_____

_____

_____

_____

_____

_____

_____

_____

_____

Under Construction

Using the lesson plan you are designing, decide on your purpose. Remember that your purpose comes from your standards and learning intentions.

Purpose:

☐ Conceptual Understanding   ☐ Procedural Fluency   ☐ Transfer

online resources Download the full Lesson-Planning Template from resources.corwin.com/mathlessonplanning/3-5
Remember that you can use the online version of the lesson plan template to begin compiling each section into the full template as your lesson plan grows.

Notes

Standards

LI and SC

Purpose

Tasks

Materials

Student Thinking

Lesson Structures

Form. Assess.

Lesson Launch

Lesson Facilitation

Closure

CHAPTER 6

CHOOSING TASKS
The Heart of a Lesson

Third-grade teachers Marvin and James were planning out their next three lessons on fractions. They were both unenthused about what they had written so far. James finally said, "Marvin, our students are really not that engaged in this fraction unit we are doing. In fact, I'm a little bored by the tasks we have been giving them."

Marvin responded, "I feel the same way. Yet the tasks are really getting to the math we want to hit, but the situations are not engaging the students. You know, I was at the movies this weekend and while I was there I saw our students, Jessie, Mayda, and Ruby, leaving that new *Wonder Woman* movie and they were all excited, chatting away. Maybe we could do something with superheroes. They are all the rage with third graders these days."

James exclaimed, "I think you are on to something! You know, we won't even need to write new tasks. The fractions tasks in our text are mathematically rich even though they are boring.

Let's try rewriting those with a superhero theme. Do you think we can do it?"

Marvin replied, "Why not? We can at least give it a try. I am getting more enthused about these lessons already!"

A worthwhile task is the heart of a lesson. In fact, selecting the task is the most important decision teachers make that affects instruction (Lappan & Briars, 1995; Smith & Stein, 2011).

This chapter will address the following questions:

- Why are tasks important?
- What is a worthwhile task?
- How do you adapt a task?
- What are some sources for worthwhile tasks?

WHY ARE TASKS IMPORTANT?

Effective teachers understand that the **tasks** they choose influence how their students make sense of mathematics. Tasks should challenge students to explore mathematical concepts; they should not be designed simply to have children work to get the right answer. Getting students to use **higher-order thinking skills,** such as those from Bloom's Taxonomy (create, evaluate, apply, etc.), is a hallmark of a worthwhile task. As you plan your lessons, be sure to select tasks to reach this goal. Consider the following two examples.

Example 1: Jennifer

Jennifer gives her fifth-grade students this challenge:

> There are 5 prize bags on the table. Each bag has 4 pieces of candy and 3 pencils. Explain why the expression 5 × 4 + 5 × 3 describes the total number of prizes in the bags? See Figure 6.1.

Figure 6.1

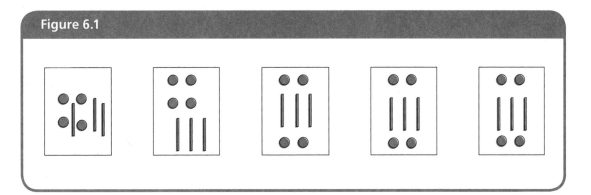

Example 2: Carlos

Carlos asks his fifth graders the following:

> Solve the following equation: 5 × 4 + 5 × 3 = ?

These two examples illustrate the types of questions that teachers ask about the distributive property. Only one is an example of a worthwhile task. The following section will identify the characteristics of a worthwhile task.

WHAT IS A WORTHWHILE TASK?

There are seven characteristics of worthwhile tasks:

1. Uses significant mathematics for the grade level
2. Rich
3. Problem solving in nature
4. Authentic/interesting

5. Equitable
6. Active
7. Connects to the Process Standards and Standards for Mathematical Practice

Let's take a look at each feature in more detail.

Uses Significant Mathematics for the Grade Level

The big ideas, essential questions, and standards from your lesson should be your guiding light for finding a worthwhile task; these three elements keep your lesson plan coherent. Tasks based on significant mathematics focus on students' understandings and skills, and they stimulate students to make sense of the mathematics they are learning. A task should take into account students' prior knowledge and the understandings and skills already taught at this grade level or previous grades.

Rich

Each task should be challenging, requiring students to use higher-order thinking skills. Smith and Stein (2011) refer to this kind of task as a **high cognitive demand** task. According to Van de Walle et al. (2016), "A high cognitive demand task is a task that requires students to engage in **productive struggle,** that challenges them to make connections to concepts and to other relevant knowledge" (p. 37). A high cognitive demand task encourages students to represent their thinking in multiple ways, explore various solution pathways, and connect procedures to mathematics. These tasks always call for some degree of higher-level thinking, and students cannot routinely solve them. Students often use multiple representations such as manipulatives or diagrams to help develop the meaning of mathematical ideas and to work through the task to develop the understanding (Smith & Stein, 2011). If students immediately know the answer, then the task was not challenging.

Problem Solving in Nature

When a task is problem solving in nature, students will not know how to immediately and routinely solve it. They will need to reason and develop a new strategy or try previously learned strategies to seek a solution. Simply applying an algorithm to arrive at the answer is not problem solving. Productive struggle is a hallmark of problem solving. This means that students wrestle with a solution strategy and must apply effort to make sense of the mathematics—to figure something out that is not obvious. The challenge may not come easy to them, but they persevere. Good problems have multiple entry points so that all students have an opportunity to learn. It is important to point out that all worthwhile tasks are problems, but not all problems are worthwhile tasks.

Authentic/Interesting

An authentic and interesting task is one that represents mathematics as a useful tool for navigating the real world. It captures students' curiosity and invites them to wonder and make conjectures. Authentic/interesting tasks prompt classroom discourse and pique student interest either through the topic or the method of engagement. This does not mean that the task must be real world. In fact, many young children are just as interested in fanciful stories that stimulate their curiosity. Think about the superheroes theme Marvin and James want to pursue from the beginning of this chapter.

Equitable

When a task is equitable, it has multiple entry points and representations so that students of all levels, abilities, and skills can access the task. NRICH (2017) from the University of Cambridge describes these kinds of tasks as having low threshold and high ceilings (LTHC), and Jo Boaler (2015) describes them as having low floors and high ceilings. Essentially, this means that when a task is equitable, "everyone in the group can begin and then work at their own level, yet the task also offers lots of possibilities for learners to do much more challenging mathematics, too" (NRICH, 2017, paragraph 6). The content can be fairly simple, but the processes and the thinking that students do are much more complex. Some students may solve a task using manipulatives or drawing pictures while others apply symbols at a more abstract level. The task is also nonbiased, meaning it does not contain information that stereotypes individuals or groups of people, and it is culturally sensitive. The teacher honors and respects all students' ideas and solutions pathways. Everyone has an opportunity to learn.

Active

With an active task, students are engaged in doing the mathematics. They are decision makers. An active task requires more than simply applying an algorithm. Students must develop reasons, offer explanations, and actively figure things out to make sense of the task and its solution.

Connects to the Process Standards and Standards for Mathematical Practice

The tasks you select should be designed to encourage students to exhibit process standards. Sometimes, teachers believe the way to challenge learners is by presenting them with higher-level content. However, this act alone does not necessarily support all students to reason, communicate mathematically, use and apply representations, see and use patterns, and recognize the underlying structure of the mathematics they are learning. By ensuring that a task incorporates opportunities for students to demonstrate the process standards, you support their learning.

To determine if a task is worthwhile for you to use in a lesson, use the rubric shown in Figure 6.2. The first column identifies the characteristic, and the next three columns allow you to rate the degree to which you feel the task has met that characteristic by checking the box, with 3 being not acceptable and 1 being a good example of that characteristic. The final column is for any comments you would like to discuss with your colleagues. Note: You may deem a task worthwhile even if you do not rate all of the characteristics as a 1. Not all worthwhile tasks will have all of the characteristics.

Figure 6.2

Determining a Worthwhile Task Rubric

Characteristic	1	2	3	Notes
Uses significant mathematics for the grade level				
Rich				
Problem solving in nature				
Authentic/interesting				
Equitable				
Active				
Connects to Standards for Mathematical Practice or Process Standards				

online resources This Determining a Worthwhile Task Rubric can be downloaded for your use at resources.corwin.com/mathlessonplanning/3-5

Thinking about Jennifer and Carlos and their tasks, rate the tasks using the checklist in Figure 6.2. Discuss your results with a colleague. Whose example is a worthwhile task and why? Note your thoughts below.

_____
_____
_____
_____
_____

In the vignette presented at the beginning of the chapter, Marvin and James wanted to develop a task that more closely aligned to their students' experiences and interests. You may also have experienced a time when you encountered a textbook or school district task that did not match the multiple needs of your learners. Like Marvin and James, many teachers choose to adapt tasks to increase the cognitive demand (Smith & Stein, 2011) and to provide more entry points for students to reason mathematically. Here are a few examples.

Example: Michaela

Michaela, a third-grade teacher, found the task in Figure 6.3 in her textbook and adapted it to incorporate the process standards.

Figure 6.3

Original Task	Adapted Task
Round 3,651 to the nearest hundred.	Leo rounded 3,651 to 3,600. Lettie rounded 3,651 to 3,700. Who rounded the number to the nearest hundred correctly? How do you know?

Example: Marty

Marty, a fourth-grade teacher, was given the task in Figure 6.4 by his school district. He wanted to design a task to provide more entry points for his students.

Figure 6.4

Original Task	Adapted Task
Margot invites three friends to her house for ice cream. She wants to give each friend $\frac{3}{4}$ cup of ice cream. How many cups of ice cream will Margot need for her friends?	Margot needs $\frac{3}{4}$ cup of ice cream for each of her three friends. She has $2\frac{1}{2}$ cups of ice cream. Will this be enough? Explain your thinking in pictures and words.

Example: Andrea

Andrea, a fifth-grade teacher, found the task in Figure 6.5 after an Internet search. She wanted a task that was more engaging than the one she found on the Internet.

Standards

LI and SC

Purpose

Tasks

Materials

Student Thinking

Lesson Structures

Form. Assess.

Lesson Launch

Lesson Facilitation

Closure

Figure 6.5

Original Task	Adapted Task
Decide if the statement is true or false. $\frac{2}{3} = \frac{6}{9}$ $\quad$ $14 = \frac{48}{4}$	Some of these equations are true and some are false. Alex says that three are true and Mariana says that four are true. Explain who is correct. $\frac{6}{8} = \frac{3}{4}$ $\qquad$ $\frac{4}{8} = \frac{8}{4}$ $\frac{4}{5} > \frac{2}{3}$ $\qquad$ $\frac{9}{8} < \frac{10}{9}$ $3\frac{3}{4} = \frac{15}{4}$ $\qquad$ $\frac{2}{6} > \frac{5}{8}$

What do you notice about how each of the teachers enhanced the task? How might you adapt your tasks to make them worthwhile? Jot a few notes below.

_____

_____

_____

_____

_____

_____

_____

_____

_____

_____

_____

_____

WHAT ARE SOME SOURCES FOR WORTHWHILE TASKS?

Tasks can be problems, short- or long-term projects, or games. In Chapter 5, we listed many tasks as they relate to learning intentions in Grades 3 through 5. Some other reliable sources for worthwhile tasks in this grade range follow.

Books

Markworth, K., McCool, J., & Kosiak, J. (2015). *Problem solving in all seasons.* Reston, VA: NCTM.

Ray-Reik, M. (2013). *Powerful problem solving: Activities for sense making with the mathematical practices.* Portsmouth, NH: Heinemann.

Schrock, C., Norris, K., Pugalee, D., Seitz, R., & Hollingshead, F. (2013). *Great tasks for mathematics, K–5.* Denver, CO: National Council of Supervisors of Mathematics.

Van de Walle, J., Karp, K., & Bay-Williams, J. (2016). *Elementary and middle school mathematics: Teaching developmentally.* New York, NY: Pearson.

Online

Graham Fletcher https://gfletchy.com/category/3-act-tasks/

Robert Kaplinsky http://robertkaplinsky.com/lessons/

Illuminations at NCTM https://illuminations.nctm.org

Illustrative Mathematics https://www.illustrativemathematics.org

Inside Mathematics, Problem of the Month http://www.insidemathematics.org/problems-of-the-month/download-problems-of-the-month

Math Forum: Primary Problems of the Week http://mathforum.org/library/problems/primary.html

Math Pickle Mathpickle.com

NRICH http://nrich.maths.org

Numberless Word Problems https://bstockus.wordpress.com/numberless-word-problems/

Open Middle: Challenging Math Problems Worth Solving (Third, Fourth, Fifth) http://www.openmiddle.com

Building Unit Coherence

Tasks are another great way to build coherence and ensure rigor throughout a unit. As you look across the unit, you can connect the tasks that you construct, select, or adapt. Some teachers do this by linking the tasks across a theme. Others do this by extending tasks over two or three days so students have plenty of time to dive into the concept.

Example: Huan

Huan, a third-grade teacher, noticed how his students were obsessed with making slime from glue. They brought him several batches to experience since he was unaware of the new fad. Capitalizing on this interest his students had, Huan decided to use slime as the topic of most of his real-world problems for his unit on fractions.

Third-Grade Snapshot

Task Selection

Saida, Julian, and Kimi are reviewing several tasks for the comparing fractions lesson. They decide they want something interactive, a task where students can apply their prior knowledge to discover new ways to use what they already know. Saida remembers playing a game called "Convince Me!" in a workshop she took over the summer. "It wasn't about fractions," she said, "but I think we can adapt it. It really made me think when I played it with place value. It was so rich. Other people in the workshop had so many different ideas. I learned so much from listening to them."

Kimi and Julian agreed. Kimi said, "Let's try it."

Task:

Convince Us!

We are going to play a game. I will put a statement on the board. With your partner, you need to convince us that what I wrote is true. You can use any materials, drawings, or reasoning that you want. We are looking for a variety of ways to convince us that the statement is true.

See the complete lesson plan in Appendix A on page 186.

 This task can be downloaded for your use at resources.corwin.com/mathlessonplanning/3-5

Why do you think this is a good third-grade task? Use the task checklist to help you decide. Write any thoughts or concerns below.

_____
_____
_____
_____
_____
_____
_____
_____
_____
_____
_____
_____
_____
_____
_____
_____
_____
_____
_____

Adrienne and Davante want a rich problem-solving task for their transfer lesson on fractions. However, they are having difficulty finding just the right one. Davante thinks aloud, "I saw one in our text last week that was OK. It was close to what we want but not exactly. We need something more open-ended."

Adrienne suggests, "Could we adapt it?"

Davante responded, "I never thought of that. Let's try!"

Task:

Carol's Cookie Corner

You are the manager of Carol's Cookie Corner. It is your busy season and almost all of your bakers are hard at work. A new order for your special Choco-oat-raisin cookies just came in and you have one baker, Sammy, who can make them. However, you only have a $\frac{1}{4}$ cup measuring cup and $\frac{1}{4}$ teaspoon handy because your other bakers are using all of your other measuring cups and spoons. Sammy needs help with fractions so you have to change all of the measures in the recipe so he can use the $\frac{1}{4}$ teaspoon and measuring cup.

You remember using a number line in school to work with fractions.

1. Rewrite all of the measures in the recipe as equivalent fractions that Sammy can use with the measurement tools you gave him.

Your business is booming and you may run out of measuring tools again. You decide to teach all of your bakers to use equivalent fractions.

2. Create a large number line on chart paper. Put the numbers from the recipe on the number line.

3. Add as many equivalent fractions as you can to the number line for each number you placed on the number line.

4. Be prepared to teach your fellow bakers about equivalent fractions. Explain in writing what you will say to them.

See the complete lesson plan in Appendix A on page 191.

 This task can be downloaded for your use at resources.corwin.com/mathlessonplanning/3-5

Why do you think this is a good fourth-grade task? Use the checklist to help you decide. Write any thoughts or concerns below.

_____

_____

_____

_____

_____

_____

_____

Fifth-Grade Snapshot

Task Selection

When the fifth-grade teachers meet to plan lessons, Chelsea shares the following:

"After our discussion about developing robust tasks, I realized that my tasks were not very robust. I would like to see how we could change some of the tasks we are using to encourage students to incorporate multiple learning intentions. I would also like the tasks to encourage the students to communicate mathematically and to develop mathematical arguments to justify their reasoning. Do you think we could set up our fraction task to do this?"

Boton agrees and says, "I think this task will also engage them in wanting to find a solution and prove they are correct."

Rodrigo exclaims, "Yes, let's do this!"

Task:

Who Ate the Most Brownies?

Twin sisters, Satthiya and Priya, each made a pan of brownies for the fifth-grade school picnic. Satthiya made chocolate chunk brownies and Priya made caramel swirl brownies. The sisters set their brownie pans on the table to cool and when they got back they noticed that someone had been eating their brownies! Satthiya's pan had only $\frac{3}{4}$ of the brownies left in the pan! Priya had $\frac{2}{3}$ of the brownies left in the pan! They had no choice but to take the brownies to the picnic and explain what happened to their teachers. After the picnic, Satthiya saw that her class had eaten $\frac{2}{3}$ of the $\frac{3}{4}$ brownies that were in the pan. Priya saw that her class had eaten $\frac{2}{4}$ of the $\frac{2}{3}$ brownies left in her pan. Now the sisters are arguing about the class that ate the most brownies! Help the sisters find out. Show a representation to prove your idea.

See the complete lesson plan in Appendix A on page 195.

 This task can be downloaded for your use at resources.corwin.com/mathlessonplanning/3-5

Why do you think this is a good fifth-grade task? Use the checklist to help you decide. Write any thoughts or concerns below.

_____

_____

_____

_____

_____

_____

_____

_____

_____

_____

_____

Under Construction

Using your lesson plan that is under construction, add a task. Be sure it follows from your previous work and matches your instructional purpose.

Task:

online resources

Download the full Lesson-Planning Template from resources.corwin.com/mathlessonplanning/3-5
Remember that you can use the online version of the lesson plan template to begin compiling each section into the full template as your lesson plan grows.

CHAPTER 7

CHOOSING MATERIALS
Representations, Manipulatives, and Other Resources

A new fifth-grade teacher, Onado, had been waiting to meet with his teammates, Evita and Anna. He could hardly contain his excitement to begin the new school year. Bulletin boards were up, and desks were organized and labeled with nametags. The classroom was ready.

Onado asked his colleagues, "What manipulatives will I have in my new classroom?"

Evita replied, "Unfortunately, we can't store the materials in our classrooms. In the past, we didn't have enough manipulatives for everyone to have them, and some people never got enough. Now we have a math supply room on the third-grade wing where we keep all of the manipulatives the school shares."

Onado then asked, "Do you have a list of all the materials in the supply closet?"

Anna replied, "I don't think I have ever seen one, although I remember that discussion coming up one time at a faculty meeting."

Evita added, "I just go down there when I am introducing a new topic and I scrounge around to find what will fit."

Onado said, "But what if we need certain things, like fraction strips? I was hoping to gather tons of different kinds of fraction material for a big fraction lesson."

Evita said, "Well, we better get up there and get what you need right now before everyone else starts collecting their manipulatives."

Resources vary. They can include anything from manipulatives, the amount of time devoted to mathematics, or your district-wide textbook. Resources can include teacher aides or special education collaborative teachers who join your class for certain lessons. Technology can vary from hardware, such as calculators, laptops, tablets, and document cameras, to software and applications. Likewise, manipulative materials can vary from school to school and from grade to grade. This chapter focuses on the resources that can help you create a rigorous and coherent set of math lessons. This chapter will answer these questions:

- What is the role of representations in mathematics lessons?

- What is a manipulative?

- How are manipulatives used?

- What are other resources?

WHAT IS THE ROLE OF REPRESENTATIONS IN MATHEMATICS LESSONS?

The Annenberg Learner Foundation (2003) offers this definition:

"Mathematical representation" refers to the wide variety of ways to capture an abstract mathematical concept or relationship. A mathematical representation may be visible, such as a number sentence, a display of manipulative materials, or a graph, but it may also be an internal way of seeing and thinking about a mathematical idea. Regardless of their form, representations can enhance students' communication, reasoning, and problem-solving abilities; help them make connections among ideas; and aid them in learning new concepts and procedures. (paragraph 2)

Since mathematical concepts are abstract, when we teach, we represent the concepts in a variety of ways. Representations can be thought of as a broad category of models. According to Van de Walle, Karp, and Bay-Williams (2016), there are seven ways to represent or model mathematical concepts:

1. Manipulatives

2. Pictures or drawings

3. Symbols

4. Language (written or spoken)

5. Real-world situations

6. Graphs

7. Tables

Selecting a representation is a vital part of your decision making while lesson planning. You must decide, "What representations will help me achieve the learning intentions of today's lesson?" Here is an example of a teacher using a representation to help students make sense of rounding.

Example: Al

When planning a lesson that involves placing fractions on a number line, Al, a third-grade teacher, told his students to place $\frac{1}{3}$ on the number line and asked, "Is $\frac{1}{3}$ closer to 0 or 1?"

Al used a number line as a representation to model the relationship of unit fractions between 0 and 1. By using this representation, students can see that $\frac{1}{3}$ is closer to 0 than 1, working toward a conceptual understanding of fractions.

The charts in Figures 7.1, 7.2, and 7.3 show examples of representations that can be used with selected standards.

Figure 7.1

Third Grade

Selected Third-Grade Standards	Representation
Explain equivalence of fractions and compare fractions by reasoning about their size.	**Fraction Strips**  **Number Line** 0 1
Understand a fraction as a number on the number line.	**Fraction Circles** 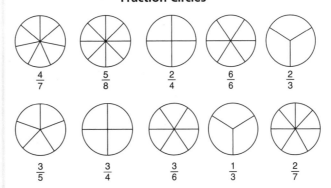
Recognize and generate simple equivalent fractions. Explain why the fractions are equivalent using a visual model.	**Two Color Counters** 

(Continued)

Standards | LI and SC | Purpose | Tasks | Materials | Student Thinking | Lesson Structures | Form. Assess. | Lesson Launch | Lesson Facilitation | Closure

Figure 7.1 (*Continued*)

Selected Third-Grade Standards	Representation
Generate measurement data by measuring length using rulers marked with halves and fourths of an inch.	**Ruler** 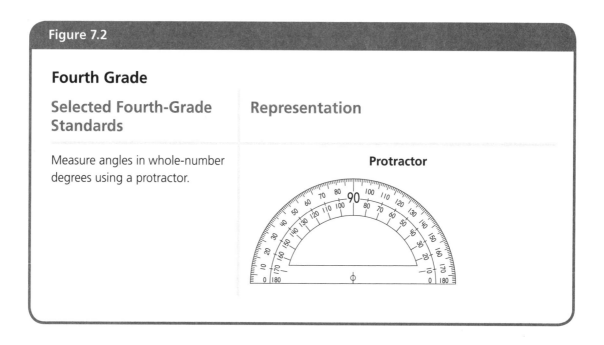
A square with side length one unit, called a unit square, is said to have one square unit of area and can be used to measure one square unit of area.	**Square Tile**
	Geoboard

Figure 7.2

Fourth Grade

Selected Fourth-Grade Standards	Representation
Measure angles in whole-number degrees using a protractor.	**Protractor**

Figure 7.2 (Continued)

Selected Fourth-Grade Standards	Representation
Determine whether a given number in the range 1 to 100 is prime or composite.	**Patterns in the Hundreds Chart** | 1	2	3	4	5	6	7	8	9	10
11	12	13	14	15	16	17	18	19	20
21	22	23	24	25	26	27	28	29	30
31	32	33	34	35	36	37	38	39	40
41	42	43	44	45	46	47	48	49	50
51	52	53	54	55	56	57	58	59	60
61	62	63	64	65	66	67	68	69	70
71	72	73	74	75	76	77	78	79	80
81	82	83	84	85	86	87	88	89	90
91	92	93	94	95	96	97	98	99	100	
Understand addition and subtraction of fractions as joining and separating parts referring to the same whole.	**Pattern Blocks** 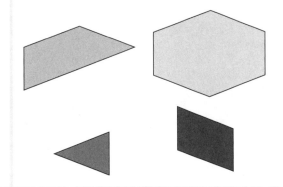
Compare two decimals by hundredths by reasoning about their size. Recognize that comparisons are only valid when the two decimals refer to the same whole.	**Base Ten Blocks** 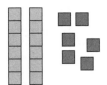

(Continued)

Figure 7.2 (*Continued*)

Selected Fourth-Grade Standards	Representation
Apply area and perimeter formulas for rectangles in real-world and mathematical problems.	**Pentominoes**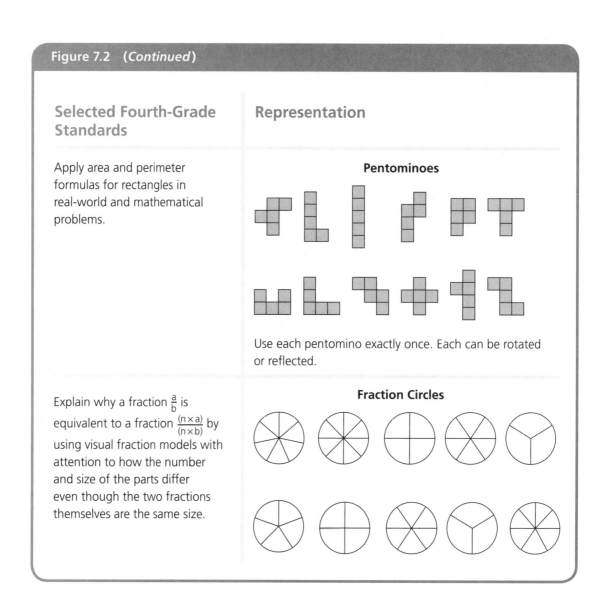Use each pentomino exactly once. Each can be rotated or reflected.
Explain why a fraction $\frac{a}{b}$ is equivalent to a fraction $\frac{(n \times a)}{(n \times b)}$ by using visual fraction models with attention to how the number and size of the parts differ even though the two fractions themselves are the same size.	**Fraction Circles**

Figure 7.3

Fifth Grade

Selected Fifth-Grade Standards	Representation
Recognize that in a multidigit number, a digit in one place represents ten times as much as it represents in the place to its right and $\frac{1}{10}$ of what it represents in its place to the left.	**Representations** Hundred thousands / Ten thousands / Thousands / Hundreds / Tens / Ones

Figure 7.3 (*Continued*)

Selected Fifth-Grade Standards	Representation
Read, write, and compare decimals to thousandths.	**Place Value Blocks**
Use place value understanding to round decimals to any place.	**Number Line** 7.0 7.1 7.2 7.3 7.4 7.5 7.6 7.7 7.8 7.9 8.0
Solve word problems involving multiplication of fractions. Use visual fraction models.	**Fraction Strips** 1 Whole; $\frac{1}{2}$; $\frac{1}{3}$; $\frac{1}{4}$; $\frac{1}{5}$; $\frac{1}{6}$; $\frac{1}{8}$; $\frac{1}{10}$; $\frac{1}{12}$ $\frac{4}{7}$ $\frac{5}{8}$ $\frac{2}{4}$ $\frac{6}{6}$ $\frac{2}{3}$ $\frac{3}{5}$ $\frac{3}{4}$ $\frac{3}{6}$ $\frac{1}{3}$ $\frac{2}{7}$

(Continued)

Standards | LI and SC | Purpose | Tasks | Materials | Student Thinking | Lesson Structures | Form. Assess. | Lesson Launch | Lesson Facilitation | Closure

Figure 7.3 (*Continued*)

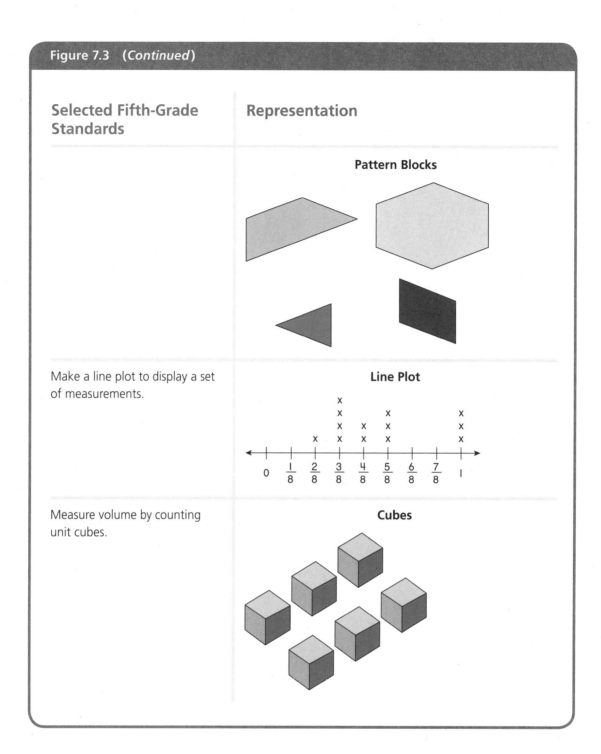

Selected Fifth-Grade Standards	Representation
	Pattern Blocks
Make a line plot to display a set of measurements.	**Line Plot**
Measure volume by counting unit cubes.	**Cubes**

WHAT IS A MANIPULATIVE?

A **manipulative** is one type of representation. Any concrete tool used to support **hands-on learning** can be considered a manipulative. Generally, manipulatives are concrete objects that students use to bring meaning to abstract mathematical ideas. Some common manipulatives used in mathematics at the intermediate level include (but are not limited to) snap cubes, pattern blocks, square tiles, GeoBlocks, and base-ten materials. Figures 7.1, 7.2, and 7.3 include some manipulatives used as representations. The chart in Figure 7.4 lists some materials available commercially.

Figure 7.4

Description	Common Use	3	4	5	Picture
Base-ten blocks: proportional representations of units, tens, and hundreds	Place value, addition and subtraction, decimals	✓	✓	✓	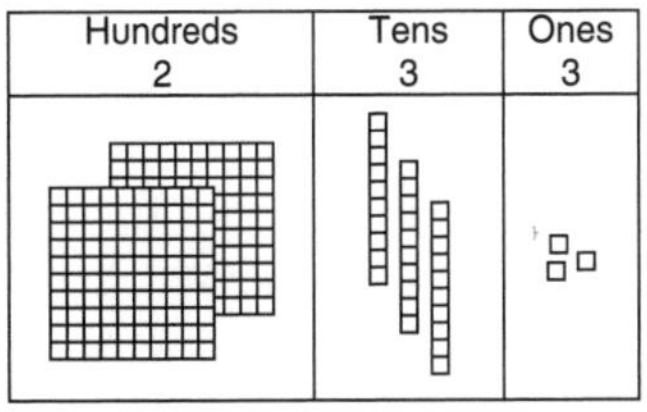
Color cubes, tiles, squares	Area, volume, perimeter	✓	✓	✓	
Fraction circles	Fractions	✓	✓	✓	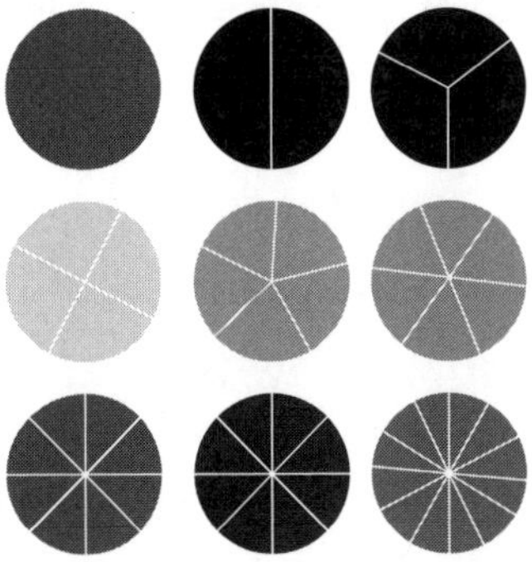
Pattern blocks: six proportional shapes in six colors	Fractions, patterning, geometry	✓	✓	✓	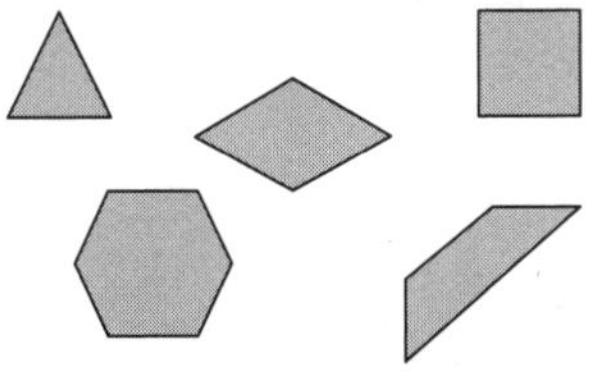
Snap cubes: interlocking plastic cubes	Physical line plots; volume			✓	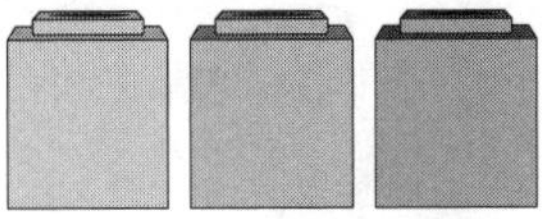
Counters: can be one color or two colors	Set model for fractions	✓	✓	✓	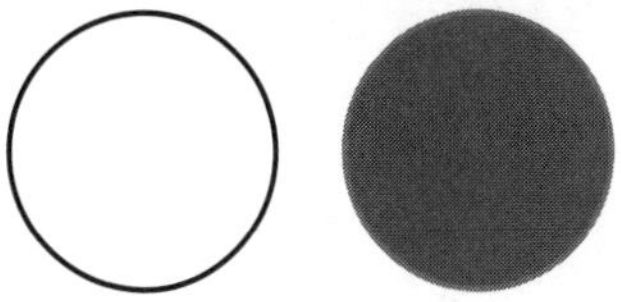

Standards

LI and SC

Purpose

Tasks

Materials

Student Thinking

Lesson Structures

Form. Assess.

Lesson Launch

Lesson Facilitation

Closure

Not all manipulatives need to be commercially produced. Beans, seashells, buttons, pennies, candy, marbles, toys, pebbles, straws, sandboxes, and so forth are all good objects to use for making sense of mathematical concepts.

Some manipulatives can be made. Examples include pattern blocks, fraction strips, and fraction circles, which can all be made using a die-cut machine available at craft stores or from templates downloaded from the Internet.

Virtual manipulatives are available online for little or no cost. These are described as "interactive, Web-based, visual representations of dynamic objects that present opportunities for constructing mathematical knowledge" (Moyer, Bolyard, & Spikell, 2002). Virtual manipulatives are not static computer pictures because they are interactive. Research has shown that virtual manipulatives are effective representations. Reimer and Moyer (2005) described a study that showed statistically significant gains in students' conceptual knowledge using virtual manipulatives. Research by Steen, Brooks, and Lyon (2006) indicates that the use of virtual manipulatives as an instructional tool was extremely effective.

Two free sources for virtual materials are the Library of Virtual Manipulatives found at http://nlvm.usu.edu/ and The Math Learning Center at https://www.mathlearningcenter.org/resources/apps.

HOW ARE MANIPULATIVES USED?

"I hear and I forget. I see and I remember. I do and I understand." This ancient quote from Confucius sums up the current beliefs about using manipulatives in mathematics. It reminds us that we need to provide learning tools to help students make sense of mathematical concepts. In 2009, the U.S. Department of Education's What Works Clearinghouse, a trusted source for scientific evidence of what works in education, made using manipulatives one of its top research-based recommendations. It is important to note that the mathematics is not *in* the manipulatives; rather, students use their interaction with a manipulative to construct the mathematical concepts. In other words, students form ideas about mathematics while working with the manipulatives. They use the manipulatives to test out hypotheses, model/create meaning for algorithms, find patterns and relationships, and so forth, all of which help them construct the abstract concepts.

When introducing a new manipulative to your class, give the students time to explore before giving them any specific instructions. Not only does this give your students a chance to explore the characteristics of the manipulative, but it also helps cut down on behavior issues where students want to play with the manipulative later instead of following instructions.

The most popular use of manipulatives is to introduce a concept. Here is an example.

Example: Eli

Eli, a fourth-grade teacher, wants to introduce the concept of equivalent fractions. She gives each student five sheets of paper, each sheet a different color cut to a different length: 2, 4, 6, 8, and 10 inches. The five sheets are stapled at the top as in a flip book. See Figure 7.5.

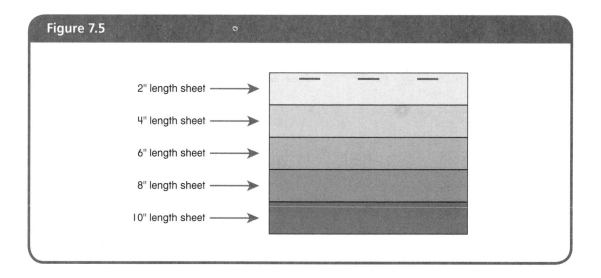

Figure 7.5

2" length sheet
4" length sheet
6" length sheet
8" length sheet
10" length sheet

Eli tells the class that the top sheet represents the whole. She asks the students to take scissors and cut the next sheet in half and demonstrates. See Figure 7.6.

Figure 7.6

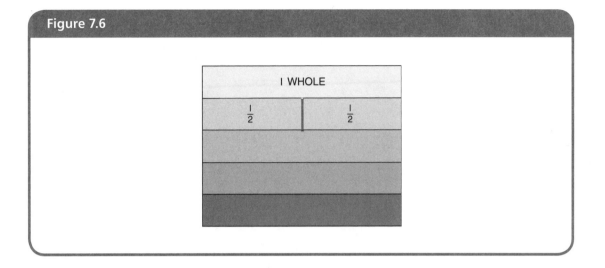

Following her lead, she asks the students to cut the next strip into fourths. Then she asks them to cut the next two strips into eighths and sixteenths, respectively. See Figure 7.7.

Figure 7.7

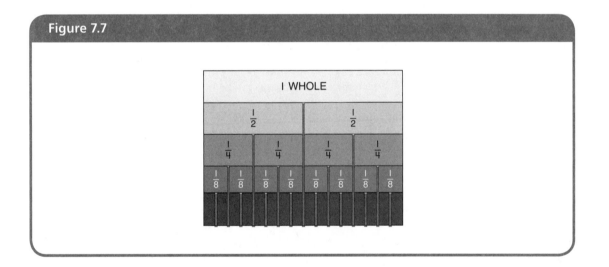

Each time the students complete a cut ($\frac{1}{4}$, $\frac{1}{8}$, $\frac{1}{16}$), Eli asks questions. For example, after students complete the $\frac{1}{4}$ cuts, she asks, "Can anyone explain how you decided where to make your cuts for $\frac{1}{4}$?" One likely response students will make is that they used the half as the guide and cut their fourths as half of the previous halves. Eli continues this line of questioning with each successive cut and encourages student dialogue by asking additional questions such as, "Can you think of a time when you might need to know that two of the $\frac{1}{4}$ pieces are the same size as the half?"

In subsequent lessons, Eli has the students draw pictures of equivalent fractions.

Finally, Eli thinks her students are ready to work abstractly with the concept of equivalent fractions. She gives them the following scenario.

Standards

LI and SC

Purpose

Tasks

Materials

Student Thinking

Lesson Structures

Form. Assess.

Lesson Launch

Lesson Facilitation

Closure

Billy and Roberto were mixing slime. The recipe called for $\frac{1}{4}$ cup of glue, $\frac{1}{4}$ cup of water, and $\frac{1}{4}$ cup of Borax. The problem is that Billy's mom only gave him a $\frac{1}{8}$ measuring cup. How can Billy and Roberto solve their problem?

In Eli's scenario, she first works concretely with students using manipulatives. Then she has them use pictures to model the concept. Finally, she assesses to see if they are understanding and applying the concept abstractly.

> Think about your school and the manipulatives available to you. Make a list of your manipulatives for teaching mathematics. Discuss the list with others in your professional learning community and decide if you have manipulatives that can be used for the concepts you want to teach. Note them in the space below.
>
> _____
>
> _____
>
> _____
>
> _____
>
> _____
>
> _____

As Eli's example shows, teachers can use representations for assessment as well as instruction because the manipulatives give insight into what students do or do not understand. You can then use this knowledge to help you make decisions about future lesson planning. To begin, you can tie these questions, suggested by NCTM past-president Skip Fennell, into your formative assessment.

- How are students using representation to model and interpret the mathematics presented?
- What do the representations that a student is using tell about that student's understanding of the mathematics?
- What do students provide when asked to use diagrams, sketches, or equations to explain their solution to a problem or task? (Fennell, 2006)

See Chapter 10 for more information on formative assessment and lesson planning.

When students can use different representations to model a concept, they demonstrate their ability to understand the concept. Conversely, when students are introduced to only one representation, their misconceptions may be enhanced. For example, students who are exposed only to fraction circles may believe that it is not possible to divide a rectangle into fractional parts. It is good practice to use multiple representations for a concept.

WHAT ARE OTHER RESOURCES?

In addition to representations, you have many other **resources** at your disposal. One of the most common is the **textbook**, but a textbook is only as good as the teacher who uses it. A skilled builder with a hammer and nails can create an architectural masterpiece. In the hands of an unskilled builder, the same blocks of wood made into furniture will fall apart in your living room. As you consider the most effective way to use your textbook for instruction, keep these suggestions in mind:

- Carefully select portions of the text for your students to use. Consider the readability level of what you select and the complexity of the explanations and the level of questions offered. Questions in textbooks are often low level (e.g., recall, carry out an algorithm).

- Discover your students' prior knowledge before preselecting any material based on lessons written for the general 3–5 population.

- Supplement your lessons with suggestions from the teacher ancillary materials that accompany your text.

Note that there will never be a textbook tailored to meet the individual needs of your students. For this reason, creating your own lessons—incorporating the best of what your textbook has to offer—can be advantageous.

Another resource you may have is a **district-wide curriculum.** Usually, district lesson plans are aligned closely to the state-required mathematics standards. Most plans are based on big ideas, conceptual understandings, real-world applications, and hands-on experiences. The district plans will likely engage your students and keep them excited about learning mathematics; these plans may even have ideas for differentiating instruction. Always prepare the district lesson plans thoroughly, using our guidelines, but in class remember to teach your students, not the plan.

The Internet is an endless source of teaching materials. A word of caution: The learning intentions and success criteria you create for your lessons should be of paramount importance. Before jumping to any website with what appear to be engaging lessons or ideas, be sure to match them with your learning intentions and success criteria and think deeply about your standards, big ideas, essential questions, and the purpose of your lesson.

Using a copy of your textbook, something you found on the Internet, or your district curriculum that you used recently in a lesson, reflect on how closely the lesson matched your big ideas, essential questions, learning intentions, and success criteria. Note your reflections here.

_____

_____

_____

_____

Building Unit Coherence

You can create coherence and appropriate rigor across a unit by carefully attending to how and when you use particular resources, particularly the manipulatives. It can be tempting to use the same manipulative throughout a unit, but students need to understand a concept through a variety of manipulatives.

Example: Eli

When Eli teaches equivalent fractions, she begins with a lesson that has students create their own fraction strips as in Figure 7.7. As she continues, she uses fraction circles and two-colored counters so that she can introduce students to area, set, and linear models.

Standards

LI and SC

Purpose

Tasks

Materials

Student Thinking

Lesson Structures

Form. Assess.

Lesson Launch

Lesson Facilitation

Closure

Saida, Julian, and Kimi are discussing their lesson on equivalent fractions, trying to decide which manipulatives to let the students use during the lesson. Kimi weighs in and says, "They are used to using fraction circles, fraction strips, and counters. Some students are drawing their own pictures. Why not let the students make their own decision during the lesson? We can make all of these materials available, and they can use whichever ones they choose. It will empower them."

"Great idea as usual, Kimi!" agrees Julian.

Materials (representations, manipulatives, other):

Fraction circles, fraction strips, two color-counters, number lines, individual student whiteboards and markers

See the complete lesson plan in Appendix A on page 186.

How does the representation for this lesson enhance or further the learning intentions and success criteria of this lesson? Write your thoughts below.

Material Selection

Davante and Adrienne are discussing whether or not to use manipulatives for their transfer lesson. Davante says, "If we make the materials available, then students who need them can use them and those who do not, won't."

"Good thinking! And we can walk around and observe who is using them and how!" agreed Adrienne.

Materials (representations, manipulatives, other):

Recipe, $\frac{1}{4}$ measuring cup, $\frac{1}{4}$ teaspoon, chart paper, markers

See the complete lesson plan in Appendix A on page 191.

How do the representations for this lesson enhance or further the learning intentions and success criteria of this lesson? Write your thoughts below.

_____

_____

_____

_____

_____

_____

_____

_____

_____

_____

_____

_____

_____

_____

_____

_____

_____

_____

_____

_____

_____

Standards

LI and SC

Purpose

Tasks

Materials

Student Thinking

Lesson Structures

Form. Assess.

Lesson Launch

Lesson Facilitation

Closure

As the fifth-grade teachers consider the manipulatives they might use for their lesson, they review all the materials they have in their closet. Boton notes, "We have so many great manipulatives for the fraction concepts, but we always seem to use the same thing over and over."

Chelsea adds, "I agree. We get stuck in a rut. I would like to see if we can think about offering more manipulatives for the students to use. I tend to use the fraction circles, but I know I should use more length models. Maybe we could provide them a choice?"

Rodrigo agrees, "Yes, I think it would also be good for them to see how particular manipulatives can be used to represent different operations and contexts."

Boton concludes, "Yes, let's work on explicitly planning for our manipulatives and discussing with the students why we chose those manipulatives. Also, let's provide them with a choice so they can start making their own decisions about which manipulatives to use."

Materials (representations, manipulatives, other):

Color tiles, one-inch graph paper, markers, chart paper

See the complete lesson plan in Appendix A on page 195.

How do the representations for this lesson enhance or further the learning intentions and success criteria of this lesson? Write your thoughts below.

Under Construction

Now it is your turn! Decide what representations will help meet your learning intentions and success criteria for the lesson you are building.

Materials (representations, manipulatives, technology):

Download the full Lesson-Planning Template from resources.corwin.com/mathlessonplanning/3-5
Remember that you can use the online version of the lesson plan template to begin compiling each section into the full template as your lesson plan grows.

LI and SC

Purpose

Tasks

Materials

Student Thinking

Lesson Structures

Form. Assess.

Lesson Launch

Lesson Facilitation

Closure

CHAPTER 8

CEMENTING THE CRACKS

Anticipating Student Thinking

A team of fourth-grade teachers was making plans for the upcoming school year while thinking about their previous year. Dion made the following comment:

> You know, I thought I was doing a great job last year focusing on geometry with the coordinate plane. We went outside to make a live coordinate graph with x and y axes. Toward the end of the year, a student named Shanna still mixed up the x and y axes.

One of his colleagues, Isabella, shared a similar experience:

> I know what you mean. I really focused on fractions last year. I know my students understood how to add and subtract with unlike denominators, but at the end of the year, Loreen was adding $\frac{2}{8} + \frac{2}{3} = \frac{4}{11}$. I was so curious about this misconception that I asked Loreen about her thinking. She said this is adding so I just added top to top and bottom to bottom.

"Right!" exclaimed Dion. "I don't understand where these ideas come from sometimes. We teach with hands-on materials and really get our students involved, and then they come up with these ideas we never taught."

Isabella added, "You know, I was with some friends this summer. We weren't discussing teaching, but the term *unintended consequences* came up in discussion. It reminds me of what we're talking about. We teach one idea, but for some reason, a few students—sometimes more than that—end up with a completely different conclusion."

Dion concluded, "It might help this year if we are more proactive on these topics that we know get turned around in their minds. Let's make a list now while we are thinking about it. Perhaps we could even plan with the student misconceptions in mind."

Dion and Isabella are frustrated about how their students' thinking, in some cases, is not aligned with what they believe the students should have learned. In this chapter, we will consider the factors that lead to these situations and explore how advance planning and anticipation can be crucial. This chapter will focus on the following questions:

- What are misconceptions, and where do they come from?

- How can you plan to minimize misconceptions?

WHAT ARE MISCONCEPTIONS, AND WHERE DO THEY COME FROM?

One problem that leads to very serious instructional issues for teachers and students is misconceptions. **Common errors** and misconceptions occur when children make incorrect or inappropriate generalizations of an idea (Resnick, 1982; Resnick & Omanson, 1987). Misconceptions may result from several sources: preconceptions, informal thinking, or poor memory.

Students do not come to school with a blank slate of knowledge. They come with background knowledge gathered from prior learning experiences both within and outside of school, such as home or the playground. Some of this knowledge relates to the topics taught in school (Bransford et al., 1999; Gelman & Lucariello, 2002; Piaget & Inhelder, 1969; Resnick, 1983). Learning builds on and is related to this prior knowledge. Prior knowledge is based on intuition, everyday experiences, and what students have previously been taught. Before beginning instruction, you need to know your students' prior knowledge. Your instruction depends on whether this knowledge is accurate or not (Lucariello, 2012).

> Example: Sean
>
> Sean, a fourth-grade teacher, always asks his students to explain their reasoning. He was surprised to see Paul, one of his students, write the following:
>
> $\frac{1}{4} > \frac{3}{5}$ because fourths are greater than fifths.
>
> Perplexed, Sean asked Paul why he used that reasoning. Paul said, "Last year I learned that the bigger the number in the denominator, the smaller the parts."
>
> Sean was surprised that Paul was overgeneralizing what he learned last year. This misconception about fractions was so strong that Paul still had the misconception after Sean's instruction. Paul continued to look only at the denominator, ignoring the numerator, even after participating in all of Sean's engaging comparing fractions activities.

Other misconceptions arrive from everyday experiences. Children form many ideas about numbers, shapes, fractions, time, and money from their environment, including talk on the playground, what they see on television, computer games they play, children's literature, and so forth. It's no wonder some children develop very interesting and perhaps incorrect ideas about mathematical concepts (Bamberger, Oberdorf, Schultz-Ferrell, & Leinwand, 2011). For example, students may read the book *The Legend of Spookley the Square Pumpkin* by Joe Troiano. In the touching story, Spookley starts out as a misfit but ends up a hero. The problem is this: Spookley is described as a square pumpkin, but all illustrations of Spookley in the book depict him as a cube. This misconception can be very hard to correct as students become emotionally attached to Spookley as a character. Mohyuddin and Khalil (2016) tell us that students become emotionally and intellectually attached to misconceptions because they have actively constructed them. They often find it difficult to accept new concepts that are different from their misconception.

Not all misconceptions come from prior knowledge. Some are the **unintended consequences** of the best-intentioned teaching. Here is an example.

> Example: Annie
>
> Annie, a third-grade teacher, asked her students to find the length of the paperclip in the picture (Figure 8.1).

Figure 8.1

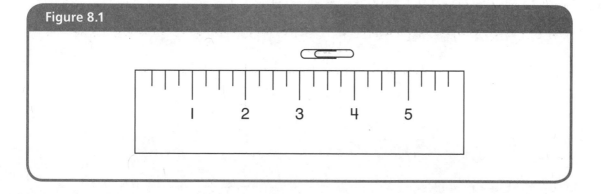

Kelly, one of her students, responded, "4 inches long."

Annie was puzzled by the answer, particularly since the class had spent a lot of time measuring a variety of objects around the classroom. She asked Kelly to explain how she arrived at her answer.

Kelly said, "The paperclip comes up to the 4 on the ruler so it is 4 inches long."

Annie was surprised at the misconception Kelly had. Kelly believed that the highest number next to the end of an object is the measure. She did not understand that the paperclip was not being measured from the beginning of the ruler. Nor did she seem to understand that an inch is a distance, no matter where you measure on the ruler. Annie felt that she had contributed to this misconception by always having her students measure from the beginning of the ruler.

To summarize, misconceptions are a problem for two reasons. First, students become emotionally and intellectually attached to the misconceptions because they have actively constructed them, as in the example with *Spookley the Square Pumpkin*. Second, they interfere with learning when students use them to interpret new experiences, as in the example with Kelly and Annie and with Sean's fourth-grade students.

For more exploration of unintended consequences, check out "The Thirteen Rules That Expire" (Karp, Bush, & Dougherty, 2014). This National Council of Teachers of Mathematics (NCTM) article highlights 13 generalizations that are often taught in elementary school because they work for the lesson at hand, but they do not hold true over the long term. For example, elementary educators often tell students that a larger number cannot be subtracted from a smaller number because they do not want to confuse students by introducing negative numbers. However, students do not have to be taught explicitly about negative numbers to know they exist. The focus of your lessons should always be on developing conceptual understanding instead of adhering to a rule.

> **How do you identify your students' common misconceptions? Note some of the main ones here.**
>
> _____
>
> _____
>
> _____
>
> _____

HOW CAN YOU PLAN TO MINIMIZE MISCONCEPTIONS?

According to Steven Leinwand (2014),

> Effective teachers have always understood that mistakes and confusion are powerful learning opportunities. Moreover, they understand that one of their critical roles is to anticipate these misconceptions in their lesson planning and have at their disposal an array of strategies to address common misunderstandings *before* they expand, solidify, and undermine confidence.

Before we can plan to minimize misconceptions (admitting they can never be eliminated totally), it is helpful to know some of the more common mathematics misconceptions that third-, fourth-, and fifth-grade students form. Note that the table in Figure 8.2 is not an exhaustive list.

Figure 8.2

Misconception	Student Example
When you multiply a number by ten, just add 0 to the end of the number.	$0.35 \times 10 = 0.350$

Figure 8.2 (Continued)

Misconception	Student Example
Subtraction is commutative.	$8 - 5 = 5 - 8$
Key words tell us which operation to perform, such as *more* and *altogether* always mean add.	John has 145 songs on his iPod and Mary has 237. Who has more songs on their iPod? Student will answer 382.
We can only add two numbers at a time.	$13 + 54 + 7 = \_\_$. Students do not know what to do since they believe we cannot add three numbers.
Equal sign means "the next number is the answer."	Students respond to $120 = \_\_ + 60$ as 180.
Multiplication makes numbers bigger.	$\frac{1}{4} \times \frac{1}{2} = \frac{1}{8}$ Students believe $\frac{1}{8}$ is bigger than $\frac{1}{4}$ or $\frac{1}{2}$.
You always divide the larger number by the smaller number.	When given the question "What is 25 divided by 100?" students will write $100 \div 25 = 4$.
When using a ruler, the markings are the inches, not the spaces between the markings.	When asked to show an inch on the ruler, the student points to the mark for 1 inch.
Multiply everything inside parentheses by the number outside parentheses.	$23 (4 \times 6) = 23 \times 4 \times 23 \times 6 = 12{,}696$.
Using English-language names for shapes as opposed to mathematical names.	Calling this shape a diamond.
Using the denominator of a fraction as a whole number to determine the relative size of a fraction.	Fourths are larger than halves because 4 is bigger than 2.
Using the term "the biggest half."	My half is bigger than yours.

Because misconceptions tend to be strongly held student beliefs, it does not work well to simply repeat a lesson or tell a student that his or her idea is a misconception. Instead, you need to include in your plan how you will uncover and diagnose student misconceptions.

You can do this through use of anticipation, formative assessment, and questioning techniques. Let's take a quick look at each of these approaches.

Standards

LI and SC

Purpose

Tasks

Materials

Student Thinking

Lesson Structures

Form. Assess.

Lesson Launch

Lesson Facilitation

Closure

Formative Assessment

Formative assessment can include techniques such as observations, interviews, show me, hinge questions, and exit tasks as explained in the book *The Formative Five* (Fennell, Kobett, & Wray, 2017). Each of these techniques can be used to uncover prior knowledge that may include misconceptions. Chapter 10 will focus on using formative assessment strategies.

Questioning

Questioning is another way to uncover misconceptions in prior knowledge. Some questioning techniques that work for this purpose include the following:

1. Prepare and pose questions that probe prior knowledge related to the lesson you are planning.

2. Avoid asking questions that require one-word answers (Kazemi & Hintz, 2014).

3. Ask follow-up questions to both correct and incorrect answers (Moyer-Packenham & Milewicz, 2002; Walsh & Sattes, 2005).

Anticipating

Anticipating misconceptions is another way to minimize them. Here are three ways you can add steps to your lesson plan to anticipate, diagnose, and correct the misconceptions.

1. Use Figure 8.2 to help you anticipate misconceptions and to help you think about those you commonly see in the content of your lessons.

2. Consider your experience with previous students.

3. Discuss the misconceptions with your colleagues to gather additional ideas on how to correct the misconceptions.

> Example: Nancy
>
> Nancy, a fourth-grade teacher, includes this word problem in her lesson plan on addition to determine if her students have any preconceived ideas about solving word problems using key words.
>
> > There are 4 plates of cookies on the table. There are 24 cookies on each plate. How many cookies are on the table altogether?

In particular, Nancy is looking to see if any students answer 28. If they do, she will follow up with additional questions, such as, "How did you get 28 for your answer? Does it make sense that there are only 28 cookies? Can you convince me that 28 is the correct answer?"

Notice that Nancy does not ask any one-word-answer questions. They are all questions that probe thinking for a specific piece of prior knowledge.

Nancy discovers that three of her students had the misconception that the key word *altogether* means *add*. To address this, she adds the following activity to her lesson the next day.

Nancy works with a small group of students who had the misconception. She tells them that they are going to act out yesterday's cookie problem. She hands each student a paper plate and a bucket of counters to represent cookies. Students complete the task of setting up the cookies on the plates as specified in the problem and determine that 28 is not the correct answer.

Nancy is deliberately providing the students with other experiences that allow them to reconstruct the concept they misunderstood. This is a necessary step for students who are truly vested in their misconceptions because they constructed them and used them successfully in the past.

Building Unit Coherence

To increase coherence, you can also identify the misconceptions that students may develop across a unit.

Mariya, a fifth-grade teacher, always jots down misconceptions that she anticipates the students may develop or have already developed. This allows her to plan lessons that will help her prevent the misconception from occurring.

Mariya developed this practice after her students insisted that dividing by $\frac{1}{2}$ is the same as dividing in half! She had to interrupt her teaching to plan a lesson that corrected the misconception. She planned a lesson where students had to perform the following two computations and compare results to see that dividing by $\frac{1}{2}$ is not the same as dividing in half. See Figure 8.3.

Now, she lists misconceptions that she anticipates for each unit before she begins teaching so she will be ready.

Figure 8.3

Dividing by $\frac{1}{2}$	$26 \div \frac{1}{2} =$
Dividing in half	$26 \div 2 =$

Notes

Standards

LI and SC

Purpose

Tasks

Materials

Student Thinking

Lesson Structures

Form. Assess.

Lesson Launch

Lesson Facilitation

Closure

Third-grade teachers Saida, Julian, and Kimi are discussing their students' fraction knowledge. Saida says, "Sometimes I notice students comparing fractions only using denominators."

Julian says, "I have had a few students like that too. I wonder if maybe we are not doing enough work with the concept of what a fraction means."

To check out whether this is a student misconception, they decide to pay extra attention to how students reason when they compare fractions in their instructional tasks.

Misconceptions or Common Errors:

- Students may confuse the meaning of *numerator* and *denominator*.
- Given the whole, the smaller the denominator, the smaller the size of the pieces.
- Students ignore the size of the whole.

See the complete lesson plan in Appendix A on page 186.

Why do you think that simply informing students of a misconception will not change their thinking? What role does anticipating a misconception play in helping you focus your lesson plan? Record your thoughts below.

Standards

LI and SC

Purpose

Tasks

Materials

Student Thinking

Lesson Structures

Form. Assess.

Lesson Launch

Lesson Facilitation

Closure

Fourth-Grade Snapshot

Student Thinking

Adrienne and Davante are planning their transfer lesson on equivalent fractions. Adrienne says, "My students can quickly find equivalent fractions by multiplication. However, I do not feel comfortable that the children really understand that two fractions with different numbers represent the same part of a whole."

Davante agrees. He adds, "I wonder what the students really know about equivalent fractions when they get to fourth grade."

Adrienne adds, "I am always wondering how well they really understand equivalence, too. Could we keep this on our minds as we teach and look for evidence?"

Misconceptions or Common Errors:

- You cannot write a fraction for a whole number.
- Fractions don't work on a number line.
- A mixed number cannot be written as an improper fraction.

See the complete lesson plan in Appendix A on page 191.

Why do you think that simply informing students of a misconception will not change their thinking? What role does anticipating a misconception play in helping you focus your lesson plan? Record your thoughts below.

At a team meeting where they are planning lessons on fractions, fifth-grade teachers Boton, Chelsea, and Rodrigo discuss how, in the past, students did not understand multiplication of fractions, recognizing that multiplying fractions results in smaller values rather than bigger values (whole-number multiplication). The teachers decide to design a lesson to help students address this misconception through a real-world scenario.

Misconceptions or Common Errors:

- Believing that multiplication always makes things bigger, and therefore the same will be true for fraction multiplication

- Believing that procedural fluency (multiplying numerators and multiplying denominators) is the same as conceptual understanding

- Believing that multiplication is the same as addition by creating common denominators

See the complete lesson plan in Appendix A on page 195.

Why do you think that simply informing students of a misconception will not change their thinking? What role does anticipating a misconception play in helping you focus your lesson plan? Record your thoughts below.

_____

_____

_____

_____

_____

_____

_____

_____

_____

_____

_____

_____

_____

_____

_____

_____

_____

_____

_____

_____

_____

Under Construction

Now it is your turn! Decide on whether you are anticipating a misconception or need to probe prior knowledge. Add it to your lesson plan.

Misconceptions or Common Errors:

online resources Download the full Lesson-Planning Template from resources.corwin.com/mathlessonplanning/3-5
Remember that you can use the online version of the lesson plan template to begin compiling each section into the full template as your lesson plan grows.

Standards

LI and SC

Purpose

Tasks

Materials

Student Thinking

Lesson Structures

Form. Assess.

Lesson Launch

Lesson Facilitation

Closure

CHAPTER 9

FRAMING THE LESSON
Formats

Imani felt like she had not been meeting all of her students' needs, particularly the stragglers, who were not working unless she was constantly reminding them, and she wanted to try some new things to engage them along with all of her students. They needed more opportunities to talk with one another and learn how to work together on problems. In order to facilitate this kind of shared experience, Imani knew that she would need to be available to monitor the students while they were working; she did not want to be tied up in an instructional group. She still believed in small-group instruction; she just felt that her students needed to be working together more often.

As Imani sat down with her team, Bonnie and Diamond, she shared the following:

"I think we really need to take a look at our lesson format. We have been using the same math rotations. I am not sure we are building enough opportunities for math discourse between the students. I know they are talking to each other in the groups, but I am not hearing much math talk. I think we need to build some more strategic tasks that we could facilitate through a combination of whole-group and small-group instruction to promote math talk among the students. What do you think?"

Diamond agreed. She said, "I would love to try some different formats. Perhaps we can begin with pairs and see how that goes. I think the students will be very excited about solving some problems together. We can also work on the social learning intentions at the same time!"

Bonnie was also on board. She said, "Let's do it!"

Lessons need structure. Lesson formats give you that structure. Lesson formats refer to how you organize your class for the lesson. Some lessons work better when students are in collaborative groups, and some are more effective when students move around to different centers. For instance, rotating stations may be a good decision for a procedural fluency lesson but not for the introductory lesson on a new concept. As you select a lesson format for a particular lesson, you should base your decision on the purpose of the lesson. Lesson format can and should vary depending on the purpose of the lesson as Imani, Diamond, and Bonnie all agree.

This chapter will address the following question:

- What are some different lesson formats?

Standards

LI and SC

Purpose

Tasks

Materials

Student Thinking

Lesson Structures

Form. Assess.

Lesson Launch

Lesson Facilitation

Closure

WHAT ARE SOME DIFFERENT LESSON FORMATS?

Seemingly, everyone has their own preferred **lesson format,** but the fact is that there is not one mathematics lesson format that should be implemented every day. Adhering to one model can be limiting, and it may not best support your students' learning because the format is taking precedence over the students' needs. Effective teachers use more than one type of lesson format. As you think about selecting lesson formats, ask yourself if the mathematics lesson structure meets the following criteria.

- Does it support student discourse?

- Does it support differentiation?

- Does it place the big ideas front and center in the lesson?

- Does it enhance opportunities for formative assessment?

As you decide on a lesson format, you will need to analyze the standards you will teach. In particular, you should consider which of the standards point to developing conceptual understanding and which ones point to procedural fluency.

The following formats are just four ways you might structure your lessons. Flexibility is the key to selecting lesson formats. You should structure your lessons with a deep consideration of your students' needs and mathematics standards. Note that these lesson formats provide many opportunities to formatively assess students, provide timely feedback, and foster student-to-student interactions.

Four-Part Lesson Plan

Structure your class using this format for problem-solving lessons. The four parts are known as *before, during, after,* and *reflection* (see Figure 9.1). This is an adaptation of the format from the book *Teaching Mathematics Developmentally K–8* by Van de Walle et al. (2016).

Figure 9.1

Before

| Teacher activates prior knowledge in students | Teacher ensures the problem is understood | Whole group |

⬇

During

| Students work | Teacher provides support | Small group |

⬇

After

| Class discussion | Students present their conclusions/conjecture | Whole group |

⬇

Reflection

| Students make sense of the lesson | Closure | Individual |

Before

In the *before* stage, your students are in a **whole group.** The goal of this part of the lesson is to prepare students for the mathematics to come by having them revisit concepts, procedures, and strategies previously learned. You can do this by focusing on vocabulary, starting with a similar problem, or having students reword, act out, or model the problem. You also introduce the problem during the before stage.

During

In the second part of the lesson, the *during* stage, students work in small groups. They work on solving the problem, and they prepare to present their ideas to the class. They can use manipulatives or any representations they choose. This is when they actively engage with the task. You can use this time to support the groups through questioning. Use several different questioning strategies to support your students' higher-order thinking, such as the following:

- Ask group members to share their strategies with other group members.
- Pose questions to provoke further thinking when groups are at an impasse.
- Ask probing questions.
- Provide extensions when appropriate.

In this part of the lesson, take note of student thinking and the strategies used so that you can begin to organize the *after* part of the lesson. Be as hands-off as possible so that your students can engage in productive struggle.

After

In the *after* part of the lesson, students come back together in a whole group to share their work. The purpose of this part of the lesson is for students to analyze their classmates' thinking. In the *during* stage, you noted the students' strategies so that you can now organize student presentations, posters, or other products in an order that leads to discourse around their work. For example, you may decide to have the students with incorrect solutions make their presentations first so you can ask the class if everyone agrees. This will allow you to start a class discussion on the effectiveness of the strategy used. Alternatively, you may have students do a gallery walk or try another method to share student thinking and encourage discourse. During the *after*, your students make sense of the mathematics. They form conjectures and link the new ideas to their previous understandings.

Reflection

Reflection refers to the process of thinking about learning. In the *reflection* piece of the lesson, students get the time they need to cement their learning individually. It is during reflection that student learning takes place. During reflection, students examine ideas and seek out evidence to support or refute ideas they have previously held. To ensure this reflection, you should provide students with a prompt they can use to reflect on the class discussion and the mathematics involved. Here are some sample prompts for reflection that you might try.

- How was your strategy different from those of your classmates?
- What was your favorite strategy, and why?
- Explain a strategy used by a classmate that was not yours.
- How did this lesson connect to what we did yesterday?

Reflection is a proactive way to support students' mathematical development. You should never skip the reflection portion of the lesson. In fact, you may wish to use reflection time as your closure (see Chapter 11).

Game Format

There are some lessons where you want students to practice what they have learned so they can make connections. The game format works well for this purpose and gives you a chance to assess your students formatively.

During planning, assign all students into groups of two or three, and decide on a game or activity for each group or pair. Select games or activities they are familiar with so they can practice the concept or skill they need. For example, if you know that three of your students all have some difficulty comparing numbers using place value, group them to play "The Place Value Game" (see Figure 9.2).

Figure 9.2

The Place Value Game

Give each group of three to four students a set of ten cards numbered 0 to 9 and a recording sheet. Students place the cards randomly face down. One student (called leader) announces the first-round goal is to create the greatest number possible and selects a digit card to show the group. Each person secretly makes a decision about whether that digit should be recorded in the ones, tens, hundreds, thousands, or ten thousands place in the number he or she is building. Once each person places the digit, it may not be changed. The leader continues and repeats the process until five digits have been recorded by each student hoping to create the greatest number. The leader then asks, "Who has the greatest number?" Students compare their numbers, order them, and decide who wins the round by discussing how they know which number is the greatest.

Students take turns being the leader of the round. The leader determines whether the goal is to create the greatest or least number possible, shuffles the digit cards and places them randomly face down, and selects the cards used in the round.

Recording Sheet

Round 1 _ 7 _ _ _ _ _

Round 2 _ _ _ _ _ _

Round 3 _ _ _ _ _ _

Round 4 _ _ _ _ _ _

Round 5 _ _ _ _ _ _

Rich games and activities such as "The Place Value Game" lend themselves well to this lesson format.

To begin a lesson structured in the game format, gather the whole group together as shown in Figure 9.3. Assign groups of two, three, or four students to games and allow them to play. Use this time for you to move from game to game, observing, formatively assessing, and joining in when necessary. Note that students remain with the same game throughout the lesson. This is not a student rotation format; instead, the teacher moves from group to group.

Standards

LI and SC

Purpose

Tasks

Materials

Student Thinking

Lesson Structures

Form. Assess.

Lesson Launch

Lesson Facilitation

Closure

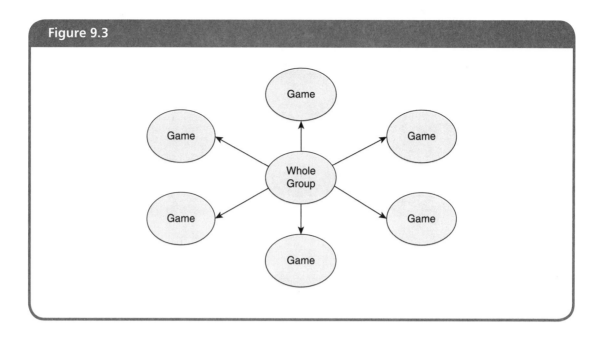

Figure 9.3

Small-Group Instruction

In this lesson format, you have the opportunity to work with small groups of students for instruction while the other groups work independently. Research shows that students who work in groups on problems, assignments, and other mathematical investigations display increased achievement (Protheroe, 2007).

You begin instruction with a whole-group mini-lesson that takes 10 to 15 minutes. For instance, you might review a previous concept, introduce a new concept or vocabulary, play a short game on the day's topic, model a game that students will play independently, and so forth.

After the mini-lesson, you ask two or three small groups to engage in independent tasks that allow students to explore, practice, apply, and/or review the topic for the lesson. Students can play games, use the computer, solve problems, or explore concepts with manipulatives. While most students are working in small groups independently, another group works with you. Be sure to form the groups in a way that makes sense for their learning. For example, you may choose to work with a small group of students with a particular misconception about multiplication that you noticed the previous day.

You can vary how you use this format. Figure 9.4 shows how you can move from a whole group into small groups and remain in those groups for the entire class time. This works well for students who need time to fill in knowledge gaps or need extra time on a concept with you. Remember that not all students learn at the same pace. Some need more instructional time to cement concepts or practice procedures. If you work with only one group during the class period, you should reconvene the whole class at the end of the lesson to share ideas from the day. You may use this time to preview the next lesson and/or review the day. See Chapter 13 for more on closure.

Standards

LI and SC

Purpose

Tasks

Materials

Student Thinking

Lesson Structures

Form. Assess.

Lesson Launch

Lesson Facilitation

Closure

Figure 9.4

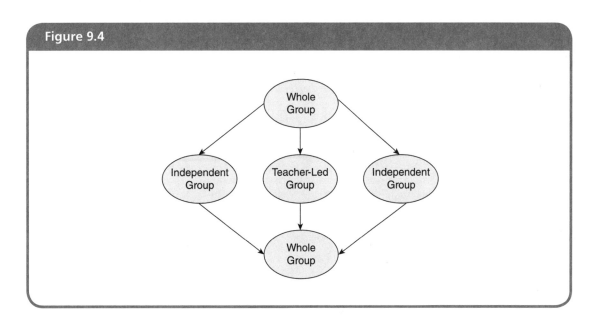

You can use this format two or three days in a row if you use the small-group instructional time to work on deepening knowledge on a topic. For example, if you work with a small group on a misconception about comparing fractions and it takes the entire class time allotted, then the next day you may work the entire class time with another group that needs work on multiplication. In this scenario, you can see one group each day for instruction with you while the others work independently. This also works if you have three or four groups and they need different levels of depth.

Alternatively, you can use the format as shown in Figure 9.5. Here you get the opportunity to work with a rotation of small groups during the class time. For example, you may decide that your introduction to place value needs to be differentiated. You group students accordingly and rotate groups during the class time so that you work with each group and can differentiate the lesson to meet the needs of the group members. Students working independently also get a chance to rotate among two or three different activities or stations.

Figure 9.5

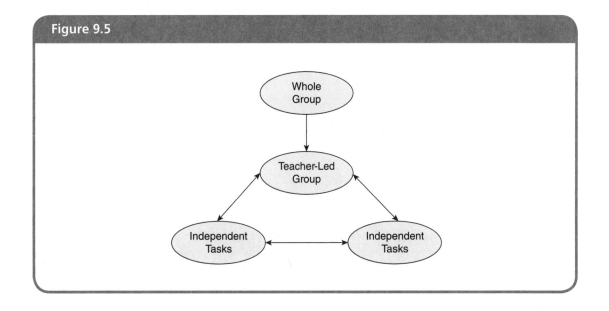

This format lends itself to procedural fluency lessons because you can use the small-group instruction time to target students who need additional scaffolding to link the concept to the procedure. On the other hand, you can use this model to reinforce a concept or to practice procedural fluency with a group of students who, based on your formative assessment from the previous day, need additional attention immediately. Students learn concepts at varying rates. Not all students make sense of mathematics at the same pace. This model provides you with the opportunity to bridge this gap.

A benefit of this model is that students are engaged at all times, either directly with you or in an independent setting. It allows your students to fluidly move within groups based on their needs. In other words, you can change the makeup of the groups often to meet specific needs.

Pairs

With this format, students work in pairs to answer questions throughout the lesson. For example, you may begin the lesson by presenting two shapes and asking the students to decide with their partners what is the same about those shapes. Then they discuss their answers as a whole group. Next, you further the discussion by asking pairs to discuss how the shapes are different. After a brief discussion, they share as a whole group. The lesson continues in this fashion. It may involve a series of short tasks or one short task that students engage in with their partner.

You can pair students of similar abilities, different abilities, differing language strengths, and so forth depending on your goals for that particular lesson. Frequently changing the way you pair students is a good practice.

This format encourages student discourse. The smaller the number of students in a group, the more the children get individual opportunities to express themselves. This structure works well for helping students build conceptual understanding.

These are just a few lesson formats. You may have a few of your own to add to the list, or you may adapt any of these presented as long as the format supports the purpose of your lesson.

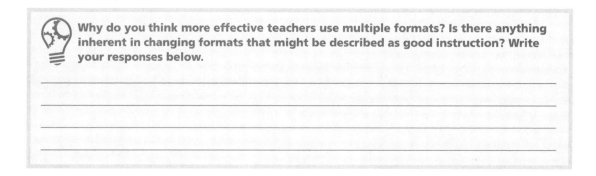

Why do you think more effective teachers use multiple formats? Is there anything inherent in changing formats that might be described as good instruction? Write your responses below.

_____

_____

_____

_____

Building Unit Coherence

When using multiple lesson formats, you often create stronger coherence because you are matching the format to the content and to your learning intentions. In other words, you are facilitating your lesson using a format that best meets the needs of your learners. Forcing lessons into the same format day after day chips away at coherence because you are trying to make the lesson fit the structure instead of deciding which structure best suits the lesson content.

Example: Chris

Chris, a fifth-grade teacher, used to teach small-group lessons every day. He rotated the students through the lessons, but he found that he did not always have enough time to develop the concept. Many days he ended up giving directions instead of asking good questions. Now, he plans the unit using multiple formats. He finds that he can develop better connections between concepts, and he can create that unit coherence he was craving.

Third-Grade Snapshot

Lesson Format

After selecting the task, Saida, Julian, and Kimi review some of the lesson elements discussed in previous chapters, including prior knowledge, big ideas, learning intentions, task selection, and misconceptions. Saida shares the following: "I would like to pair the students for this lesson. I really think it will be good for them to work on the task with partners to give them an opportunity to discuss their ideas. I can also determine places where I can differentiate if needed. What do you both think?"

Julian says, "I have really been wanting to do this, too. I think my ELL students will love the opportunity to share their ideas in the safety of a pair."

Kimi agrees.

Format:

☐ Four-Part Lesson   ☐ Game Format   ☐ Small-Group Instruction

☑ Pairs   ☐ Other_____

See the complete lesson plan in Appendix A on page 186.

Think of a lesson you recently taught. What kind of format might best meet the purpose of that lesson? Record your thoughts below.

_____
_____
_____
_____
_____
_____
_____
_____
_____
_____
_____
_____
_____
_____
_____
_____
_____
_____

Adrienne and Davante discuss different types of structures that they might begin implementing in their fourth-grade classrooms. Davante shares the following:

"I have to admit, I think we are stuck in a bit of a rut. We tend to teach using math rotations every day, no matter what content we are using. We need to think about how we can use these classroom formats to better meet our students' learning needs and align those needs to the content we are teaching. Whole group can work if students are working in small groups most of the time. Are you ready to try the four-part lesson plan format?"

Adrienne responds, "Let's do it!"

Format:

☑ Four-Part Lesson   ☐ Game Format   ☐ Small-Group Instruction

☐ Pairs   ☐ Other_____

See the complete lesson plan in Appendix A on page 191.

Think of a lesson you recently taught. What kind of format might best meet the purpose of that lesson? Record your thoughts below.

_____

_____

_____

_____

_____

_____

_____

_____

_____

_____

_____

_____

_____

_____

_____

_____

_____

Lesson Format

Chelsea tells her fifth-grade colleagues, "I would like to make heterogeneous groups for this lesson. I want them to spend time developing their understanding and have them share their ideas with others."

Boton adds, "I like this idea because they can hear each other's perspectives and develop mathematical arguments to explain their reasoning."

Rodrigo agrees. He says, "If we use the four-part lesson structure, we can monitor the groups and encourage them to collaborate to share their ideas and then strategically connect their thinking to the multiplication of fractions."

Format:

☑ Four-Part Lesson ☐ Game Format ☐ Small-Group Instruction

☐ Pairs ☐ Other_____

See the complete lesson plan in Appendix A on page 195.

Think of a lesson you recently taught. What kind of format might best meet the purpose of that lesson? Record your thoughts below.

_____

_____

_____

_____

_____

_____

_____

_____

_____

_____

_____

_____

_____

_____

_____

Standards | LI and SC | Purpose | Tasks | Materials | Student Thinking | Lesson Structures | Form. Assess. | Lesson Launch | Lesson Facilitation | Closure

Now it is your turn! Select the lesson format you would like to use for your lesson that is under construction. Be able to justify for yourself how this format supports the purpose of the lesson.

Format:

☐ Four-Part Lesson ☐ Game Format ☐ Small-Group Instruction

☐ Pairs ☐ Other_____

online resources Download the full Lesson-Planning Template from resources.corwin.com/mathlessonplanning/3-5
Remember that you can use the online version of the lesson plan template to begin compiling each section into the full template as your lesson plan grows.

Notes

CHAPTER 10

EVALUATING IMPACT
Formative Assessment

Iyana, a third-grade teacher, glanced at her observation checklist and noted that she hadn't been able to record observations for Roberto and Anna in almost two weeks. She liked to gather observation evidence on every student at least once a week. She had always observed what students were doing, of course, but this new more formalized observation practice had truly empowered her teaching. She was making better decisions in the moment of teaching and could adjust her instruction using the information she was gathering. Today she was going to use the Show Me technique (Fennell et al., 2017) and capture students' work with pictures during small-group instruction. She had family conferences coming up and thought it would be helpful to be able to show pictures of the students' work.

She planned to pose this question: "How many arrays can you make for the product 36? Please show me." She anticipated that students would make guesses and perhaps quickly identify 6 × 6. She asked this open-ended performance-based prompt because she wanted students to wrestle with the arrays that demonstrate the commutative property. She wondered if they would consider 4 × 8 as the same or differently than 8 × 4.

Iyana began by asking the students to make predictions. She recorded the predictions next to their names on the board. She then posed the question and gave the students connecting cubes and a piece of one-inch graph paper to record the arrays.

As the students worked, Iyana noted that Mariella and Nuhad worked systematically through the arrays. She was fascinated to see that Mariella began by making a 36 × 1 array, turned it, and made a 1 × 36 array. Next, she broke the 36 connecting cubes in half and made a 2 × 18 array, turned it, and made an 18 × 2 array. She asked Mariella to tell her about her arrays and explain how she was finding all the arrays.

Mariella answered, "I wanted to start with the long one row of 36 one first. Then, I moved to two rows of 18. Next, I am going to go with three rows and see how many are in the row. If I find the arrays like this, I won't leave any out."

Iyana was thrilled to see Mariella attack this problem with organization.

Nuhad began making her arrays by starting with the 6 × 6 array first. She then gathered 36 more cubes and began arranging them to find a new array.

Iyana asked, "How will you know when you have found all the arrays?"

Nuhad replied, "I will know when I can't make any more arrays!"

Iyana took photos using her phone and uploaded them to the recording sheet. Then she adjusted her instruction to help the students focus on using the commutative property to find all of the arrays. She asked, "How can you use the commutative property to find all the arrays for the product 36?"

> Iyana used formative assessment to design a prompt to understand her students' thinking, gather assessment data, adjust instruction using that data, and communicate the information to the students' families. This chapter will explore the following questions:
>
> - What is formative assessment?
> - What are specific formative assessment techniques?

WHAT IS FORMATIVE ASSESSMENT?

Formative assessment, also called **formative evaluation** (Hattie, 2009), focuses on collecting information about student learning in the moment—as it is happening—and responding to that information by adapting instruction to improve learning. Consistent and thoughtful formative evaluation can be leveraged to produce the largest student-learning gains (Hattie, 2009). Formative assessment can be thought of as *assessment for learning* because teachers adjust their teaching practices in response to what they learn about student understanding. On the flip side, *assessment of learning* may also be called *summative learning*. Schools use **summative assessment** to determine students' achievement levels at particular points in time, particularly at the end of units, quarters, and even entire grade levels. Wiliam and Thompson (2008) recommend the following five key formative assessment strategies:

1. *Clarifying and sharing learning intentions and criteria for success.* The first step in formative assessment involves letting your students know what they will learn and what it means when they have learned it. This is a critical but often misunderstood part of formative assessment. You will recall from Chapter 4 the importance of establishing and communicating learning intentions and success criteria for every student. When you let students know what they are supposed to be learning and help them determine or self-evaluate their own success, you empower them!

2. *Engineering effective classroom discussions, questions, and learning tasks that elicit evidence of learning.* By posing questions, responding to students' thinking, and designing and conducting tasks that prompt deep mathematical thinking, you set the stage for responsive formative assessment. Chapters 6 (tasks), 8 (student thinking), and 12 (facilitating lessons) emphasize the need for and importance of eliciting student thinking. As the engineer, you carefully plan for these opportunities to formatively assess and adapt your instruction.

3. *Providing feedback that moves learning forward.* Feedback that is built upon student thinking and reasoning is powerful because you are targeting exactly the next right instructional move for your particular students. You are charged with evaluating your students to give some type of grade or score, but grades are not actionable feedback. You take the daily collection of student evidence to the next level by offering explicit feedback to students that builds on prior learning, stretches their thinking, and unpacks misconceptions. This feedback is a key component to formative assessment because you are meeting students where they are and advancing their learning during the lesson without delay. Feedback is not a punitive opportunity to catch students when they are wrong but an opportunity to uncover interesting thinking.

   Consider the following examples:

   > Great job explaining what a multiple is, Aidan!

   > Lin, I like how you explained that a multiple is the number you get when you multiply a number by another number. You also said that multiples are also patterns. Can you show me what you mean by giving the class an example?

   Note how the second example provides explicit feedback to the student and asks for further clarification from the student to represent his thinking using an example. Elementary teachers are so very positive with their students! Extend your current warm, positive, and inviting approach by specifically linking your feedback to what students do and say.

4. *Activating students as instructional resources for one another.* Students can and do provide each other with instructional support. They often recognize each other's misconceptions and can remediate confusion naturally and effortlessly. Other times, they work together through shared learning and serve as instructional supports to each other by asking questions. They also clarify their own understanding by explaining their thinking to others. When you build this kind of co-construction of learning in your classroom, you empower your entire learning community by equally distributing the responsibility of learning to everyone.

5. *Activating students as the owners of their own learning.* When you stimulate students to own their learning, you communicate confidence to them about their ability to advocate for themselves. Students become "in tune" with their own understanding and can convey their levels of understanding to their classmates, teachers, and families.

Example: **Misha**

Fourth-grade teacher Misha distributes the image of a stoplight (Figure 10.1) to her students during small-group instruction. At strategic points, she asks students to place a cube on the stoplight to show their readiness to move on in the lesson. When Misha first introduced this approach, her fourth graders expressed reticence to evaluate their own understanding, but she persevered and encouraged them to self-evaluate. Now, they are quite comfortable sharing. One of the students, Lucas, explains, "I was nervous to say I didn't understand. Now I know that Ms. Cohen wants to know if we are confused. She just smiles and doesn't get mad at us."

Figure 10.1

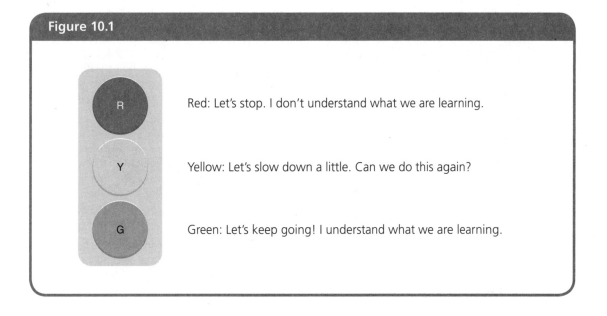

Red: Let's stop. I don't understand what we are learning.

Yellow: Let's slow down a little. Can we do this again?

Green: Let's keep going! I understand what we are learning.

As you review these strategies, you may note the shared responsibility that teachers and students hold in the mathematics learning community. You and the students work together to build one another's understanding and probe each other to clarify reasoning. Be sure to communicate that misconceptions are a normal part of every lesson that should be expected and celebrated (Hattie et al., 2016), and express appreciation for their efforts. Also ensure that students understand that they are expected to explain and show their mathematical thinking, ask questions, and evaluate their own understanding.

Which of the formative assessment strategies described so far in this chapter are you currently practicing? Which strategy would you like to develop? Write your intentions below.

_____

_____

_____

_____

_____

_____

_____

Standards
LI and SC
Purpose
Tasks
Materials
Student Thinking
Lesson Structures
Form. Assess.
Lesson Launch
Lesson Facilitation
Closure

The Formative 5 assessment techniques (Fennell et al., 2017) include the following:

- Observation
- Interview
- Show Me
- Hinge questions
- Exit tasks

Each of these techniques includes five important phases:

1. Anticipating student responses
2. Implementing the technique
3. Collecting evidence
4. Adjusting instruction
5. Providing feedback to students

Let's take a close look at each technique, including the five different phases, so you can determine how to implement them in your classroom.

Observation

You observe your students every day! **Observation** is perhaps the most comfortable of all the classroom-based formative assessment strategies because you are constantly informally observing your students as they engage in mathematics activities. Observational evidence is particularly powerful when you document what you observe to inform your instruction (Fennell et al., 2017).

Anticipating Student Responses: How might students respond to the mathematics concepts you are teaching? What will students do during the lessons? What kinds of behaviors or actions will you observe? Think about potential misconceptions (Chapter 8) students might make (Figure 10.2).

Figure 10.2

Mathematics Standard	Anticipate	
	Observations	**Misconceptions**
Determine the unknown whole number in a multiplication or division equation relating three whole numbers. For example: $9 \times 9 = \underline{}$ $7 \times \underline{} = 56$ $12 = \underline{} \div 3$	Students will vary in their use of different strategies to find the unknown. Students will use primarily one or two strategies.	Students will not consider the operation to find the unknown. They may incorrectly apply the commutative property to division. They may assume that the equals sign always belongs at the end of an equation.

Implementing the Observations: How and when will you conduct the observation during your lesson? Consider the strategic points during the lesson to conduct observations and collect data.

Collecting Evidence: What kind of tool will you use to record your observations? As you conduct the observation, you will want to use a simple recording tool. Figure 10.3 shows a completed example of a form that third-grade teacher Vivian used to collect evidence during a lesson.

Figure 10.3

Standard:	Determine the unknown whole number in a multiplication or division equation relating three whole numbers.
Prompt:	$7 \times \underline{\hspace{1cm}} = 56$
Names	**Observations**
Kevin	Could determine the unknown only for multiplication examples.
Marta	Could not solve the problems that began with the equals sign and said, "This does not make sense to me."

Adjusting Instruction: How will you immediately adjust instruction using the feedback from the observation? For example, using the evidence collected in Figure 10.3, Vivian prompted Kevin to see if he could use what he knows about multiplication to solve the unknown division problems. She asked, "How could you use multiplication to find the unknown in this division example? What multiplication fact is related to this division fact?"

For Marta, Viviane leaned over and asked, "What does the equals sign mean to you?" She then grabbed some cubes, drew an equals sign and asked Marta to make an equal amount on the opposite side of her equals sign. She asked, "I have 6 blue cubes and 4 red cubes on my side of the equals sign. You have 5 blue cubes and 5 red cubes on your side of the equals sign. What does that mean?"

Providing Feedback to Students: How will you do this during the lesson to move learning forward? It's important to give feedback swiftly, after students have supplied evidence of their learning. Immediate feedback helps students positively connect the feedback with their explanation or representation. You also need to ensure that the feedback is explicit and connects specifically to the student's learning needs. In Viviane's example, she said to Marta, "I can see that you made a different way to make ten that is still equal to the way I made ten. I am wondering what this number sentence would look like if we began it as $10 = \underline{\hspace{0.5cm}} + \underline{\hspace{0.5cm}}$."

Viviane positively reinforced Marta's knowledge of a way to find two equivalent representations for ten. She then prompted her to use this information to write it with the equals sign positioned at the beginning (after the total) of the number sentence.

Viviane's feedback to Marta was also careful and thoughtful. She said, "Marta, you are very good at identifying things that don't make sense to you. You insist that the mathematics you are learning makes sense, which is an important characteristic of good mathematicians. Now that you found a way to use the equals sign with addition, how can you use what you know about the equals sign to see if you can find the unknown value in this multiplication equation, $24 = \underline{\hspace{0.5cm}} \times 8$."

Once again, Viviane gave explicit feedback to Marta and then deftly positioned a new task to move her thinking along. If teachers wait too long to give feedback to students, the magical moment can be lost, and students will not be able to connect the feedback to their actions.

Interview

The formative assessment **interview** is a brief interview that you tuck into a lesson when you want to collect more information about a student's thinking. The interview is brief, is on the spot, and can be conducted as a response to something you observed students doing. Interviews can help you dig deeper into the source of student misconceptions.

Anticipating Student Responses: Consider the kinds of responses students might give you during the interview. You can decide ahead of time that you will interview particular students or a group of students. You might also decide to interview students who respond in particular ways to the lesson. Interview questions include these:

Why did you decide to solve it that way?

What representations help you understand this concept?

Can you explain your thinking?

Implementing the Interview: When and how will you conduct it? You can also plan to tuck interviews in a lesson during small-group instruction.

Collecting Evidence: You gather student data to inform your instructional decisions. For example, Ariana, a fifth-grade teacher, designed an interview recording sheet for each of her small groups (Figure 10.4). Although she only meets with her small groups twice a week, she finds that this is the best time to conduct the interview because she can concentrate on her students' thinking.

Figure 10.4

Group:

Date	Name	Interview Question	Interview Notes

Adjusting Instruction: As you interview students, you can gain insight into those sticky misconceptions that prevent students from learning. For example, during an interview about decimal place value, Ariana interviewed Hunter by asking him to represent 2.34 using place value blocks and explain his thinking. Hunter showed her the following:

Figure 10.5

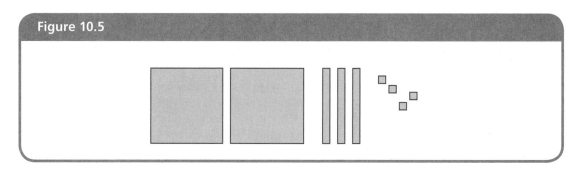

Ariana replied, "Now tell me about the value of each of the digits in two and thirty-four hundredths, and show me where the value is represented in the place value blocks."

Hunter explained, "Well, there are two wholes [pointing to the two large squares], and three tenths [pointing to the three tenths], and there are four hundredths [pointing to the four hundredths]."

Ariana asked, "You said that there are three tenths and four hundredths, but when you read the decimal, you said two and thirty-four hundredths. How can three tenths and four hundredths be the same value?"

Hunter responded, "Well they are the same amount. Just like 34 ones is the same as three tens and four ones! We just read it as hundredths because you say the place value of the last digit. It is kind of funny, but I noticed it is the opposite with whole numbers. Like if we see [writes 3,675], we read it as three thousand, six hundred seventy-five. If this same number is a decimal [writes 3.675], we read the whole number first and then the value is the smallest place value so I would read it as three and six hundred seventy-five thousandths because the 5 is in the thousandths place."

Ariana asked, "When did you notice the difference between how we read whole numbers and decimals, and how does this help you read decimals?

Hunter responded, "I noticed right away in fourth grade when we started decimals, but I didn't tell anyone because I wasn't sure if it was true."

Ariana replied, "Hunter, you are thinking like a mathematician because you are noticing patterns and then applying those patterns. You noticed something important about the way we read whole numbers and decimals and how this connects to the value. I would like you to share your ideas with the class because I think it will help everyone understand decimal place value."

Ariana's interview revealed Hunter's advanced understanding of place value and his ability to make connections and see patterns between whole numbers and decimal place value. If she had not interviewed Hunter, she might never have known that he was thinking this deeply about his learning.

Providing Feedback: Once again, timely *feedback* is critical. However, note that in Ariana's interview, she did not start providing feedback to Hunter before she gathered evidence of his thinking. She needed to fully understand the extent of his understanding in order to provide appropriate feedback.

Ariana next said to Hunter, "You explained to me that the decimal values are named by the smallest value. What is the relationship of each of the place values as you move to the right of the decimal point and how is it alike or different from how the values change to the left of the decimal point?"

In this example, Ariana reflected back what Hunter said and did in the interview, and then she asked a question to prompt more thinking. While it would have been easier for Ariana simply to tell Hunter the pattern, she knew that providing feedback by reflecting back to Hunter about his own thinking would promote new learning.

Show Me

The **Show Me** technique is "a performance response by a student or group of students that extends and often deepens what was observed and what might have been asked within an interview" (Fennell et al., 2017). This technique is nicely suited for elementary teachers because you can easily integrate the Show Me technique into lessons by asking students to show understanding using manipulatives and/or drawings, digit cards, whiteboards, and/or response cards.

Anticipating Student Responses: As you plan to use the Show Me technique, think about the potential responses students might provide. For example, Gerald, a fourth-grade teacher, gave each student a set of pattern blocks. He planned to ask the students to show a representation of the fraction in mixed fraction form and as an improper fraction using the pattern blocks as he named it (Figure 10.6). He anticipated that some students would struggle and prepared some pattern block outlines of the pattern block hexagon so that students could focus on how they were representing the whole region in the mixed fraction. He decided that he would allow the students to choose the hexagon outlines.

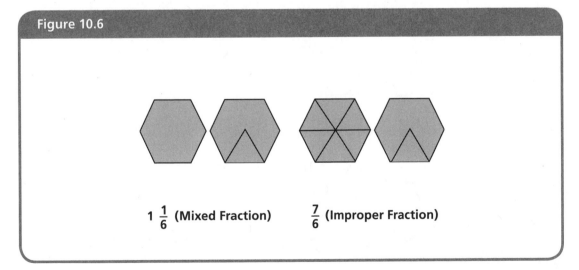

Figure 10.6

$1\frac{1}{6}$ **(Mixed Fraction)** $\frac{7}{6}$ **(Improper Fraction)**

Standards

LI and SC

Purpose

Tasks

Materials

Student Thinking

Lesson Structures

Form. Assess.

Lesson Launch

Lesson Facilitation

Closure

Implementing Show Me: Consider at what points you will want to use it. Gerald planned to implement the Show Me technique during the brief whole-group lesson. He hoped to give them several prompts and ask them probing questions to explain their representations.

Collecting Evidence: You can collect evidence using the Show Me technique by taking photographs, jotting down notes, and using technology applications like Go Formative (Goformative.com), which collects representations of individual students' work. Gerald often snaps a photo of the students as they are showing their work.

Adjusting Instruction: As you conduct the Show Me technique, consider how you will adjust instruction using the evidence you are collecting. Show Me prompts, in particular, often reveal trends in student thinking because you can see everyone's response at one time. For example, as Gerald was prompting the students with the Show Me mixed and improper fractions, he noted that a few students were not able to show the improper fraction. He decided to have the students first show the improper fraction and then show the mixed fraction that matched it. He thought that this adjustment would help the students focus on one fraction at a time and see that while the fraction representations were different, the two fractions were equal.

Providing Feedback: The Show Me formative assessment offers the perfect opportunity for students to provide feedback to each other by explaining their own thinking and probing each other's thinking. For instance, as Gerald scanned the room, he noticed that Alethea quickly showed the two fraction representations almost before he even posed the prompt. While she waited for her classmates, she created more mixed and improper fractions. Gerald decided to put the students in pairs while he posed the prompts so they could explain their thinking to each other. He purposely paired Alethea with Terry because he noticed that Terry was struggling to show the mixed fraction. He heard Alethea say, "Terry, when Mr. Raymond says the fraction, imagine it in your head. The first thing he is going to say is how many wholes there are—that will equal the same number of hexagons."

Hinge Questions

As a teacher, you craft and ask hundreds of questions throughout the course of one day! The **hinge question** is a special kind of question that essentially provides a check for understanding at a pivotal moment in your lesson (Wiliam, 2011). In other words, the next part of your lesson hinges on how students respond. According to Wiliam (2011), students should respond in one minute or less. Fennell et al. (2017) suggest that this could be expanded to two or three minutes, particularly as you consider the developmental needs of your primary students.

Anticipating Student Responses: The key to writing a good hinge question is to anticipate the possible interpretations or incorrect responses that students might give. Hinge questions take several forms, including multiple choices and short, open-ended prompts. For example, Kendra, a fourth-grade teacher, developed a multiple-choice hinge question for the following standard:

> Read and write multi-digit whole numbers using base ten numerals, number names, and expanded form. Compare two multi-digit numbers based on meanings of the digits in each place, using <, =, and > symbols to record the results of comparisons.

Here is Kendra's hinge question:

> Circle the following numbers that are correctly ordered from least to greatest.
>
> A. 345   3,045   3,154   3,545
>
> B. 279   297   209   290
>
> C. 608   619   698   699
>
> D. 1,034 1,056   1,064   1,604

Kendra anticipated that all or most of her students would select A. She wanted to see if the students would recognize the C and D as also correct.

Implementing Hinge Questions: To implement hinge questions, you can pose them at the beginning, middle, or end of the lesson. The key idea is to pose the question at a strategic point to assess if students are ready to move on to the next concept. For example, Kendra decided to ask her question after a task on comparing numbers when zero was in the tens or hundreds place, which was at the midpoint of her lesson.

Collecting Evidence: You can collect evidence of students' responses to the hinge questions by using small slips of paper, journals, or technology. For example, Kendra displayed the prompt for her students on a whiteboard and distributed small slips of paper with the same prompt for students to circle.

Adjusting Instruction: Many teachers choose to regroup students to adjust instruction after collecting evidence from the hinge question. For example, Kendra planned to move her students into math stations so she could provide additional instruction for her struggling students in a small group while the other students rotated through the stations, which included a task with comparing values of numbers. Kendra used the hinge question to flexibly group her students, using real evidence from the lesson. She loved that she was immediately responding to the students' learning needs.

Providing Feedback: You can provide feedback on the hinge question in many ways. Some teachers reveal the correct answer and have students gather in pairs or small groups to discuss the solutions. Other teachers, like Kendra, use the hinge question to provide explicit instructional feedback to the students during the lesson, either in small groups or individually. The key is to take an immediate call to action based on the evidence.

Exit Task

The **exit task** is a "capstone problem or task that captures the major focus of the lesson for that day or perhaps the last several days and provides a sampling of student performance" (Fennell et al., 2017, p. 109). You may be familiar with the term **exit ticket** or **exit slip.** However, an exit task extends beyond a simple question that may assess only a small portion of the student's understanding. Instead, the exit task is a high-cognitive task (see Chapter 6) that includes opportunities for students to connect procedures to concepts, explore mathematical relationships, use representations, and apply self-monitoring and self-regulation skills as they work to solve the problem (Smith & Stein, 2011).

Bryan, a fifth-grade teacher, considered the prompts in Figure 10.7 for his exit task.

Figure 10.7

Task A	Task B
Convert 5 miles to feet. Write your answer.	Juanita was training to run a marathon. On Saturday, Juanita ran 17 miles in 3 hours. If she ran the same distance every hour, how far did she run in one hour? Juanita's goal was to run at least 26,400 feet per hour. Did she make her goal? If yes, by how much? If no, by how much? Show your evidence.

Bryan chose Task B because he wanted the students to use reasoning and provide mathematical evidence to show their thinking. Task A wasn't going to give him good information about the students' understanding of conversions.

Anticipating Student Responses: Once again, it is critical to *anticipate* the results of the formative assessment, particularly as you consider how you will assess your students' understanding of the concept you just taught. You can also differentiate the exit task or design it so that students can enter into the task from different points. For example, students could begin with the total miles or with Juanita's goal to solve Task B in Figure 10.7. Bryan can also determine how students solved it by examining their work to see if they were able to make sense of the conversions.

Standards

LI and SC

Purpose

Tasks

Materials

Student Thinking

Lesson Structures

Form. Assess.

Lesson Launch

Lesson Facilitation

Closure

Implementing Exit Tasks: As the description of the task indicated, you can implement an exit task at the end of a concept or lesson. Some teachers design exit tasks to reflect standards that they have been teaching for a long time. Other teachers design and conduct exit tasks toward the end of the lesson. The key is to make sure you give students plenty of time to solve the task!

Collecting Evidence: Review the students' responses to the exit task to collect evidence for overall trends in their understanding. After that, you can examine each group for individual strengths and needs. For example, Bryan likes to use an exit task summary sheet (Figure 10.8) to analyze student work from the whole class. He uses the same format for each exit task and supplies the specific criteria for each task. He then records the names of the students below the appropriate criteria.

Figure 10.8

Exit Task: Juanita was training to run a marathon! On Saturday, Juanita ran 17 miles in three hours. If she ran the same distance every hour, how far did she run in one hour? Juanita's goal was to run at least 26,400 feet per hour. Did she make her goal? If yes, by how much? If no, by how much? Show your evidence!

Does Not Meet Expectations (Describe)	Meets Expectations (Describe)	Exceeds Expectations (Describe)
Provides incomplete or incorrect conversions.	Provides accurate conversion and explanation.	Provides accurate conversions and includes thorough explanation.
Rico	Josh	Sophia
Mia	Kaylee	Lince

Adjusting Instruction: Your exit task evidence is quite important in deciding how you will adjust instruction. For instance, you may decide that your students are ready to move on or, perhaps, that they need additional, targeted instruction. The exit task is particularly suited to differentiation as you see the particular needs of your students. You may be tempted to divide them into same-ability groups, but you might also wish to consider mixed-ability groups, which allow students to share strategies and construct new ideas together. The key is to use student evidence to make your decisions about how you will adjust instruction.

Providing Feedback to the Students: Since the exit task is often conducted at the end of the lesson or series of lessons, you will want to provide feedback that is directly connected to the success criteria. You can do this when you move to your next instructional step, whether you choose to work with students individually, in small groups, or in large groups. Exit task data are also great to share with families. For example, Bryan collects five exit tasks per quarter to place in the students' portfolios for family conferences. In his school, students lead the conferences by sharing their work, thus providing even more opportunities to receive feedback.

As you can see, formative assessment is intricately tied to your planning and teaching. If you are just beginning to use formative assessment techniques, begin with those that are most comfortable for you and build your repertoire as you develop ease with the techniques.

Which of the formative assessment techniques will you try first? Why? How will you begin integrating this technique into your teaching practice? Record your ideas below.

_____

_____

_____

_____

_____

_____

_____

_____

_____

_____

_____

Building Unit Coherence

As you design and collect daily formative assessment evidence, you develop comprehensive knowledge of your students' mathematical understanding. You can support unit coherence by varying the techniques and kinds of formative assessment data you collect.

Example: Isabel

Isabel, a third-grade teacher, realizes that she is primarily using the observation technique for her students. This technique produces a lot of anecdotal evidence, but although it is rich in detail, she wants to use more student work evidence. Consequently, she decides to incorporate more Show Me assessment prompts over the course of the unit. She feels that the combination of anecdotal notes and student work nicely captures her students' mathematical understanding and, over the course of the unit, creates a coherent picture of all of the students' learning.

Standards

LI and SC

Purpose

Tasks

Materials

Student Thinking

Lesson Structures

Form. Assess.

Lesson Launch

Lesson Facilitation

Closure

The third-grade teachers are deciding which formative assessment technique to use in their lesson. Saida suggests, "Since we are planning for a lot of conversation and students' sharing their own ideas, I would like to use a hinge question in the middle of the lesson to be sure everyone understands the concept of comparing fractions." "Good idea," says Julian. "Sometimes in large-group discussions, I find it hard to determine if I should move on because I am not sure everyone has the concept."

Formative Assessment:

Hinge question used after students compare fractions with same denominators: Here are two fractions.

$$\frac{3}{8} \text{ or } \frac{5}{8}$$

On your whiteboard, write the fraction that is greater and draw a picture to back up your thinking.

If students answer this correctly, continue playing "Convince Us!" using fractions with same numerators and different denominators.

See the complete lesson plan in Appendix A on page 186.

💡 **Think of a lesson you taught recently where a hinge question would have been useful. Note the question below.**

Fourth-Grade Snapshot

Formative Assessment

Adrienne and Davante are planning for their transfer lesson on fractions. Adrienne asks, "Since this is a final lesson on comparing fractions, do you think it would be appropriate to use observation for an informal assessment?" "Sure," says Julian. "We can informally observe as they are working and listen for the key concepts and vocabulary we focused on in the previous lessons."

Formative Assessment:

Use the observation checklist to observe the following:
- Partners listening to one another
- Ordering of fractions on the number line
- Strategies/models selected to find equivalent fractions
- Number of equivalent fractions on the number line (including fraction forms of whole and mixed numbers)

See the complete lesson plan in Appendix A on page 191.

How might you capture students' work while using the Show Me formative assessment technique?

Boton, Chelsea, and Rodrigo are working to develop brief formative assessment interviews to use with their fifth graders. Rodrigo explains, "The interviews we have been conducting have been incredible! I feel like I have a much better idea about their understanding. I am able to adjust my instruction in the moment!"

Boton agrees, "Yes, I have also noticed how much they love to be interviewed, too! I am able to give them specific feedback that really seems to make a difference."

They decide they will interview individual students and/or student pairs about their solutions.

Formative Assessment:

Individual and paired interviews: Ask students, "How does your representation show multiplication of fractions?"

See the complete lesson plan in Appendix A on page 195.

How could you integrate brief formative assessment interviews into your practice? Note your ideas below.

_____

_____

_____

_____

_____

_____

_____

_____

_____

_____

_____

_____

_____

_____

_____

_____

_____

_____

_____

_____

_____

Standards

LI and SC

Purpose

Tasks

Materials

Student Thinking

Lesson Structures

Form. Assess.

Lesson Launch

Lesson Facilitation

Closure

Under Construction

Now it is your turn! Decide on the formative assessment(s) that will best suit the lesson you are building.

Formative Assessment:

online resources
Download the full Lesson-Planning Template from resources.corwin.com/mathlessonplanning/3-5
Remember that you can use the online version of the lesson plan template to begin compiling each section into the full template as your lesson plan grows.

PART III

PULLING ALL THE PIECES TOGETHER

CHAPTER 11

PLANNING TO LAUNCH THE LESSON

Sally, a third-grade teacher, began her lesson by displaying the first picture in a series of three pictures (Figure 11.1).

She told her students that she would give them one minute to See, Think, and Wonder (Ritchhart, Church, & Morrison, 2011) about the picture. After a minute of silence, she told the students to find their Turn and Talk Buddies to discuss what they see, think, and wonder about the picture. The classroom buzzed with productive mathematics talk. Sally noticed some of the students pointing and counting as they looked at the picture. She then revealed two more pictures (Figure 11.2).

Once again, she gave the students a minute of silence to observe the pictures and then asked them to turn and talk with each other. As she surveyed the room, she noted that every single student appeared to be engaged.

Sally asked, "What do you notice about the pictures? Please raise your hands and let me know about something your Turn and Talk Buddy noticed."

Hands waved wildly in the air as students strained to share their partners' observations. Sally wrote quickly to include what they saw. Then she asked her students to share their think and wonders (Figure 11.3).

Figure 11.1

Figure 11.2

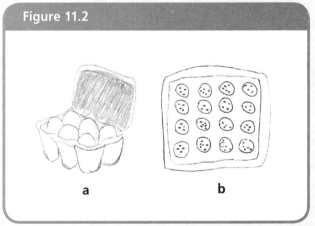

a   b

Figure 11.3

See	Think and Wonder
• It looks like candy!	• I am trying to figure out how they are related.
• The first picture is a group, but the second and third pictures are organized.	• Are they all things that would be at a party?
• I think the first picture looks like 20.	• Are we going to group things?
• The skeletons are in a row.	• Are we going to put things in a row?
• It looks like a pattern.	• Is this going to be about multiplication?
• There are groups of four.	
• There are rows and columns.	

Sally announced that today they would be exploring ways to group objects equally. She asked, "How many ways can you arrange 24 objects in equal groups? How many in each group?"

She then directed the students to review their learning intentions and success criteria for the lesson.

This chapter explores ways to begin your lesson. We will explore the following questions:

- What is a lesson launch?
- How can you launch a problem-solving lesson?
- What kinds of lesson launches focus on mathematics concepts?
- What are number routine lesson launches?
- What do you anticipate students will do?

WHAT IS A LESSON LAUNCH?

Imagine you are opening to the first page of a book or turning to a new television show. How quickly do you decide whether you will continue to read or watch or abandon? In a similar way, students may also make conscious or unconscious decisions about whether they will engage in a lesson. This possibility highlights the importance of the **lesson launch.**

Your lesson launch can be implemented in many ways and should be designed with just as much purpose and planning as the main body of your lesson. For example, lesson launches may include a number sense routine to help students think and talk about numbers, equations, and computation. Or, your lesson launch might introduce a specific problem-solving task. Your lesson launch can be tied directly to the big idea and learning intention for the day, particularly if you plan to use the lesson launch to set up the lesson you are about to teach. Or you might use the lesson launch to circle back to a big idea or concept that the students previously learned because you want to make sure the children continue to build understanding of that concept. This is called **interleaving,** and it increases the students' retention and performance on assessments (Rohrer, 2012).

The way that you construct how your lesson will be launched will depend greatly on your students' learning needs, the content standards, Standards for Mathematical Practice or process standards, learning intentions, and lesson purpose. Lessons can be launched by creating interest around a problem-solving task (like in the vignette at the start of this chapter), connecting to prior knowledge or previous lessons, or implementing a **number routine.** Lesson launches can be facilitated in 5 to 15 minutes and are typically conducted in a whole-group setting.

Many teachers use the same routine, like a warmup, to launch a lesson every day. While there are benefits to building a routine into your mathematics lesson, such as a warmup, teachers report that most students passively watch one or two students answer the warmup exercises. Rather than beginning your mathematics lesson in the same way every day, vary your lesson launch as it connects to the students' learning and math content needs. As you read this chapter, consider ways you might launch your mathematics lessons to stimulate *all* students' interests and boost conceptual understanding.

HOW CAN YOU LAUNCH A PROBLEM-SOLVING LESSON?

Launching a lesson with a focus on problem solving gives you an opportunity to help students unpack a problem before trying to solve it. The following problem-solving lesson launches also nicely connect to the Standards for Mathematical Practice or process standards. You can focus on helping students make sense of problems, develop ways to communicate their ideas, ask questions of their peers, and critique each other's reasoning and thinking.

See, Think, and Wonder Lesson Launch

The See, Think, and Wonder (STW) (Ritchhart et al., 2011) routine summons students to carefully observe, make some predictions, and expand the predictions into questions. Along with Notice and Wonder (Math Forum, 2015), which is described later in this chapter, STW capitalizes on students' keen observational skills and natural curiosity about what they are learning. When you use this launch, you invite students to bring their own thoughts and questions forward before you instruct them to engage in particular ways with the content. Both strategies can help students draw on prior knowledge, and they motivate students to reason before receiving formal instruction, which is particularly useful for English Language Learners (ELLs) or other learners who struggle. The two strategies have slight but important variations.

Example: Marcy

Marcy, a third-grade teacher, has always noticed that her third graders are very inquisitive, and she likes to engage their curiosity as much as possible. Instead of giving the students the definition of quadrilaterals and then perfect models of a triangle and then directly telling them the definition of a quadrilateral, she decides to capitalize on their natural curiosity to engage and motivate them.

To launch the lesson, Marcy shows students the illustration in Figure 11.4 and asks them to SEE quietly.

Figure 11.4

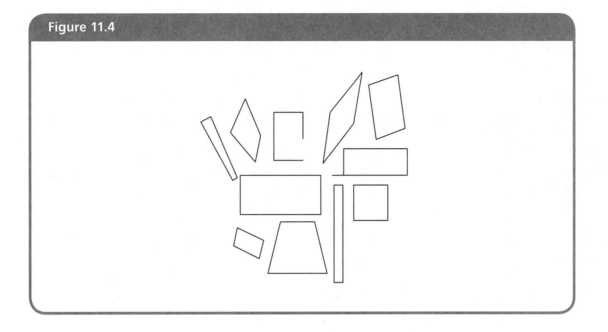

This quiet reflection time allows students an opportunity to make observations without being hindered by another student's thoughts. Marcy makes sure that students have enough time to notice important details in the picture. She then asks the students to share with a partner what they saw. She reminds them that she wants them to share by making "I SEE" statements. She then asks the student pairs to share something their partners noticed that they didn't. She records their answers in a chart that everyone can view (Figure 11.5).

Figure 11.5

I SEE

Nine shapes.

A square.

A skinny rectangle.

A diamond on a point.

Someone dropped shapes on a table.

A rectangle with a piece of a line on it.

A rectangle with a hole in it.

Shapes with four sides.

Shapes with four angles.

Some of the shapes are the same but bigger than each other.

Marcy then asks the students to THINK. To remind her students that this is when they make predictions about what they are seeing, she says, "Using what you observe, make a prediction about what you are seeing. What do you think is going on here?" She again gives them quiet time to think. This time she calls on students to share their ideas. Then she records their answers (Figure 11.6).

Figure 11.6

I THINK

There are a bunch of shapes.

Some are rectangles but some are not.

They all have four sides.

They all have four angles.

Some are not real shapes like a square or a rectangle.

Marcy then asks students what they WONDER after Seeing and Thinking about the shapes. She records the Wonders (Figure 11.7). Students may also record their own Wonders on individual whiteboards and then post them for everyone to see.

Figure 11.7

I WONDER

If we are going to make them.

If we will find out who drew them.

If the shapes have a name.

If we can touch them.

If the shapes fit together.

Marcy then uses the Wonders to launch into her lesson about the shared attributes of quadrilaterals. She gives the students the shapes to sort, describe, and finally name and define. By igniting their curiosity, Marcy is able to build on what they already know to advance their understanding of geometry.

Notice and Wonder Lesson Launch

While similar to the See, Think, and Wonder approach, the Notice and Wonder protocol, developed by the Math Forum (2015), simplifies the process into two distinct steps. It was originally designed to focus students on unpacking word problems to enhance students' understanding of "the story, the quantities, and the relationships in the problem" (p. 2). The Math Forum suggests the following steps:

Notice

- Display or read a portion or complete problem to students.

- Ask the students, "What do you notice?" Be sure to encourage wait time.

- Record all of the students' ideas without commenting.

Wonder

- Ask the students, "What are you wondering?"

- Record all of the students' ideas without commenting.

- Ask the students if they have additional questions or clarifications.

At the conclusion of the Notice and Wonder, you can encourage students to tell the story in partners or small groups before solving the problem.

Example: Lince

Fourth-grade teacher Lince often uses Notice and Wonder to introduce routine and nonroutine word problems. Her students are so accustomed to this approach that they can even conduct their own Notice and Wonder sessions in small groups. One day she shares the following problem with her fourth graders:

Patsy traveled 376 miles to pick up her niece. The entire trip took 9 hours. She traveled 50 miles the first hour. She traveled 32 miles the last hour. Patsy traveled an equal number of miles for each hour in between the first and the last hour. ██? (Note that the question is covered.)

The fourth graders notice the following:

- She had to travel 376 miles.

- She traveled more miles the first hour than the last hour.

- She traveled 82 miles the first and last hour.

They wondered the following:

- Why did it take so long?

- Where was her niece?

- What would they do?

- How many more miles did she travel in the first hour than the second?

- How many miles did she travel in the middle?

- How many miles did she travel each hour?

Lince then reveals the question: "How many miles did she travel each hour in between the first and last hour?" to the cheers of the fourth graders! They clap for themselves, excited that they have once again wondered the question in the word problem.

Lince often uses the Notice and Wonder technique to encourage the students to engage with the problem before seeing the question. She notices that the students often ask the question in the problem themselves, which enhances student comprehension and heightens their interest in solving the problem.

Numberless Word Problem Lesson Launch

Students may be so distracted by the numbers in the word problem that they are tempted to perform any operation regardless of what makes sense. The **numberless word problem** launch encourages the students to make sense of the word problem without the numbers.

Example: Torrence

Torrence, a fourth-grade teacher, displays and reads the following problem to his students:

Standards

Ll and SC

Purpose

Tasks

Materials

Student Thinking

Lesson Structures

Form. Assess.

Lesson Launch

Lesson Facilitation

Closure

Gabriella and Isabel are saving to buy their grandmother a special birthday present. Gabriella saved some money. The amount of money Isabel saved is many times more than her little sister. They need a certain amount to buy the present. Did they save enough money? Why or why not?

Torrence has purposely selected a word problem with the word *more* in it because he has noticed that many students think that they need to automatically add when they see the word *more*. Torrence asks student pairs to talk with each other and share their ideas about what is happening in the word problem. As he looks around the classroom, he notices that the students are excitedly talking about how much money each sister might have saved. He has purposely paired the students for the discussion because there are two students in the word problem. Prior to the lesson, he anticipated that the students might supply numbers and begin trying to solve the problem.

After about five minutes of paired discussion, Torrence asks, "What is this word problem asking us to solve?" Here are the students' replies.

Mary: I think we are adding something to Gabriella's amount, but Kevin does not think we should do that.

Ari: We thought that too, but then we realized that Isabel saved a certain amount times more than Gabriella so we have to find how much more money Isabel saved than Gabriella.

Rosie: Yes, if Gabriella saved $2 and then Isabel saved five times as much, then they saved $10 together because five times two equals ten.

Torrence smiles. This is exactly the kind of discussion he had hoped to elicit. Without the numbers in the problem, the students are able to reason about the problem and even supply their own numbers to prove their ideas.

What do you notice about the lesson launches? How might you integrate these kinds of lesson launches into your lesson planning? Record some of your ideas here.

_____

_____

_____

_____

_____

WHAT KINDS OF LESSON LAUNCHES FOCUS ON MATHEMATICS CONCEPTS?

You can use the following lesson launch routines to focus students on recalling, using, and applying prior knowledge; using, developing, and applying appropriate vocabulary; and noticing and examining the structure of mathematics.

One of These Things Is Not Like the Others

You may remember the old *Sesame Street* song:

> One of these things is not like the others,
> One of these things just doesn't belong. (Raposo & Stone, 1972)

In this lesson launch, students examine three related numbers or pictures and one unrelated number or picture and try to determine why one of the choices does not belong. Students must select one of the options and then construct a viable argument about why they believe a particular picture or number does not belong. The key to this launch is to provide examples that offer different entry points for students.

Example: **Dee**

Dee's students have been working diligently on representing decimal numbers using place value materials and have recently been comparing decimals. She wants to see if the students will recognize decimal equivalencies when presented in different forms.

Dee designs the prompt in Figure 11.8 to elicit conversation about decimal place value, equivalencies, and expanded form. Whenever Dee uses this type of prompt, she typically displays it and then gives the students time to think about and prepare a mathematical argument for which one is not like the others. Sometimes she even challenges the students to create a mathematical argument for all of the choices. In this case, she ensures that any of the choices can be selected as the one not like the others if students can explain their reasoning.

Figure 11.8

847 hundredths	847 tenths
$8 + 0.4 + 0.07$	$(8 \times 1) + (1 \times \frac{4}{10}) + (8 \times \frac{7}{100})$

Dee asks, "Which one of these things is not like the others?"

Dee's students quickly notice that two show the value in word form. Only a few notice that 847 hundredths is equal to the others. Some recognize that 847 tenths is not equal to the others. Others believe that $(8 \times 1) + (1 \times \frac{4}{10}) + (8 \times \frac{7}{100})$ is not the same because the decimals are written in fraction form. While all the values of this example are the same, the students are able to think about the meaning of equivalent decimal values.

This lesson launch offers Dee good insight into her students' thinking about decimal place value. She is able to use the student work from this lesson launch to transition to her lesson that focuses on multiple ways to represent a number.

You can also tailor this lesson launch to focus on particular kinds of reasoning that your students exhibit. For more examples like this, you can check out the Which One Doesn't Belong website (http://wodb.ca) created by Mary Barousa with contributions by teachers from all over the country. Also, check out Christopher Danielson's (2016) book, *Which One Doesn't Belong?* which focuses on shapes, numbers, and other mathematics concepts.

WHAT ARE NUMBER SENSE ROUTINE LESSON LAUNCHES?

Number sense routines focus on strategies that help students understand number concepts and build computational fluency. Most important, you are providing opportunities for students to derive their own strategies, hear the strategies their peers use, and develop fluency using those strategies. Number sense routines also offer opportunities for students to engage in **spaced practice,** which occurs when you expose students to an idea over several days and then *space* opportunities to practice the learned skill (Hattie et al., 2016). Select your number sense routines purposely, either as a launch to link to the content you are about to teach or as an opportunity to provide spaced practice. The following number sense routine lesson launches encourage the students to develop understanding and reasoning about numbers, flexibility with numbers, and number fluency.

Standards

LI and SC

Purpose

Tasks

Materials

Student Thinking

Lesson Structures

Form. Assess.

Lesson Launch

Lesson Facilitation

Closure

Example: Leo

Leo, a fourth-grade teacher, uses estimation both as a lesson launch and as a station in his classroom. He uses estimation as a launch when he wants to create a discussion with students about efficient ways to multiply and divide whole numbers. For a lesson on multiplication of ten, Leo launches the lesson by distributing laminated pictures of seniors graduating from high school throwing their caps in the air to pairs of students (Figure 11.9).

Figure 11.9

He first asks them to estimate how many total caps are in the air and write it on a sticky note. He posts the sticky notes in order from least to greatest. Then he asks the students to use the dry erase marker to circle ten caps on the laminated picture and use the new information to make a new estimate and record it on a sticky note (Figure 11.10). He posts the new sticky notes from least to greatest and asks the students to make observations about the new estimates. Students quickly note that the new estimates are in multiples of ten. They also notice that their estimates are now much closer together. This launch sets the stage perfectly for Leo to build on the power of multiplying by ten!

Figure 11.10

For more estimation examples, pictures, and lessons for Grades 3, 4, and 5, check out the Estimation 180 website (http://www.estimation180.com/lessons.html) created by Andrew Stadel.

Number Lines

The number line is ideally suited to support students as they develop meaning about whole numbers and fractions and understanding about number and fraction relationships. The number line offers endless opportunities to differentiate according to students' content and learning needs. You can change the start and end points, include particular benchmarks, and provide or encourage students to connect concrete or pictorial representations to the placement of values on the number line.

You can use the number line in a number sense launch routine to help students construct conceptual understanding, reason about number patterns and relationships, and develop fluency.

Example: Amelia

Third-grade teacher Amelia uses a number line to encourage students to reason about where the fractions $\frac{1}{3}$, $\frac{1}{2}$, $\frac{1}{4}$, and $\frac{1}{6}$ are placed on a number line. She poses the prompt and distributes laminated number lines and fraction manipulatives to the students. Students then record their thinking using dry erase markers. Finally, she posts the students' ideas and has the students discuss what they notice about the placement of the fractions (Figure 11.11).

Happily, she notes that many students are thinking about the unit fraction and noticing that the greater the number of parts in the fraction, the smaller the unit fraction.

Standards

LI and SC

Purpose

Tasks

Materials

Student Thinking

Lesson Structures

Form. Assess.

Lesson Launch

Lesson Facilitation

Closure

Figure 11.11

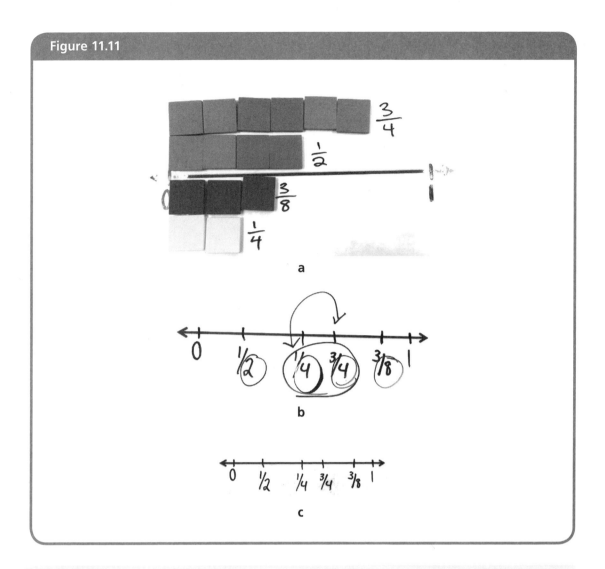

a

b

c

Clothesline Math

Clothesline Math number lines are interactive number lines that can be conducted as a whole-class lesson launch. Armed with string, tape, or a fastener to hold the string, clothespins, and index cards, Sean decides to conduct a fraction clothesline to help his students compare fractions with the same numerator but different denominators. He posts four clotheslines in different stations around the room. At each clothesline, he posts a different set of fraction cards, manipulatives, and paper for drawing representations. As student groups decide how they will organize the fractions, Sean walks around and asks students to explain their reasoning. After student groups have completed the fraction clotheslines, he asked each group to share their fraction placements and provide feedback to the other groups (Figure 11.12).

Figure 11.12

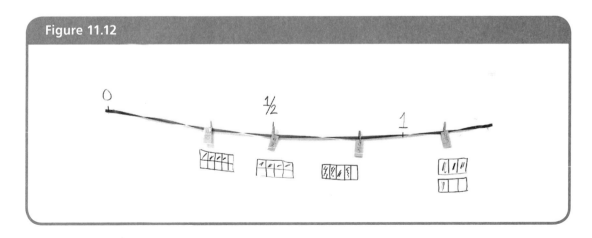

Splats

Developed by Steve Wyborney, Splats are visual number sense routines that build students' mathematical reasoning by presenting them with a combination of visual **subitizing,** visual patterns, and hidden values. Jeremy uses Splats to foster understanding about multiplication, division, and fractions.

> ### Example: Jeremy
>
> Jeremy wants his students to find the hidden value under the splat by using multiplication and addition or subtraction when given the total. He presents the Splat to the students and reminds them that when the splat is the same color, the hidden values are the same (Figure 11.13).
>
> **Figure 11.13**
>
>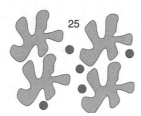
>
> Jeremy asks, "What value is under the Splat?" and "What would a number sentence look like for this Splat?"
>
> Jeremy's students notice that there are four Splats and five dots showing.
>
> Amir says, "I see 25 is the total so first I subtract the 5 and get 20. Then I know there are four Splats that are equal, so this means I am going to divide. Twenty divided by 4 equals 5."
>
> Jeremy writes 25 − 5 = 20 and then 20 ÷ 4 = 5 and says, "You were able to subtract and then use your knowledge of division to find the Splat value."
>
> Lori says, "I kinda did it the opposite way. I guessed a couple of times by multiplying. First, I tried 3 and 'timesed it' by 4 to get 12 and then added the 5 to get 17." As Lori explains, Jeremy records Lori's thinking on the board: 3 × 4 = 12, 12 + 5 = 17. She continues, "Then I thought it had to be 5 so I multiplied 5 by 4 and got 20." (Jeremy writes 5 × 4 = 20.) "Then, I added 5 more and got 25." (Jeremy writes 20 + 5 = 25.)
>
> Jeremy is pleased with both strategies. Although Amir's is most efficient, Lori's strategy demonstrates her reasoning and emerging fluency skills.

Number Talk

A **number talk,** also called a **math talk,** is a brief classroom routine that focuses on number relationships, mathematical structures, and strategies to build computational fluency. During a number talk, you present students with one or more computation problems to solve mentally. Then you encourage them to explain and justify their strategy while you record their ideas for the rest of the class to see. These explanations help the students work toward accurate, efficient, and flexible strategies (Parrish, 2011). You may conduct a number talk by following these important steps.

1. Present the number problem to your students. You might display subitizing cards, rekenreks, manipulatives, written math equations, and word problems.

2. Give students time to think about the solution. Encourage your students to think quietly. Some teachers encourage students to signal when they are ready to share a strategy.

3. Elicit students' strategies. Record the students' strategies as they explain their thinking. You may also want to record the students' names next to each strategy.

Standards

LI and SC

Purpose

Tasks

Materials

Student Thinking

Lesson Structures

Form. Assess.

Lesson Launch

Lesson Facilitation

Closure

4. Encourage students to ask clarifying questions. You can also ask students to determine efficient and flexible strategies.

5. Repeat with a new problem if there is time.

Example: Kenze

Kenze (Ms. Reynolds), a third-grade teacher, conducts number talks at least twice a week with her students. One day, she displays the following prompt and waits for the students to think of at least one strategy:

$$5 \times 26 =$$

Students begin holding one finger up to show that they have at least one strategy. Some students show two or three fingers, indicating that they have two or three strategies. Kenze calls on Sande to share a strategy.

Sande: Well, I just break 26 into 20 and 6. So I multiply 5 times 20, which is 100. Next, I multiply 5 times 6, which equals 30. So then I add 100 and 30, which equals 130.

Ms. Reynolds: You used place value, Sande! How many of you also used the place value strategy? Sara, do you have a strategy to share?

Sara: First, I broke 26 into 25 and 1. Then I times 25 times 5 and got 125 because that is like having five quarters! Then I times the 1, left over from the 25, times 1, which equals 5. After that, I added 125 plus 5, which equals 130!

Ms. Reynolds: Sara, you made 26 a friendly number before multiplying and you thought about money. How many of you also used friendly numbers? We have time for one more person to share. Misha, it looks like you have a strategy.

Misha: Yes, I decided that I didn't like 26 so I rounded it to 30. Then I multiplied 30 times 5 and got 150. But then I had to subtract because I rounded up. So, first I multiplied 4 times 5, which equals 20. Then I subtracted the 20 from 150 to get 130.

Ms. Reynolds: How come you subtracted 20?

Misha: I had to subtract the 20 because I added it in the beginning when I rounded 26 to 30 in the beginning. I had to make sure that I subtracted it in the end.

Kenze is pleased with the number talk. She notices that many students are using the place value strategy. She is also excited about Sara's solution. She had hoped that a student might introduce the idea of flexibly changing the number to make it easier to add or subtract. Even though place value was a good way to unpack this problem, this has been a great opportunity for students to think about this strategy and hear Sara's thinking.

What do you notice about the number routine lesson launches? How might these kinds of number routine lesson launches be integrated into your lesson planning? Note your responses below.

_____

_____

_____

_____

_____

_____

_____

_____

WHAT DO YOU ANTICIPATE STUDENTS WILL DO?

As you plan your lesson launch, it is critical to anticipate how your students will respond to the launch you have designed. Consider the information in Chapter 1. As you plan instructional activities for your class, anticipate how individual students will react to particular activities. This can help you respond in a way that moves your students' learning forward. If you anticipate and include some typical student responses in your lesson plan, you can also plan for your next instructional move.

How do you anticipate your students' responses to your instructional activities? Note your response below.

_____

_____

_____

_____

_____

_____

_____

_____

_____

Building Unit Coherence

While your lesson launches should be connected to the content you are teaching, you can support unit coherence by varying your lesson launches to reflect different Standards for Mathematical Practice and mathematical habits of mind. You can also use the lesson launch to anchor the current lesson within the unit. You can connect the lesson you are currently teaching to prior learning and forecast what you will be teaching next. Students can then eagerly engage in the launch knowing fully the place this lesson has within the unit.

The launch is also a great point to showcase rigorous tasks. The way you choose to launch the lesson should invite students with varying abilities to enter into the task with confidence.

Example: Bianca

Fifth-grade teacher Bianca regularly chooses the See, Think, and Wonder and Notice and Wonder lesson launches because they invite her English Language Learners to talk and share ideas with partners. She ensures that they have multiple opportunities to talk their partners. She believes that this supports them in making connections from one lesson to another.

Standards

LI and SC

Purpose

Tasks

Materials

Student Thinking

Lesson Structures

Form. Assess.

Lesson Launch

Lesson Facilitation

Closure

Saida, Julian, and Kimi are working on their lesson launch. They decide that since this lesson will introduce new ways of thinking about comparing fractions, they want to launch the lesson by cycling back to previously learned concepts, particularly the whole, numerator, and denominator. They decide to launch the lesson with a short pizza problem to get everyone onboard.

Launch:

Present students with a problem that will activate their prior knowledge about fractions before beginning to play "Convince Us!"

Distribute copies of the following problem:

Mark was asked to draw a picture to compare two fractions: $\frac{4}{5}$ and $\frac{2}{3}$. He drew the following:

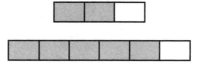

Mark said that $\frac{2}{3}$ is the same size as $\frac{4}{5}$. There is a mistake in Mark's thinking and drawing. Tell your group what you think Mark's error is.

As students work on this problem in small groups, walk around and listen to student reasoning. Have students share their responses with the class after sharing with their groups.

Anticipate student responses:

- Mark did not make his wholes the same size.
- All the pieces are different sizes.
- Mark does not understand that four out of five pieces should be more than two out of three when the wholes are the same size.
- A larger number in the denominator means a larger fraction.

See the complete lesson plan in Appendix A on page 186.

💡 **Think about how you launched a recent lesson. Record your thoughts below.**

_____

_____

_____

_____

_____

_____

_____

_____

Launch the Lesson

Since they have chosen a problem as the lesson task, Davante and Adrienne decide to launch the lesson by unpacking the task. Since students will be taking on a job in the task, this will be fun way to get the students involved.

Launch:

Introduce the first part of the problem with a discussion about the importance of precise measures in baking. Ask students questions such as:

- What happens when you do not use the precise measures called for in a recipe?
- How do you measure amounts when you cook? What tools do you use?
- Can you think of any other situations where precise measures are needed?
- What are some situations where you may need equivalent fractions?
- What is Carol's problem with her measuring tools?

Introduce the second part of the problem:

You remember using a number line in school to work with fractions.

1. Rewrite all of the measures in the recipe as equivalent fractions that Sammy can use with the measurement tools you gave him.

Your business is booming and you may run out of measuring tools again. You decide to teach all of your bakers to use equivalent fractions.

2. Create a large number line on chart paper. Put the numbers from the recipe on the number line.

3. Add as many equivalent fractions as you can to the number line for each number you placed on the number line.

4. Be prepared to teach your fellow bakers about equivalent fractions. Explain in writing what you will say to them.

Ask the students to identify what they need to do to solve the problem. Discuss any questions they may have.

Share success criteria.

See the complete lesson plan in Appendix A on page 191.

Think about how you launched a recent lesson. Record your thoughts below.

_____

_____

_____

_____

_____

_____

Standards
LI and SC
Purpose
Tasks
Materials
Student Thinking
Lesson Structures
Form. Assess.
Lesson Launch
Lesson Facilitation
Closure

Boton, Chelsea, and Rodrigo are discussing their lesson launch for their multiplication of fraction lessons. Chelsea says, "I really want to build curiosity about the task. What if we use the Notice and Wonder technique, but use pictures first, and then reveal parts of the task like we are telling a story?" Boton chimes in. "Yes, that will get them excited and interested in solving the problem." Rodrigo agrees, "Let's also have them make predictions. This always gets them engaged."

Launch:

Reveal this picture to the students and conduct a Notice and Wonder:

1. Record the students' Notices and Wonders. (Students might notice that the brownie pans are not full. Students might also notice that the brownie pans have different kinds of brownies and the brownie pans show different amounts.)

2. Introduce the first part of the problem to the students and ask them to add to the Notice and Wonder. They might notice that $\frac{3}{4}$ is greater than $\frac{2}{3}$.

    Twin sisters, Satthiya and Priya, each made a pan of brownies for the fifth-grade school picnic. Satthiya made chocolate chunk brownies and Priya made caramel swirl brownies. The sisters set their brownie pans on the table to cool and when they got back they noticed that someone had been eating their brownies!

    Satthiya's pan had only $\frac{3}{4}$ of the brownies left in the pan! Priya had $\frac{2}{3}$ of the brownies left in the pan!

    They had no choice but to take the brownies to the picnic and explain what happened to their teachers.

3. Reveal the last part of the problem:

    After the picnic, Satthiya saw that her class had eaten $\frac{2}{3}$ of the $\frac{3}{4}$ brownies that were in the pan. Priya saw that her class had eaten $\frac{2}{4}$ of the $\frac{2}{3}$ brownies left in her pan. Now the sisters are arguing about the class that ate the most brownies! Help the sisters find out. Show a representation to prove your idea.

4. Share and discuss the language and social learning intentions. Do not reveal the mathematical intentions because this is an inquiry lesson.

See the complete lesson plan in Appendix A on page 195.

 How can you use the Notice and Wonder technique as a lesson launch?

_____

_____

_____

_____

Under Construction

Now it is your turn! Develop a lesson launch and anticipate how your students will respond.

Launch:

online resources
Download the full Lesson-Planning Template from resources.corwin.com/mathlessonplanning/3-5
Remember that you can use the online version of the lesson plan template to begin compiling each section into the full template as your lesson plan grows.

PLANNING TO FACILITATE THE LESSON

Barbara, a third-grade teacher, had always imagined herself as an educator. As a child, she collected worksheets from her teachers and stored them in her basement, which she set up as a school. She cajoled neighborhood friends into playing school with her for hours on end.

By the time that Barbara actually started teaching, she knew that the approach to education had shifted from her own days as a student. She recognized the need to encourage her students to construct meaning through carefully planned activities and to allow her students to talk to each other, explain their thinking, and even productively struggle, but she still felt conflicted with how to best support her students' communication skills. She hated to watch them struggle, even a little bit. She frequently found herself falling right into the trap of saving a student way too early instead of asking a question or providing a suggestion. Just the other day, one of her students, Justin, had asked for help, and she had picked up a pencil and started showing him what to do. She hadn't even realized it until she glanced at him and caught him grinning from ear to ear!

Barbara shared her concerns with her co-teacher, Dominic, and they decided that they would help each other by specifically planning how they would facilitate lessons so there would be more chances for students to explain and justify their thinking, more questioning from both students and teachers, and more opportunities for students to productively struggle.

As they began their planning, their math coach suggested that Barbara and Dominic think about a lesson that had gone well because students were actively engaged in mathematical discourse as inspiration for their planning. Both Barbara and Dominic agreed that a good example was the lesson in which the students designed the reading nook for the media center.

The lesson had developed after the media specialist had told them that they would be constructing a new reading nook in the media center. She had explained that they were trying to decide how to organize or block off the space in the best way. The students were very excited about the new reading nook and asked the media specialist if they could propose some designs. For this lesson, the students were presented with the following problem:

Mrs. Petry has been given permission to design a reading nook that has area that equals 400 square feet. Prepare a proposal for Mrs. Petry. Include the design, measurements, and prepare a mathematical argument why you think this is the best design.

Both Barbara and Dominic had been amazed at how well the fourth graders had worked on the project, particularly as they had negotiated decisions about the best design for the reading nook. Barbara and Dominic had spent all of their time supporting the students and questioning them as they worked.

As the teachers discussed this lesson with their math coach, Dominic asked, "So how can we capture that kind of energy and student-centered learning every day?"

> **Capturing those moments when students are engaged productively in mathematical thinking, reasoning, and communication is so exciting to see. Sometimes they just happen, but most likely they happen when all of your hard work in planning comes together. Planning to facilitate a lesson incorporates the selection of effective instructional activities and strategically planning how you will support and facilitate student learning during the instructional activities. Good tasks, problems, games, and activities are only just that—good—until you mindfully use care and purpose to design a teaching and learning environment that supports your students' learning through discourse and appropriate and productive struggle. This chapter will discuss the following questions:**
>
> ● What is mathematical communication?
>
> ● How do you facilitate meaningful mathematical discourse?
>
> ● How do you plan for and pose purposeful questions?
>
> ● How do you facilitate productive struggle?

WHAT IS MATHEMATICAL COMMUNICATION?

Communication is an essential part of mathematics and mathematical education. *Principles to Action: Ensuring Success for All* (National Council of Teachers of Mathematics [NCTM], 2014b) notes that "effective teaching of mathematics facilitates discourse among students to build shared understanding of mathematical ideas by analyzing and comparing student approaches and arguments" (p. 29). Students need multiple opportunities to exchange ideas, explain and defend their reasoning, use mathematical vocabulary, and consider one another's ideas (NCTM, 1991, 2000, 2014a). There are several facets to good mathematical communication, including the following:

- *Precise use of vocabulary*. Teachers must use precise mathematical vocabulary consistently and facilitate students' use of mathematical language to promote mathematical understanding. This means that all students learn and use the correct mathematics vocabulary, even when first learning new mathematical concepts.

- Some teachers may want to focus on key words or simplify the language by using simple terms, but that can ultimately confuse students. For example, teaching students that they should always add when they see *in all* in a word problem will lead students to believe that this will always work, when in reality it will work only in particular situations and cannot be transferred to all word problems.

- *Verbal discussion or **mathematical discourse***. Mathematical discourse occurs when students talk about the mathematics they are learning with each other and the teacher. During this discussion, they demonstrate their understanding and reveal their reasoning. Teachers should plan for and facilitate multiple opportunities for discourse throughout the lesson to provide students many different ways to engage in conversation about the mathematics they are learning. Often, the most powerful mathematical conversations occur between students as they reason with each other to make sense of their learning.

- *Writing*. Writing in the mathematics classroom allows students to record their thinking so they can remember how they thought through a problem or how they solved it. Writing helps students focus on and build precise mathematical language, whereas words "disappear" once spoken. For students who feel shy when talking aloud, writing gives them the opportunity to explain their thinking.

- If some of your students have difficulty with writing, give them sentence starters such as, "I think the answer is ____ because____" or allow them to use pictures and diagrams in their written explanations. These approaches will help them fully participate. In addition, you can show students examples of writing to help them improve their discourse skills. To do this, you can use student work on chart paper or under a document camera to show examples of what you mean by phrases like "Use pictures to explain your solution."

What are some strategies you use to facilitate discourse? List a few below.

_____

_____

_____

_____

HOW DO YOU FACILITATE MEANINGFUL MATHEMATICAL DISCOURSE?

Providing for and teaching mathematical communication requires explicit attention to planning lessons (Walshaw & Anthony, 2008). Building a classroom community that supports discourse requires some shifts in the traditional student and teacher roles. In particular, the students assume greater responsibility for their learning and the teacher no longer serves as the primary source of mathematical authority. Instead, the teacher consistently encourages student engagement and strategically uses questioning to position students as mathematical leaders in the classroom. *Principles to Action* (NCTM, 2014b) notes the critical roles by considering what teachers and students are *doing* in classrooms where rich mathematical discourse is occurring. For example, teachers are designing learning activities that prompt students to use multiple representations, describe their solutions, and explain their reasoning. Teachers also strategically facilitate conversations among students about the mathematics they are learning. When teachers are promoting mathematical discourse, a peek inside these classrooms shows students presenting their ideas to other students while other students are listening and asking questions.

You can promote effective discourse by monitoring and responding to the students as they work. You can ask particular questions that will support students to explain their thinking and reasoning. Here are some sample questions you may wish to ask:

- Was this the first strategy you tried? Why did you give up on the first strategy?

- How did you decide what to do?

- Did you try something that did not work? How did you figure out it was not going to work?

- How does what you are doing make sense to you?

The questions help students reflect on their work but also give you more information to determine which of the student strategies you want to select for the class discussion. In this way, you can plan a purposeful discussion on the strategy or strategies to focus on in the lesson. Once you make the decision about which student work you will present to the class (one, some, all), you also decide the order in which they will be presented. This purposeful planning of the discussion allows concepts to unfold in a coherent manner that you predetermine to match the learning intention (Smith & Stein, 2011). Once the students are presenting their work, you facilitate the discussion through questions that connect the strategies and concepts studied. Here are some additional sample questions:

- Is there anything in Graham's strategy that is like something we have done before?

- What mathematical words did he use that we have learned?

- Is there something in this solution that reminds you of anything we did yesterday in class?

- How is Graham's solution like or different from Gail's solution?

You should also encourage the students to ask questions of one another, thus promoting student-to-student interaction and engagement in constructing viable arguments and critiquing the reasoning of others (National Governors Association Center for Best Practices & Council of Chief State School Officers, 2010). You can encourage classroom discourse by establishing an environment and expectation for students to engage in some type of discourse every day (Rasmussen, Yackel, & King, 2003; Wood, Williams, & McNeal, 2006; Yackel & Cobb, 1996).

Many teachers of elementary students find it helpful to **unpack** what it means to be in a mathematics **learning community.** You can do this by holding classroom discussions about what math talk looks like in your classroom. You may also find it helpful to explicitly teach students how to share their ideas, actively listen, and give appropriate responses to peers (Wagganer, 2015).

Here are some additional suggestions:

- Encourage student-to-student discourse by asking students to address each other's questions: "Antonia, can you answer Jamal's question?" Or "Jamal, did you understand Antonia's solution? You can ask her a question to help her explain what she meant."

- Use a Think Aloud technique to model your own thinking and reasoning through a problem that focuses on mathematical thinking that you want your students to develop (Trocki, Taylor, Starling, Sztajn, & Heck, 2015).

- Model how to ask questions and instruct students to ask questions of each other. You can show students that it is okay to be confused and to ask for an explanation. Model a question you would like students to ask: "Class, I am confused about this problem. Can someone help me?" Or "Jamal, why don't you ask Antonia a question about the solution?"

- Ask follow-up questions when students respond with a right or wrong answer that will lead them back to the conceptual understanding. For example, you might ask, "Can you start at the beginning and explain your thinking?"

- Use sentence stems (Wagganer, 2015) to jumpstart student thinking and student-to-student discourse. This is helpful for all students, but especially for English Language Learners. Here are some sentence stems you might try with your students:

  - I agree with _____ because …

  - This is what I think …

- I have a different perspective because …

- I made a connection with what _____ said because …

- When I thought about that question, I remembered …

- I chose this method because …

- Use language frames to scaffold math talk (Hattie et al., 2016) and enhance student conversations while collaborating. Some language frames for mathematics include the following:

  - Another way to solve this would be …

  - In order to solve this problem, I need to know …

  - We think this answer is reasonable because …

  - If I change _____, my answer would be different because …

  - I can check my answer by …

Like most communication, mathematics discourse is messy. Elementary-aged students, in particular, may struggle to find the right words to explain their thinking and reasoning. Your patience and willingness to let students participate in lots of discourse is the key to building a rich discourse community.

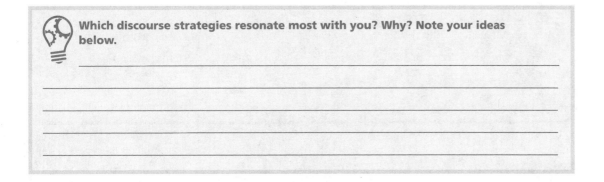

Which discourse strategies resonate most with you? Why? Note your ideas below.

_____

_____

_____

_____

HOW DO YOU PLAN FOR AND POSE PURPOSEFUL QUESTIONS?

Questioning is at the heart of effective mathematical discourse. The NCTM's (2014b) *Principles to Action: Ensuring Mathematical Success for All* states, "Effective teaching of mathematics uses purposeful questions to assess and advance students' reasoning and sense making about important mathematical ideas and relationships" (p. 35). When you plan questions to ask during a lesson, you also increase access and engagement for all students because you are mindful about whom you will be calling on.

The roles of both the teacher and the students are important as teachers pose purposeful questions that advance students' mathematical understanding (NCTM, 2014b). As a teacher, you must be intentional in your planning, consider what you are doing as you ask questions, and consider what your students are doing in response to your questions. Plan and ask higher-level questions that prompt your students to provide explanations, justifications, and reasoning about the mathematics they are learning. Also be sure to provide plenty of wait time for students to ponder, reflect, and make sense of the question. When you take these actions, your students provide deeper responses and justify their thinking with evidence. They also ask you questions to clarify and build new understanding (NCTM, 2014b).

The questions a teacher asks are the key to orchestrating positive and productive classroom discourse. As you formulate questions to challenge students to think deeply, draw conclusions, and extend the student inquiry in the lesson (Van de Walle et al., 2016), consider the purpose and type of question. The *Principles to Action: Ensuring Mathematical Success for All* (NCTM, 2014b) organized question types into four distinct categories: gathering information, probing thinking, making the mathematics visible, and encouraging reflection and justification. NCTM's (2017) publication, *Taking Action: Implementing Effective Teaching Practices*, introduced a fifth category: engaging with the reasoning of others. The question types can also be connected to the Standards for Mathematical Practice (National Governors Association Center for Best Practices & Council of Chief State School Officers, 2010). Let's briefly look at each type of question in more detail.

Standards

LI and SC

Purpose

Tasks

Materials

Student Thinking

Lesson Structures

Form. Assess.

Lesson Launch

Lesson Facilitation

Closure

Gathering Information

Teachers ask these types of questions to elicit procedural information by asking "what is" and "how to" questions. Some examples appear in Figure 12.1. When students answer probing questions, they provide factual information or steps. You can also use this type of question to elicit students' precise use of mathematics vocabulary. Typically, these kinds of questions elicit right or wrong answers.

Figure 12.1

Teachers	Students
What is the product of 5 × 9 = ____?	45
What is the value of the number in the tenths place? 2.54	The value of the number in the tenths place is 5 tenths.
How did you find the perimeter of that figure? 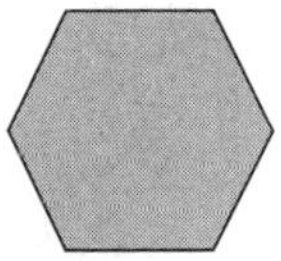	I counted the number of sides.

Probing Thinking

Teachers ask these kinds of questions to encourage students to explain their thinking and demonstrate their reasoning. Figure 12.2 gives some examples.

Figure 12.2

Teachers	Students
Why did you decide to add all the hundreds together first in this equation? 234 + 417 + 276 =	I knew automatically that the sum would be greater than 800 because I quickly added all the hundreds.
Can you tell me about how you solved this problem? If 24 cookies are arranged into equal rows of 6 cookies, how many rows will there be?	When I saw that the problem started with *cookies are arranged in equal rows of 6 cookies,* I knew that I didn't know how many rows there would be. So, I drew two rows of 6 cookies and saw there were 12. Then I knew there would be four rows because I doubled the 12 to get 24.

Figure 12.2 (Continued)

Teachers	Students
How did drawing a bar model help you solve this problem? A concert ticket costs \$24 and a movie ticket costs \$8. How many times as much does the movie ticket cost as the concert ticket?	First I drew the bar for the concert ticket, and then I drew one of the movie ticket bars. Then I saw that I needed two more movie ticket bars to equal 24. 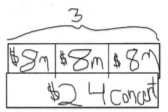

Making the Mathematics Visible

Teachers ask these kinds of questions to help the students build connections between mathematical ideas, see patterns, and understand the underlying structure of mathematical ideas. Figure 12.3 gives some examples.

Figure 12.3

Teachers	Students
What patterns do you notice in the following? 6 × 6, 8 × 8, 10 × 10, 12 × 12	All of those use the same number to multiply. So if you made a model, it would be a square. The numbers go up by 2. The products make a pattern: 36, 64, 100, and 144! The differences between the products also make a pattern! The differences are 28, 36, and 44. The differences increase by 8.
How are addition and multiplication related?	Multiplication is repeated addition. When you skip count, it is like multiplication.

Encouraging Reflection and Justification

Teachers ask these kinds of questions when they want to encourage students to develop mathematical arguments and justify their solutions with thorough explanations. Figure 12.4 includes some examples.

Figure 12.4

Teachers	Students
How do you know that $\frac{2}{12}$ is closer to 0 on the number line? 0—$\frac{2}{12}$———————1	I put $\frac{2}{12}$ on the number line in that spot because $\frac{2}{12}$ is two $\frac{1}{12}$s. This means that there are 12 parts in the whole. There are only two parts in $\frac{2}{12}$ so that means it is closer to zero.
How many ways can you represent 4.38?	I can represent the decimal using place value materials. I can show 4.38 in money. I can rename 4.38 as 438 hundredths.
Why did you use that representation to explain your solution?	I used pattern blocks to show $\frac{1}{2}+\frac{1}{3}$ because I can change the half to sixths and also change the $\frac{1}{3}$ to sixths and then add them up.

Engage With the Reasoning of Others

Teachers ask these kinds of questions when they want to encourage students to explain their own thinking, construct a viable argument, and listen to the reasoning of their peers. They also ask these types of questions to encourage students to ask questions of each other. Figure 12.5 shows some examples.

Figure 12.5

Teachers	Students
I am noticing that you and Maria solved the problem in different ways. Explain Maria's solution, and tell why you think Maria solved it that way. $60 \div 12 =$	Maria solved the problem by subtracting 12 over and over again until she reached 0. I think she did this because she can then subtract it easily.

Figure 12.5 (*Continued*)

Teachers	Students
Do you agree or disagree with Maria's idea? Why or why not?	I agree that Maria's solution works, but I would like to use multiplication on a number line. See how I use the number line to skip count by twelves until I reach 60. 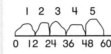

Without strategic planning, teachers tend to ask most questions at the lowest cognitive level (fact, recall, or knowledge) and wait less than one second before calling on a student after asking a question (Walsh & Sattes, 2005). Instead, you should strive to ask higher-level questions that require students to explain and elaborate on their ideas, make the mathematics visible, and encourage justification. For example, consider the questions that Alanna Martinique, a fifth-grade teacher, asks in the following scenario.

> Mrs. Martinique: What happens when you multiply a whole number and fraction?
>
> Marilee: Well, you get a product? Something bigger—like in whole numbers.
>
> Mrs. Martinique: Hmmmm. Can you show me the representation for 4×2 and $4 \times \frac{1}{2}$ and tell me how they are alike and different? (Figure 12.6)
>
> Marilee: Well, first I drew four people times two cookies. My question is: If four people get two cookies each, how many cookies do I need? Then my second question is, "If four people get $\frac{1}{2}$ cookie each, how many cookies do I need?"

Figure 12.6

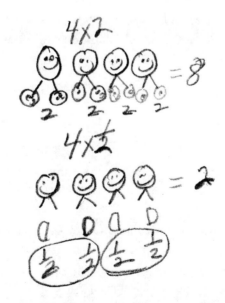

So, I noticed something different than when we multiply whole numbers, but I can't figure out why it is happening.

Mrs. Martinique: Marilee, tell us more about your thinking.

Marilee: Yes, if I multiply 4 times one half, I end up with 2! The answer is smaller than when I multiplied times 2!

Mrs. Martinique: Do you think this happens all the time when we multiply whole numbers times fractions or just some of the time?

Emma: I think it is all of the time! I think that is because the one half is smaller than a whole so the answer is always going to be smaller. I think there is a pattern!

Mrs. Martinique: Hmmmm… . What an interesting idea! Can anyone else offer an idea or a representation? Let's turn and talk to our partners. In a few minutes, I am going to ask you to be ready to add to the ideas you heard and tell whether you agree or disagree with Marilee and Emma's ideas and why.

The first question, "What happens when you multiply a whole number and fraction?" is at the gathering information level. The teacher continues to raise the level of the students' thinking by encouraging a conversation about multiplication of whole numbers times fractions; this occurs when she asks Marilee follow-up questions and then engages the whole class in the discussion.

Have you ever asked a question, called on a student who gave the correct answer, and watched all hands disappear quickly? Good questions prompt students to provide more than answers. Note how Alanna was able to move the discussion forward instead of closing it down. When you pose purposeful questions, you promote student understanding because you ask students to make connections by building upon what they know.

Teachers tend to use two kinds of main questioning techniques: funneling (Herbel-Eisenmann & Breyfogle, 2005) and focusing (Herbel-Eisenmann, 2010; NCTM, 2014b).

- *Funneling questions* lead students in a particular direction to provide evidence of student learning; for this reason, they can squash students' thinking because the teacher is asking questions with a particular answer in mind. These kinds of questions often provide only a superficial assessment of what students know.

- *Focusing questions*, on the other hand, encourage students to think on their own and provide explanations and justifications. While the teacher has an end point in mind, the students' reasoning is most important.

Consider the questions in Figure 12.7 and note how a funneling question can be opened up to become a focusing question. Anticipate the different kinds of responses each type of question will elicit.

Figure 12.7

Funneling	Focusing
What is the value of the 6 in 0.726?	Is 0.726 closer to a 0 or 1 and how do you know?
Is 23 prime or composite?	Convince me why a number is prime or composite.

As you plan to facilitate your lesson, it is important to consider how you will plan for and implement purposeful and rich questions that support rich student thinking.

Standards

LI and SC

Purpose

Tasks

Materials

Student Thinking

Lesson Structures

Form. Assess.

Lesson Launch

Lesson Facilitation

Closure

> Think of a time when you used funneling questions, and think of a time when you used focusing questions. What were the results? Note some of the differences below.
>
> _____
>
> _____
>
> _____
>
> _____

HOW DO YOU FACILITATE PRODUCTIVE STRUGGLE?

By consistently providing students with high-quality, engaging mathematics instruction, you will also invite them to productively struggle because they will be actively involved in making sense of the mathematics they are learning (NCTM, 2014b). Your students will be better able to apply their learning to new situations if you routinely ensure that they participate in mathematics learning that stretches their thinking and promotes opportunities to make and analyze their mistakes (Boaler, 2015) and that prompts them to engage in higher-level thinking (Kapur, 2010).

As you construct lessons to engage students in productive struggle, you must keep the needs of your own learners in mind. While it is tempting to rescue students by giving them answers or by overscaffolding lessons, this does not, in the long run, support their learning. On the other hand, you also do not want to send your students into an unproductive spiral of struggle. Simply telling students to try harder does not promote productive struggle when students feel that they are, in fact, trying very hard.

Creating this "sweet spot" of productive struggle for your students can be challenging, which is why it is critical to consider how you will create an environment that promotes productive struggle during the planning process. You can do this by following these steps:

1. Be explicit about what struggle looks like and feels like so students understand that it will help them.

2. Discuss perseverance with students, and actively recognize when students demonstrate it.

3. Provide plenty of time for students to struggle with tasks and move through the struggle so they know what it feels like on the other side of the struggle.

4. Plan for how you will respond when students are struggling by asking scaffolding questions.

5. Celebrate and use confusion and mistakes (yours and theirs) as an opportunity for furthering and deepening understanding.

6. Create opportunities for students to ask questions, help each other, and share how they moved through a struggle.

7. Reflect on how you respond to student confusion and struggle and plan strategic moves to use in the classroom.

Example: Fatima

Fatima, a fifth-grade teacher, doesn't like to watch her students struggle, even a tiny bit, but she knows that she needs to make this a class focus for the year. She recently watched Jo Boaler's (2017) video, _Brains Grow and Change,_ and she wants to be able to translate that information to her fifth graders. She knows that many of them worry about getting all the answers correct.

She decides to begin the school year by making each student a small, laminated nametag in the shape of the brain. She tells them that "mistakes grow your brain" and that she wants to be able to know when their brains are growing. She encourages the students to make a tally mark on the laminated nametags every time they make a mistake. She also provides time for the students to unpack their mistakes during discussions by asking the students to answer this prompt: "I used to think _____, but now I know _____ because _____."

At the end of the week, they count up the totals from the whole class and celebrate their growing brains. Then she has students share their "Favorite Mistake" of the week. She also keeps track of the weekly tallies during the year.

Fatima is surprised by the positive impact of this effort on her classroom environment as students become relaxed and thoughtful about their mistakes. One of the students, Jordan, tells her, "At first I thought my mistakes were bad and I should hide them away. But then I found out that my mistakes tell me I am learning. They aren't bad at all."

> **How might you integrate conversations about productive struggle in your own classroom? Write a few notes here.**
>
> _____
>
> _____
>
> _____
>
> _____

HOW DO YOU MAKE SURE YOU ENGAGE STUDENTS IN THE PROCESS STANDARDS AS YOU FACILITATE THE LESSON?

The examples throughout this chapter show many ways that you can engage students in communicating mathematically, developing problem-solving behaviors, demonstrating reasoning, making connections between and among mathematical ideas, and using representations to explain and justify thinking. You can ensure that you are encouraging students to demonstrate the process standards by planning for one or two process standards for each lesson. As you plan to facilitate your lesson, consider the questions you will ask and the task you design or select that will elicit particular student mathematical behaviors. For example, Jeanic wants her fourth graders to notice and use mathematical structures and designs a word problem sorting task. She gives students eight word problems and tells them they must not solve the problems. She explains that she wants them to read the word problems and then group word problems that are alike together and explain how they are alike. Jeanie's students quickly notice that particular word problems represent multiplication while others might be solved using multiplication or division.

> **How can you make sure to incorporate questioning that will support students in engaging in the process standards?**
>
> _____
>
> _____
>
> _____
>
> _____

Building Unit Coherence

Similar to the launch, the lesson facilitation shapes coherence because you are constantly connecting prior learning to new learning. You ask questions and invite robust discourse that stimulates mathematical learning. You can do this by asking students to record their ideas and explain their thinking to peers. You can post their ideas and refer to them throughout the unit. Each new lesson offers opportunities for you to call upon students' ideas and work samples to support new mathematical concepts. With this combination of teaching moves, you create coherence because students begin to connect and link their ideas from one day to the next. Every day, you may also wish to ask the students, "Why are we learning this?" This question can help them understand that the mathematics they are learning is connected to their lives and to the new mathematics they will learn.

Third-Grade Snapshot

Facilitate the Lesson

Saida, Julian, and Kimi know that discourse must be the heart of their "Convince Me!" lesson. Knowing that they want the students to enter the task at their own level, they decide that they will need focusing questions to keep the lesson moving and to tie different student strategies to others. Together, they walk themselves through the lesson examples they plan to use and they write a list of questions they anticipate will be appropriate, keeping in mind common misconceptions about fractions and their students' particular needs.

Facilitate:

1. After the launch problem, explain to the class that today they are going to work with a partner and play a game called "Convince Us!"

   a. I am going to write a statement on the board. You will work with your partner to convince us that it is true. You can use any materials in the room you wish including your white board.

   b. Here is our first statement: $\frac{3}{5} > \frac{1}{5}$

2. Our whole for this game is one large cheese pizza. Walk around and listen to student thinking. Note which students are using different strategies/tools to model their thinking. Pay attention to students who are not using materials but trying to work abstractly.

3. After sufficient time to work, ask student pairs who have used drawings to share their work using a document camera. They will explain why $\frac{3}{5}$ is greater than $\frac{1}{5}$ in pictures and words. Record their strategies.

4. Allow students who did not use materials but thought about the equation abstractly to share their ideas and explain how they know $\frac{3}{5}$ is greater. These students will likely use logical reasoning stating something like, "We know that the pizza is in five pieces and three pieces are more than one piece."

5. Follow up with questions to clarify this thinking for all students such as:

   a. Oh, so what can you tell me about the size of each slice of pizza?

   b. What clue tells you about the size of the slices?

   c. Can anyone else explain what Ginger just said in a different way?

   d. How does Ginger's explanation match what Jamie did with the fraction circles?

6. Repeat with another true statement and follow the same procedure and questioning. Each time a student gives the explanation abstractly, praise this explanation and ask others to explain it to show that they understand it. Point out how quickly a person can tell if one fraction is larger than the other just using the reasoning.

7. Repeat with true statements where the denominators are the same as many times as needed until you feel that the students have the understanding that when two fractions have the same denominator, the size of the pieces being compared is the same, so you look at the numerator to tell how many pieces each fraction represents.

8. Ask the hinge question when you think students have the understanding. If the answers to the hinge question indicate students have the concept, repeat the game using fractions with the same numerator such as $\frac{4}{6} < \frac{4}{5}$.

9. Repeat with fractions that have the same numerator until you feel that the students have the concept: When fractions have the same numerator (same number of pieces), you can compare the size of the pieces using the denominator.

(Continued)

Anticipating student responses:

Expect some students to be confused about numerators and denominators. Use the launch problem to help clarify before beginning the game.

During "Convince Us!" some students may want to rely heavily on fraction circles or fraction strips for their explanations. When you notice this, have students connect the abstract explanations to the manipulatives to demonstrate the concept.

Some students try to repeat an abstract explanation when they really do not understand the concept. Ask students to give the explanation in their own words, or interview them with a different equation to see if they truly understand.

See the complete lesson plan in Appendix A on page 186.

What do you notice about the opportunities for student discourse? Record your response below.

Facilitate the Lesson

Adrienne and Davante are thinking about facilitating their lesson. They have a problem-solving task and the students will work in groups to solve it. They want to be sure everyone in each group is contributing to the discussion. They create a list of teacher questions that they can use/adapt as they walk around the room and encourage conversation in each group, such as the following: *Tim, do you agree with what Mario just said? Sue, can you explain what Jose just said? I don't think I understand. Jimmy just said, _____. Do you think that is always true? Why?*

Facilitate:

1. Students work in pairs to solve the problem after the launch discussion.

2. Pairs are given a copy of the recipe, chart paper, and $\frac{1}{4}$ teaspoons and measuring cups to complete the task.

3. As the pairs work together, monitor their work by asking questions such as these:

   How will you get started?

   What ideas did your partner have?

   What would a manager say to his or her bakers?

   What do you think bakers need to know about equivalent fractions to include in your talk?

   What strategy or strategies are you using to find equivalent fractions?

4. Encourage students to share their explanations to the bakers (read to the class).

5. Pose the second part of the problem.

   1. Rewrite all of the measures in the recipe as equivalent fractions that Sammy can use with the measurement tools you gave him.

   Your business is booming and you may run out of measuring tools again. You decide to teach all of your bakers to use equivalent fractions.

6. Create a PowerPoint or video to teach your bakers about equivalent fractions. You can create a large number line on chart paper and add the numbers from the recipe on the number line. You decide how to use the number line in your PowerPoint or video.

See the complete lesson plan in Appendix A on page 191.

What are some of the questions you use to encourage discourse in your classroom? Write them below.

_____

_____

_____

_____

_____

_____

_____

_____

_____

Standards

LI and SC

Purpose

Tasks

Materials

Student Thinking

Lesson Structures

Form. Assess.

Lesson Launch

Lesson Facilitation

Closure

Fifth-grade teachers Boton, Chelsea, and Rodrigo anticipate that the students might want to work independently rather than collaboratively. They plan to monitor the students closely to encourage discussion and collaboration. They decide to plan some focusing questions to support student collaboration.

- What are some ideas your group members have suggested?

- How did your model help another group member understand your idea?

- Can you explain _____'s thinking?

Facilitate:

1. Ask the students to turn and talk to a partner about the brownie problem. Then have the students make a prediction about whose class ate the most brownies. Record their predictions.

2. Arrange the students into groups of four and distribute chart paper to the students.

3. Tell the students that they must decide which of the sister's classes ate the most brownies. They will need to find out how much of Satthiya's and Priya's brownie pans is left over after the picnic. Tell the students that they must represent their thinking using manipulatives and/or drawings. Offer graph paper, color tiles, and markers for the students to use.

4. As the students are working, monitor the groups as they solve. Ask questions and encourage the students to talk to each other and show their thinking. If students struggle, encourage them to show the amount of brownies in each pan first by creating an array.

   Satthiya started with $\frac{2}{3}$ of the brownie pan. Priya started with $\frac{3}{4}$ of the brownie pan.

   $\frac{2}{3}$ $\frac{3}{4}$

   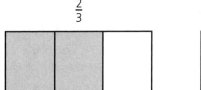   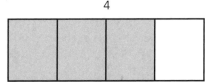

5. Then ask, "How can you show how much of the brownie pan was eaten by the class?" Encourage the students to share their ideas and represent their thinking using representations. Students might also use color tiles to represent the amount of the brownie pan eaten.

6. Continue to monitor the students as they work. Ask:

   - How could an array model help you?

   - How can you represent each pan's value?

   - How can you represent $\frac{2}{4}$ of $\frac{2}{3}$? What does that look like?

   - How can you represent $\frac{2}{3}$ of $\frac{3}{4}$? What does that look like?

   - How can you explain your reasoning to each other?

   - How can drawing a math picture help you solve this problem?

   - Convince a classmate about your thinking and reasoning.

7. After the students have completed the posters, ask the students to hang their posters for a gallery walk.

8. Give each student two sticky notes and tell them to examine the posters and give two pieces of feedback to two different groups. Explain to the students that the feedback must be specific and constructive. While the students are giving feedback, select two to three groups' posters and ask those groups to share during the whole-group closure.

See the complete lesson plan in Appendix A on page 195.

How can you facilitate effective student collaboration? Record your response below.

Chapter 12 ■ Planning to Facilitate the Lesson **167**

Now it is your turn! What will you do to facilitate your lesson?

Facilitate:

CHAPTER 13

PLANNING TO CLOSE THE LESSON

The fifth-grade team members at Hollins Elementary School were discussing some of their closure experiences.

"Closure?" questioned Abe, a third-year teacher. "I hardly ever get a chance for closure. My lessons always go to the last minute and sometimes even run over into recess."

"I have that problem sometimes," chimed in Jane, the veteran teacher in the group. "I am getting better, but last week my class had to remind me to stop because it was time for lunch! My goal for this year is to improve my closure. I'm working on it."

Cilia, a second-year teacher, spoke up. "I went to a workshop this summer and they talked about how important closure is to determine how students are grasping a lesson. I have been trying some of the suggestions. I like using exit slips, and my kids seem to like them. I let them write me notes at the end of the lesson to tell me if there was anything they didn't understand. I have been using those notes to help me launch my next lesson."

"Exit slips? And you have time to fit them in?" asked Abe.

Cilia replied, "Most days but not every day."

Jane said, "It's funny that you mentioned a workshop. I went to a workshop about closure two years ago. We discussed how closure is about reflection. And we used exit slips too, but we learned that there are other things you can do, like pair sharing. Another option is to do a more in-depth exit task, like we learned in the formative assessment workshop."

"Stop keeping all these ideas a secret!" Abe said. Then he smiled and added, "You two need to do a closure workshop for me!"

If you have ever looked at the clock and realized that you not only lack time for closure but also have run overtime, you are not alone. Abe, Jane, and Cilia have been working on closure for a few years and continue to struggle to fit it all in. Planning for closure is the first step in using it in your classroom. This chapter will discuss closure and several different closure formats while answering the following questions:

- Why do you need closure in a lesson?
- What are some different closure activities?
- What is an extended closure?

WHY DO YOU NEED CLOSURE IN A LESSON?

Closure is widely accepted as an important feature of lesson planning (Ganske, 2017), yet it is often neglected as a teaching practice because it gets sacrificed for critical instructional time. By making time for this essential lesson feature, you can help students solidify learning.

While the word *closure* indicates an ending, it is more like a pause in the learning so students can reflect on or demonstrate what they learned, and teachers can collect feedback to determine next steps for learning.

Closure has two purposes—one for the teacher and one for the students. For the teacher, closure helps determine what students have learned, and it gives direction as to where to go next: reteach, correct misconceptions, or move on. Through closure activities, you collect formative assessment information to inform instructional decision making and provide valuable feedback to students (Wiliam & Thompson, 2008). For the students, closure is a cognitive activity that helps them focus on what they learned and whether the learning made sense and had meaning (Sousa, 2014) by connecting to the learning intentions and success criteria (Hattie et al., 2016).

During closure, you help students circle back to clarify the learning intentions and success criteria to focus students on the intended learning for the lesson. Closure provides the opportunity to reorganize the information from a lesson in a meaningful way by asking them to summarize, review, and demonstrate understanding of the big ideas from the lesson. Students may reflect on what occurred in the lesson, make sense of it, and link ideas to prior knowledge. An effective closure helps students increase retention and internalize what they have learned (Pollock, 2007). Closure activities that require students to think, respond, write, and discuss concepts improve learning (Cavanaugh, Heward, & Donelson, 1996).

To ensure that closure is effective and benefits both you and your students, you need to devote enough time to it because it is a reflective process that every learner must experience to make sense of the lesson. It can seldom be done in one hurried minute before recess or lunch. You must also be mindful of the format you use, because many closure formats require students to work in pairs or small groups. In these situations, you need to be sure every student has a chance to make meaning from the lesson.

You must also attend to the students' responses. It is not enough to just collect their work as with an exit slip. When you collect any reflection/closure response in writing, use a two-pile protocol. You sort the students' responses into two piles. The first pile is for student responses that show an understanding of the lesson. The second pile for student responses that indicate additional instruction is needed. You can then decide where you go next with your lesson, how you organize grouping, and other lesson options based on these piles. For example, if a pile indicates that more than half of the students need more help, then you may choose to reteach the entire lesson using a different representation. If a pile reveals that only a few students need more help, you can plan to use a lesson format to reach these individuals and correct their misconceptions or misunderstandings. Note that closure activities should not be graded.

WHAT ARE SOME DIFFERENT CLOSURE ACTIVITIES?

There are too many different lesson closure activities to name all of them here. However, the chart in Figure 13.1 provides a sampling that you can use in Grades 3 to 5.

Figure 13.1

Name and Description	Sample Prompts
Exit slips: Students respond in writing to a prompt and hand in these responses.	Write about one idea you learned in class today and one idea you still need help with.

Figure 13.1 (*Continued*)

Name and Description	Sample Prompts
Journal entries: Students respond to a prompt using numbers, symbols, pictures, or words in their journals. This activity takes more time as the prompt requires a deeper explanation than one required on an exit slip.	Jerry argued that 0.23 is less than 0.230 because 0.230 has more digits. Explain to Jerry why his reasoning is incorrect.
Selfie: Students engage in self-reflection that allows them to assess their own learning. This can be as simple as a checklist for students to complete.	Check the statement that tells how you feel about today's lesson: _____ I got it! _____ I kinda got it. _____ I need more help. _____ I am lost!
3-2-1: Students have the opportunity to express thoughts about specific learning from the lesson.	• Write three things you learned today about measuring. • Write two different examples of when you use measuring. • Write one thing you want me to know about your learning and measuring.
Text message: This approach allows students to share what they learned with a specific audience. Use a template of a cell phone screen for students to write their message.	Provide the template with a prompt such as the following: Create a text to your parents about what you learned in math today about comparing decimals.
Play teacher: Students play the role of teacher by writing a math quiz.	Create a five-question quiz on the material from today's lesson.
Exit task: A short task that allows students to demonstrate learning from the lesson.	$\frac{1}{2} > \frac{4}{6}$ Explain why this statement is not true.
The 3 Whats: On a prepared sheet, ask students to reflect on specific questions. Teachers can tailor the "whats."	*What?* (What did I learn today about graphing?) *So what?* (Why is graphing important?) *Now what?* (Where have you seen graphs outside of school?)

(Continued)

Standards | LI and SC | Purpose | Tasks | Materials | Student Thinking | Lesson Structures | Form. Assess. | Lesson Launch | Lesson Facilitation | Closure

Figure 13.1 (*Continued*)

Name and Description	Sample Prompts
Pair/share: Students each tell their partner the answer to a specific question about the lesson. Then each of the pairs shares with the class. The teacher can take notes for the two-pile protocol.	Tell your partner the most important thing you learned today about right triangles.
Whip-around: While tossing a ball around the room, students who get the ball respond with one thing about today's class. It can be a fact (e.g., right triangles have one right angle) or a self-reflection (e.g., I am good at adding fractions). This is a fast-paced activity. The teacher should allow students a minute or two to think of what they want to say prior to starting the activity. The teacher can take notes for the two-pile protocol.	• Name a fact. • Share a self-reflection.
S-T-O-P: Students summarize the lesson orally or in writing by finishing sentence starters.	We **S**tarted the lesson _____. Our **T**opic was ____. **O**pportunities to do the math included __. The **P**urpose of the lesson was ___.
Footprint: Students each receive a cutout footprint and then use words, pictures, or symbols to show what they will *walk away* from the lesson with.	What will you walk away from the lesson with?

What Is an Extended Closure?

Some lessons may call for a more in-depth closure than the ones previously listed. This is called an extended closure.

When you teach a rich problem-based task that invites students to engage deeply with conceptual understanding, you will want to provide plenty of time for students to make sense of each other's work, connect representations, construct viable arguments, and link new learning to the learning intentions. During the lesson facilitation, you monitor the students as they work to represent their solutions and ask probing questions along the way. Just as you provide ample time for your students to work on the rich task, you will also want to make sure you leave plenty of time for your closure. During this time, you will want to strategically connect the students' solutions to the learning intention. Many teachers conduct a gallery walk to invite student feedback before formally closing the lesson.

Megan poses a rich fraction task by asking students to examine popular sports jerseys, estimate the fractional amount of red in the jerseys, and then order the jerseys by the fractional amount by gluing the jerseys to a large poster. While the students are working, Megan also thinks about how she will select and sequence the students' work (Smith & Stein, 2011) to best facilitate her students' conceptual understanding during the closure. As the student groups complete their work, Megan hangs their posters around the room and hands each student five green and five yellow sticky dots. She asks them to place a green sticky dot on solutions that are the same or similar to their solutions. She also asks them to place a yellow sticky dot on student work that they have a question about.

When the gallery walk is complete, Megan directs her students' attention to the posters and asks, "I am noticing a lot of green stickers on several posters. What strategies did many of you use to figure out a fraction for the amount of red in the jersey?"

Thomas: "Lots of us put fraction pieces on the jersey to match it up."

Megan had previously selected one of the groups that used fraction pieces to share their solution strategy and asks them to present their solution to the group.

Bertie: "We got a bunch of the fraction tiles and just started covering up the jersey with the tiles. Then we compared it to the part that wasn't covered up. We could tell if the jersey had more or less, but we weren't sure how to name it after that because there were lots of different pieces in the red part."

Megan: "Hmmmm. I see what you mean. You had a $\frac{1}{3}$ piece, a $\frac{1}{4}$ piece, and $\frac{1}{6}$ piece in the red part of the jersey."

Bertie: "Ya. So then we thought we should add that up together and ran into a big problem."

Megan: "What was that big problem?"

Bertie: "Well, that was when we noticed that the fraction tile for the whole was not the same size as the jersey so we couldn't really compare them."

Megan smiled. This is exactly what she wanted the students to understand. The extended closure allowed time for her to use the students' work for this particular concept. She then said, "Nice work, you realized that in order to compare fractional parts, the wholes must be the same size. I noticed that many of you put yellow stickers on this poster because this group used a strategy different than you. Let's have this group share their solution."

Malachi: "Well, we tried fraction circle pieces first and that was terrible because nothing was matching up! So, we decided to fold the jerseys into equal parts so we could compare the jerseys! We started folding them into fourths and then eighths. We liked the eighths better because we needed the smaller parts to be able to compare them."

Megan: "I like how the folding helped you compare the jerseys to each other."

Malachi: "Yes, because then we were comparing the same parts."

Megan asked, "These are very nice explanations because the groups are explaining their ideas and the representations on the posters help us understand our thinking. From this lesson, we can see how important it is to compare fractions when the wholes are the same size! Let's take a look at our learning intention and reflect on our learning for today."

Megan facilitates the extended closure to highlight and use the students' representations and build conceptual understanding. She explicitly states the mathematical concept that she wants to learn after they have had lots of time exploring and explaining their ideas.

 You may have seen other ideas for closure. With your team, compile a list of more closure activities that are appropriate for your grade level. Be sure each meets the purpose for the teacher and the student. Record the ones you would like to try first.

_____

_____

_____

Standards

LI and SC

Purpose

Tasks

Materials

Student Thinking

Lesson Structures

Form. Assess.

Lesson Launch

Lesson Facilitation

Closure

Closure provides a perfect opportunity for you to build coherence among your lessons. You can connect student reflection on the day's lesson to previous lessons to help your students make sense of the big idea/essential question that is the thread throughout the unit. For example, asking students to team up with a partner to answer the question, "How is the problem we looked at today different from or the same as the problem we looked at yesterday?" is an effective and simple way to tie lessons together and build the big ideas across the unit.

Notes

Third-Grade Snapshot

Close the Lesson

Saida, Julian, and Kimi decide to use an exit task. Since the lesson is their first one on comparing fractions, they want to know if the students grasped the concept of comparing two fractions with the same denominators. Julian offers to write the exit task and have them ready for the lesson.

Closure:

Distribute copies of the cellphone template so that students may answer this question:

Tell your friend in a text message how you know $\frac{3}{5} < \frac{4}{5}$.

Source: iStock.com/drogatne

See the complete lesson plan in Appendix A on page 186.

How does the closure activity in this lesson satisfy the purpose for closure for the teacher and student? Note your ideas below.

_____

_____

_____

_____

_____

_____

_____

_____

_____

Davante and Adrienne decide to have their students use journals to conduct closure activities. They believe that this record will provide them with valuable information about their students. They decide that even though they will give all of the children the same prompt, they will adjust the prompt as needed depending on the students' learning needs.

Closure:

Footprint—distribute cut out footprints to each student. Ask students to think about and then write what they are walking away with from their unit on equivalent fractions.

See the complete lesson plan in Appendix A on page 191.

How does the closure activity in this lesson satisfy the purpose for closure for the teacher and student?

_____

_____

_____

_____

_____

_____

_____

_____

_____

_____

_____

_____

_____

_____

_____

_____

_____

_____

_____

_____

_____

_____

_____

_____

_____

_____

Fifth-Grade Snapshot

Close the Lesson

Boton, Chelsea, and Rodrigo are discussing the closure for their multiplication of fractions lesson. Boton suggests, "I really think we need to build more time into our lesson for closure. We want to make sure that the students have time to hear each other's ideas."

"Yes!" Chelsea agrees. "Let's also make sure we sequence the students' work as we share to make sure that the students understand the multiplication of fraction array representation."

Rodrigo says, "Good point. Why don't we have the students also do a gallery walk and provide feedback to each other? I think this will encourage them to focus on the students' representations."

Closure:

1. Ask the students to look at their original predictions. Ask:
   - What do you notice about our predictions?
   - If you were to make a new prediction, what might you think about?

2. Ask the groups to share their solutions with the whole class. Sequence the groups' sharing from least sophisticated solution to most sophisticated solution. The prior gallery walk should have provided the students with an opportunity to give feedback and familiarize the students with their classmates' thinking. As the groups share, provide the following prompts:
   - What representation did you use to show multiplication of fractions?
   - What did you notice about fraction multiplication?
   - How is fraction multiplication same as/different from whole-number multiplication?
   - How did the array model help you figure out which sister's class ate the most brownies?

3. Connect the students' work to the learning intentions and success criteria by asking the students to look at the learning intentions and success criteria:

   I know I am successful when I:
   - Use a model to show multiplication of fractions
   - Use a model to multiply fractional side lengths to find the area

   Ask the students to turn and talk with each other to answer the prompts:
   - How did you use a model to show multiplication of fractions?
   - What is one thing you can do to improve your success?

See the complete lesson plan in Appendix A on page 195.

How does the closure activity in this lesson satisfy the purpose for closure for the teacher and student? Note your ideas below.

_____

_____

_____

_____

Standards

LI and SC

Purpose

Tasks

Materials

Student Thinking

Lesson Structures

Form. Assess.

Lesson Launch

Lesson Facilitation

Closure

Now it is your turn! Add an appropriate closure activity to your lesson plan that is under construction.

Closure:

Download the full Lesson-Planning Template from resources.corwin.com/mathlessonplanning/3-5
Remember that you can use the online version of the lesson plan template to begin compiling each section into the full template as your lesson plan grows.

178   The Mathematics Lesson-Planning Handbook, Grades 3–5

CHAPTER 14

SURVEYING YOUR RESULTS
Lesson Reflection

Fourth-grade teacher Jenna sat down at her desk after the last bell rang. She was tired as always, but it was a good tired. As usual, she allowed herself an extra 10 to 15 minutes to reflect on the day before moving on to the next thing. She didn't always get this time when there were after-school meetings, but she had learned that this brief period to reflect was very important to her professional practice. Before she had built reflective practice into her teaching, she had found herself getting burned out and focusing on only the hard things that had happened during the day. A mentor had shared her own reflection practice with Jenna before she retired, and Jenna was pretty sure it had changed her professional life.

Jenna mentally went through the day and took a couple of notes. Her mentor had suggested that she always start with successes. Jenna thought about her math lesson that day. Her students had been so excited to work in pairs and showcase their work during the gallery walk. The students' understanding of equivalence of fractions and addition of fractions was coming along nicely.

Knowing that this standard crossed over two instructional quarters helped her feel less panicked about staying on a particular schedule. She just about had the students working in pairs smoothly, an approach she had been working on since the beginning of the year.

As she continued to reflect on the day, she decided that she would move two of the students, Bryce and Kara, to work with different partners. Bryce struggled with some math anxiety and Kara still had trouble getting along with others unless the group did what she wanted.

Jenna was also pleased to note that the students were settling nicely into the number talk routine. A couple things nagged her, though. First, she recognized that she still couldn't conduct the number talk in a timely fashion. As she reflected on the situation, she decided to make sure she adheres to the time constraints and also lets the students know that they will be stopping at a certain time.

Second, she reminded herself that she needs to think about her questions more—an issue she had been working on steadily ever since she noticed that she often slips back into funneling questions with students who struggle. She recognized that her good intentions to help her students can actually interfere with their learning. She decided to ask her teammate, Diedra, who seemed to have an endless supply of good questions.

Jenna's teammates had learned not to disturb her reflection now. Now Diedra called into her classroom, "Your 10 minutes are up, Jenna!"

"Perfect," Jenna thought. "Maybe I will have a few minutes to talk to Diedra about my questioning before our meeting starts."

No doubt your day is filled with endless decisions and lots of rushing from one thing to the next. Teaching elementary learners does not allow much space for thinking about the day. However, teaching is an emotional and often physical challenge that requires deep processing. This chapter will consider the following questions:

- Why is it important to reflect upon lessons?
- What kind of reflection cycle supports teacher growth?

WHY IS IT IMPORTANT TO REFLECT UPON LESSONS?

Teachers can use reflection as a way to focus on what works, recognize challenges, and move forward in productive ways. Your reflection should be centered on a healthy curiosity about student learning that helps you better understand and learn about your teaching practice (Danielson, 2008; Smyth, 1992). You can reflect as you are teaching, which is called **reflecting in action** (Schön, 1983), to monitor and adjust to the ebb and flow of your learners' needs. You can also reflect after you have taught, which is called **reflecting on action** (Schön, 1983), by thinking about your students and instruction after a lesson ends.

You are probably already asked to reflect as a formal part of your professional practice. Many teacher evaluation systems require some sort of reflection about teaching. These reflection prompts formalize what good teachers already do every day and focus on established criteria.

Perhaps the most powerful reflection occurs when teachers pose their own questions about their teaching because those questions help them make meaningful connections between their teaching decisions and student learning. In an analysis of John Dewey's (1933, 1944) writing on the importance of reflection, Carol Rodgers (2002) extracted four essential criteria that define effective reflection.

1. *Reflection is a meaning-making process.* Your reflection should support your ability to make connections. As it moves beyond ruminating, hashing over, or contemplating the day's events, your reflection should support a deeper understanding of your teaching choices and your students' response to those choices.

2. *Reflection is a rigorous, disciplined way of thinking, with its roots in scientific inquiry.* Your reflection should always begin with a question that probes and pushes your thinking. Inquiry nudges teachers to tell their teaching stories in new ways. Consider these questions:

    * What do I believe about how students learn? How is this reflected in my instructional planning?

    * What kinds of questions did I ask during this lesson? How was student learning affected?

    * How does planning my questioning affect my lesson facilitation?

    * What does student-centered teaching mean to me?

    * How do I know my students are learning?

    * What data did I collect today that were most powerful?

3. *Reflection needs to happen in a community, in interaction with others.* Personal reflection is important and necessary. However, reflection that happens in a community of teachers is also powerful as other teachers provide unique perspectives, ask questions, and offer insight that can reveal new ways of thinking about teaching.

4. *Reflection requires attitudes that value your personal and professional growth as well as the personal and professional growth of other teachers and leaders.* Reflection is cathartic and powerful. Without it, learning and change are not likely to happen. Making time to reflect is essential to maintaining your professional health, and this approach will support you in making good decisions about teaching and learning (Constantino & De Lorenzo, 2001; Day, 1999; Harris, Bruster, Peterson, & Shutt, 2010).

> **Describe your reflective practice. When, how, and with whom do you reflect? Write your response here.**
>
> _____
>
> _____
>
> _____
>
> _____
>
> _____

WHAT KIND OF REFLECTION CYCLE SUPPORTS TEACHER GROWTH?

When you take time to mindfully unpack your professional teaching practice, you can gain insight into improving your future practice. If you focus on successes before challenges, you can gain new understandings about the factors that promote success and shape new teaching decisions. Consider the reflection cycle in Figure 14.1.

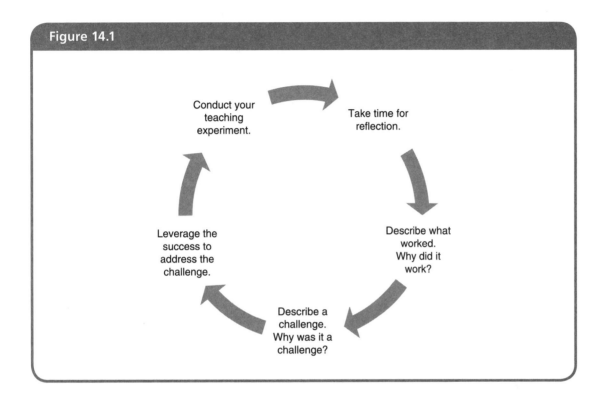

Figure 14.1

Let's look at each component of the reflecting cycle in more detail.

Take Time for Reflection

Unless you set a designated time for reflection, it can be difficult to move beyond musings about the day. Teachers are very hard on themselves and tend to focus on those most difficult moments or the problems of the day. Making time for reflection, using a specific cycle, can help you work through successes and challenges and strategically design next instructional steps. Think about how to schedule time to reflect alone and with trusted colleagues. Some teachers plan regular reflection time during professional learning meetings.

Describe What Worked

Reflect on what worked during the lesson, and describe what you and the students were doing that contributed to the success. When you ask yourself these questions, you heighten your awareness and positive potential for change (Cooperrider & Whitney, 2005). By focusing on what has worked and dissecting those elements that contributed to success, you can identify what aspects to repeat (Hammond, 1998).

Some teachers like to chart these ideas in two columns to help them discover connections (see example in Figure 14.2). This process is a key component for moving forward. Often, your inspiration about tackling challenges will come from your understanding of why a particular teaching practice was successful.

Figure 14.2

What Worked	Why
Numberless Word Problem	• Students were relaxed.
	• Students were curious.
	• Students immediately started putting numbers into the word problem to make sense of the problem.
	• Students were not encumbered with a right or wrong answer.
	• Students were allowed to collaborate and work together.

Describe the Challenge

By describing a challenge that you experienced in the lesson, you can begin to imagine how you can leverage your success to tackle your challenge. This could be something that is significant to this particular lesson, or it could be something that you have noticed as a pattern in your daily lessons. As the example in Figure 14.3 shows, it can be helpful to unpack the challenge by considering potential reasons why it exists (Figure 14.3).

Figure 14.3

Challenge	Why
Supporting students' productive struggle	• I am worried about pushing students too hard, and I think they know this.
	• I need to be better prepared with scaffolding questions.
	• I need to make sure that I am providing an environment that helps the students feel safe.
	• Some students are exhibiting learned helplessness.
	• Students are worried about being right and/or getting wrong answers.

Leverage the Success to Address the Challenge

By examining the elements of the success alongside the challenge, you can often uncover contributing elements of the success that you can leverage to help you with the challenge. For example, if you note your success with a numberless word problem but also your challenge with supporting productive struggle with some of your students, the details might prompt you to recognize that the numberless word problem was so successful because the students knew that there was not a correct answer. Based on this reflection, you might decide to use more open-ended problems with multiple solutions. This approach would also help you focus your students more on the process of solving, rather than on the answers.

Conduct Your Teaching Experiment

You conduct **teaching experiments** all the time! A teaching experiment occurs when you pose a question, try out an idea, reflect, and adjust based on the results (Tschannen-Moran & Tschannen-Moran, 2010). Teachers who share challenges often enjoy collaborating on teaching experiments and celebrating the results.

The first step in conducting your teaching experiment is to think about how to design your experiment. Consider the following questions:

- What would you like to pay more attention to in your mathematics classroom?
- What changes do you think your students would really appreciate?
- What changes would increase achievement?
- What things can you imagine doing differently?
- How might your mathematics teaching be different a few months from now?
- What changes would you like to experiment with in your mathematics teaching?

The next step is to describe your experiment and make a design plan for implementation. Consider the timeline, materials, and resources you will need to conduct your teaching experiment.

- Will you need to talk with other teachers, gain permission from your principal, or read new information to conduct your teaching experiment?
- What activities will you implement?
- What kinds of evidence will you collect?

Finally, you will need to reflect on your experiment.

- How will you know if your teaching experiment is successful?
- How will you revise your experiment?
- How will you integrate your experiment into your daily practice?
- How will you share the results of your experiment with your colleagues and leadership?

> **How can you use your reflection to design a teaching experiment through lesson planning? Record your responses here.**
>
> _____
>
> _____
>
> _____
>
> _____
>
> _____

Epilogue

You began this lesson-planning process by thinking about and examining your students' needs and considering the important ideas of coherence, rigor, and purpose. By now, we hope you have come to see the many important facets of building purposeful and cohesive mathematics lessons and maybe even fully engaged in the lesson-planning process, using the sections of this book as your guide, and filling in the lesson-planning template! Likewise, we hope you and your students are reaping the benefits of thorough planning, or at the very least getting a taste of the success yet to come. Whether you have designed a lesson fully from scratch, adapted a lesson, or even just read a few sections of this book, you have likely thought about the lesson-planning process with a new perspective that has deepened your knowledge about your own choices and decisions. The teachers we work with tell us that when they study and engage in the lesson-planning process, they

- become more confident and intentional in their teaching;

- are able to listen and respond to their students more authentically and react to their students' understandings with clarity and purpose;

- find greater meaning in the lessons because they have made sense of large and small teaching decisions, including task selection or adaptation, lesson purpose, lesson format, and lesson launch, facilitation, and closure; and

- report a renewed confidence and find they are energized and excited by the lesson-planning and implementation cycle.

As you have hopefully experienced, lesson planning builds cohesion for both students and yourself (Jensen, 2001). Thorough lessons, strategically planned, support students' ability to build connections among and between mathematical ideas (Panasuk, Stone, & Todd, 2002). This is, after all, our goal. Teachers and students see and understand how today's learning connects to yesterday's, last week's, even last year's learning *and* forecasts future learning.

You may have also noticed that the lesson-planning process can help you clarify your own understanding of the mathematics content, standard, and potential student misconceptions. This is perhaps one of the most powerful teacher benefits of lesson planning—a benefit that will extend beyond any one lesson you teach. The teachers we work with report that they experience new insight about the mathematics they are teaching, which, in turn, helps them to strategically facilitate their students' learning.

As you continue this journey, we recommend that you do the following:

Start slowly. Select a few pieces of the lesson-planning process to focus on, and then build from there. Start with what is most comfortable for you, and then extend or add new pieces to your planning repertoire. Before you know it, you will be able to spend your time on the parts of the lesson that need your attention the most.

Find planning partners. Search for other teachers to plan with regularly. They don't necessarily have to be in your school or grade level. Online platforms support co-creation and sharing across the country. Simply having an opportunity to share your planning decisions with others can be immensely rewarding and satisfying. Make sure you share your successes as well as your challenges.

Determine how you will organize and store your lessons. Many teachers store the lessons for each grade level by using online formats. This organization will support you in the future and reduce planning time in subsequent years. Storing lessons will also help you track revisions as you respond to the particular needs of your students. Don't forget to record reflections or thoughts about the lesson!

Communicate with leaders. As you know, planning lessons takes time and perseverance. Invite school and district leaders to participate in your planning sessions. Engage them in your process as you plan, implement, and reflect on your teaching successes and challenges.

Celebrate and showcase your success. So much of teaching is privately shared between students and teachers. Publicly sharing your lessons with teammates and school leaders can inspire others to plan and innovate powerful lessons. Organize opportunities for colleagues to share successful lessons that affected student learning.

Always remember that you are the architect of your classroom. You have the fortune to design and implement lessons that help children learn mathematics. You get to establish the learning environment you want to foster, and you have not only the opportunity but also the responsibility to build the best foundation and best structure for your learners as possible. We wish you every success.

Appendix A

Complete Lesson Plans

Big Idea(s):

Fractions with different numerators or different denominators can represent the same part of a whole.

Essential Question(s):

How do we know when two fractions are equivalent?

Content Standard(s):

Compare two fractions with the same numerator or denominator by reasoning about their size. Recognize that comparisons are valid only when the two fractions refer to the same whole.

Mathematical Practice or Process Standard(s):

Construct viable arguments and critique the reasoning of others.

Make sense of problems and persevere in solving them.

Learning Intention(s):
Mathematical Learning Intentions

We are learning to:
* Compare fractions when the numerators are the same
* Compare fractions when the denominators are the same
* Know that sometimes fractions are equivalent
* Know that to compare fractions, they must come from the same whole

Language Learning Intentions

We are learning to:
* Explain how fractions compare using the words numerator, denominator, and equivalent

Social Learning Intentions

We are learning to:
* Listen to each other's explanations about fraction comparisons
* Ask questions about other students' thinking
* Politely challenge or disagree with explanations
* Stick to a problem to solve it

Success Criteria
(written in student voice):

I know that I am successful when I can:
* Determine which fraction is greater than another
* Determine if two fractions are equivalent
* Talk about fractions using the words numerator, denominator, and equivalent correctly
* Listen to my classmates' explanations about fractions
* Politely offer a different way of thinking about comparing fractions
* Stick to a problem to solve it

Purpose:

☑ Conceptual Understanding   ☐ Procedural Fluency   ☐ Transfer

Task:

Convince Us!

We are going to play a game. I will put a statement on the board. With your partner, you need to convince us that what I wrote is true. You can use any materials, drawings, or reasoning that you want. We are looking for a variety of ways to convince us that the statement is true.

Materials (representations, manipulatives, other):

Fraction circles, fraction strips, two color-counters, number lines, individual student whiteboards and markers

Misconceptions or Common Errors:

*   Students may confuse the meaning of numerator and denominator.
*   Given the whole, the smaller the denominator, the smaller the size of the pieces.
*   Students ignore the size of the whole.

Format:

☐ Four-Part Lesson   ☐ Game Format   ☐ Small-Group Instruction

☑ Pairs   Other_____

Formative Assessment:

Hinge question used after students compare fractions with same denominators: Here are two fractions.

$$\frac{3}{8} \text{ or } \frac{5}{8}$$

On your whiteboard, write the fraction that is greater and draw a picture to back up your thinking.

If students answer this correctly, continue playing "Convince Us!" using fractions with same numerators and different denominators.

(Continued)

Launch:

Present students with a problem that will activate their prior knowledge about fractions before beginning to play "Convince Us!"

Distribute copies of the following problem:

Mark was asked to draw a picture to compare two fractions: $\frac{4}{5}$ and $\frac{2}{3}$. He drew the following:

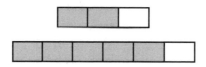

Mark said that $\frac{2}{3}$ is the same size as $\frac{4}{5}$. There is a mistake in Mark's thinking and drawing. Tell your group what you think Mark's error is.

As students work on this problem in small groups, walk around and listen to student reasoning. Have students share their responses with the class after sharing with their groups.

Anticipate student responses:

- Mark did not make his wholes the same size.

- All the pieces are different sizes.

- Mark does not understand that four out of five pieces should be more than two out of three when the wholes are the same size.

- A larger number in the denominator means a larger fraction.

Facilitate:

1. After the launch problem, explain to the class that today they are going to work with a partner and play a game called "Convince Us!"

    a. I am going to write a statement on the board. You will work with your partner to convince us that it is true. You can use any materials in the room you wish including your white board.

    b. Here is our first statement: $\frac{3}{5} > \frac{1}{5}$

2. Our whole for this game is one large cheese pizza. Walk around and listen to student thinking. Note which students are using different strategies/tools to model their thinking. Pay attention to students who are not using materials but trying to work abstractly.

3. After sufficient time to work, ask student pairs who have used drawings to share their work using a document camera. They will explain why $\frac{3}{5}$ is greater than $\frac{1}{5}$ in pictures and words. Record their strategies.

4. Allow students who did not use materials but thought about the equation abstractly to share their ideas and explain how they know $\frac{3}{5}$ is greater. These students will likely use logical reasoning stating something like, "We know that the pizza is in five pieces and three pieces are more than one piece."

5. Follow up with questions to clarify this thinking for all students such as:

    a. Oh, so what can you tell me about the size of each slice of pizza?

    b. What clue tells you about the size of the slices?

    c. Can anyone else explain what Ginger just said in a different way?

    d. How does Ginger's explanation match what Jamie did with the fraction circles?

6. Repeat with another true statement and follow the same procedure and questioning. Each time a student gives the explanation abstractly, praise this explanation and ask others to explain it to show that they understand it. Point out how quickly a person can tell if one fraction is larger than the other just using the reasoning.

7. Repeat with true statements where the denominators are the same as many times as needed until you feel that the students have the understanding that when two fractions have the same denominator, the size of the pieces being compared is the same, so you look at the numerator to tell how many pieces each fraction represents.

8. Ask the hinge question when you think students have the understanding. If the answers to the hinge question indicate students have the concept, repeat the game using fractions with the same numerator such as $\frac{4}{6} < \frac{4}{5}$.

9. Repeat with fractions that have the same numerator until you feel that the students have the concept. When fractions have the same numerator (same number of pieces), you can compare the size of the pieces using the denominator.

Anticipating student responses:

Expect some students to be confused about numerators and denominators. Use the launch problem to help clarify before beginning the game.

During "Convince Us!" some students may want to rely heavily on fraction circles or fraction strips for their explanations. When you notice this, have students connect the abstract explanations to the manipulatives to demonstrate the concept.

Some students try to repeat an abstract explanation when they really do not understand the concept. Ask students to give the explanation in their own words, or interview them with a different equation to see if they truly understand.

(Continued)

Closure:

Distribute copies of the cellphone template so that students may answer this question:

Tell your friend in a text message how you know $\frac{3}{5} < \frac{4}{5}$.

Source: iStock.com/drogatnev

 Download the complete third-grade lesson plan from resources.corwin.com/mathlessonplanning/3-5

Big Idea(s):

Fractions with different numerators and denominators can represent the same part of a whole.

Essential Question(s):

How do we know when two fractions are equivalent?

Content Standard(s):

Explain why a fraction $\frac{a}{b}$ is equivalent to a fraction $\frac{(n \times a)}{(n \times b)}$ by using visual fraction models, with attention to how the number and size of the parts differ even though the two fractions themselves are the same size. Use this principle to recognize and generate equivalent fractions.

Mathematical Practice or Process Standard(s):

Model with mathematics.

Look and make use of structure.

Learning Intention(s):

Mathematical Learning Intentions

We are learning to:
- Use a model to demonstrate how two fractions are equivalent
- Create fractions that are equivalent to another fraction

Language Learning Intentions

We are learning to:
- Explain why two fractions are equivalent using the words for the parts of the fraction (numerator, denominator)

Social Learning Intentions

We are learning to:
- Listen to each other's explanations about equivalence
- Ask questions about other students' thinking
- Politely challenge or disagree with explanations
- Apply my reasoning about equivalence to different kinds of fraction models

Success Criteria (written in student voice):

I know I am successful when I can:
- Show equivalent fractions with models
- Recognize that two fractions are equivalent
- Find a fraction that is equivalent to another fraction
- Use the correct words to describe why two fractions are equivalent
- Participate in a class discussion about equivalent fractions
- Use the rules I found for equivalent fractions with several different models

Purpose:

☐ Conceptual Understanding   ☐ Procedural Fluency   ☑ Transfer

(Continued)

Task:

Carol's Cookie Corner

You are the manager of Carol's Cookie Corner. It is your busy season and almost all of your bakers are hard at work. A new order for your special Choco-oat-raisin cookies just came in and you have one baker, Sammy, who can make them. However, you only have a $\frac{1}{4}$ cup measuring cup and $\frac{1}{4}$ teaspoon handy because your other bakers are using all of your other measuring cups and spoons. Sammy needs help with fractions so you have to change all of the measures in the recipe so he can use the $\frac{1}{4}$ teaspoon and measuring cup.

You remember using a number line in school to work with fractions.

1. Rewrite all of the measures in the recipe as equivalent fractions that Sammy can use with the measurement tools you gave him.

Your business is booming and you may run out of measuring tools again. You decide to teach all of your bakers to use equivalent fractions.

2. Create a large number line on chart paper. Put the numbers from the recipe on the number line.

3. Add as many equivalent fractions as you can to the number line for each number you placed on the number line.

4. Be prepared to teach your fellow bakers about equivalent fractions. Explain in writing what you will say to them.

Materials (representations, manipulatives, other):

Recipe, $\frac{1}{4}$ measuring cup, $\frac{1}{4}$ teaspoon, chart paper, markers

Misconceptions or Common Errors:

- You cannot write a fraction for a whole number.
- Fractions don't work on a number line.
- A mixed number cannot be written as an improper fraction.

Format:

☑ Four-Part Lesson   ☐ Game Format   ☐ Small-Group Instruction

☐ Pairs   ☐ Other_____

Formative Assessment:

Use the observation checklist to observe the following:

- Partners listening to one another
- Ordering of fractions on the number line
- Strategies/models selected to find equivalent fractions
- Number of equivalent fractions on the number line (including fraction forms of whole and mixed numbers)

Launch:

Introduce the first part of the problem with a discussion about the importance of precise measures in baking. Ask students questions such as:

- What happens when you do not use the precise measures called for in a recipe?
- How do you measure amounts when you cook? What tools do you use?
- Can you think of any other situations where precise measures are needed?
- What are some situations where you may need equivalent fractions?
- What is Carol's problem with her measuring tools?

Introduce the second part of the problem:
You remember using a number line in school to work with fractions.

1. Rewrite all of the measures in the recipe as equivalent fractions that Sammy can use with the measurement tools you gave him.

Your business is booming and you may run out of measuring tools again. You decide to teach all of your bakers to use equivalent fractions.

2. Create a large number line on chart paper. Put the numbers from the recipe on the number line.
3. Add as many equivalent fractions as you can to the number line for each number you placed on the number line.
4. Be prepared to teach your fellow bakers about equivalent fractions. Explain in writing what you will say to them.

Ask the students to identify what they need to do to solve the problem. Discuss any questions they may have.

Share success criteria.

Facilitate:

1. Students work in pairs to solve the problem after the launch discussion.
2. Pairs are given a copy of the recipe, chart paper, and $\frac{1}{4}$ teaspoons and measuring cups to complete the task.
3. As the pairs work together, monitor their work by asking questions such as these:
   How will you get started?
   What ideas did your partner have?
   What would a manager say to his or her bakers?
   What do you think bakers need to know about equivalent fractions to include in your talk?
   What strategy or strategies are you using to find equivalent fractions?
4. Encourage students to share their explanations to the bakers (read to the class).
5. Pose the second part of the problem.

   1. Rewrite all of the measures in the recipe as equivalent fractions that Sammy can use with the measurement tools you gave him.

   Your business is booming and you may run out of measuring tools again. You decide to teach all of your bakers to use equivalent fractions.

(Continued)

6. Create a PowerPoint or video to teach your bakers about equivalent fractions. You can create a large number line on chart paper and add the numbers from the recipe on the number line. You decide how to use the number line in your PowerPoint or video.

Closure:

Footprint—distribute cut out footprints to each student. Ask students to think about and then write what they are walking away with from their unit on equivalent fractions.

Recipe for Choco-oat-raisin Cookies
(Makes about 4 dozen cookies)

_____ 1 cup butter

_____ $1\frac{1}{4}$ cup brown sugar

_____ $\frac{1}{4}$ cup of granulated sugar

_____ 2 eggs

_____ $1\frac{1}{2}$ teaspoon vanilla

_____ $1\frac{1}{2}$ cups flour

_____ 1 teaspoon baking soda

_____ $\frac{1}{2}$ teaspoon cinnamon

_____ $\frac{1}{2}$ teaspoon salt

_____ 3 cups uncooked oatmeal

_____ $1\frac{1}{2}$ cup raisins

_____ $\frac{2}{8}$ cup chocolate chips

1. Heat oven to 350°F.

2. Beat together butter and sugars.

3. Add eggs and vanilla and beat well.

4. Add flour, baking soda, cinnamon, and salt and combine well.

5. Stir in oats, raisins, and chocolate chips. Mix well.

6. Drop by rounded tablespoons onto ungreased cookie sheet.

7. Bake 10 to 12 minutes.

8. Cool one minute on cookie sheet.

Write your equivalent fractions on the line next to each measure.
Remember you only have a $\frac{1}{4}$ measuring cup and a $\frac{1}{4}$ teaspoon.

online resources ➤ Download the complete fourth-grade lesson plan and the recipe handout from resources.corwin.com/mathlessonplanning/3-5

Complete Lesson Plan

Big Idea(s):

Multiplication with fractions is similar to multiplication with whole numbers. Students grapple with similarities and differences between multiplication of whole numbers and fractions.

Essential Question(s):

What does it mean to multiply fractions?

Content Standard(s):

Apply and extend previous understandings of multiplication to multiply a fraction or whole number by a fraction.

a. Interpret the product $\left(\frac{a}{b}\right) \times q$ as a part of a partition of q into b equal parts; equivalently, as the result of a sequence of operations $a \times q \div b$. For example, use a visual fraction model to show $\left(\frac{2}{3}\right) \times 4 = \frac{8}{3}$, and create a story context for this equation. Do the same with $\left(\frac{2}{3}\right) \times \left(\frac{4}{5}\right) = \frac{8}{15}$ (In general, $\left(\frac{a}{b}\right) \times \left(\frac{c}{d}\right) = \frac{ac}{bd}$)

b. Find the area of a rectangle with fractional side lengths by tiling it with unit squares of the appropriate unit fraction side lengths, and show that the area is the same as would be found by multiplying the side lengths. Multiply fractional side lengths to find areas of rectangles, and represent fraction products as rectangular areas.

Mathematical Practice or Process Standard(s):

Students make sense of problems and persevere while solving them.

Students construct viable arguments and critique the reasoning of others.

Learning Intention(s):
Mathematical Learning Intentions

We are learning to:

- Multiply a fraction by a fraction
- Multiply fractional side lengths to find areas of rectangles

Language Learning Intentions

We are learning to:

- Explain what happens to the product when multiplying fractions

Success Criteria:
(written in student voice)

I know I am successful when I can:
- Use a model to show multiplication of fractions
- Use a model to multiply fractional side lengths to find the area
- Use mathematics vocabulary to explain my reasoning
- Convince others of my thinking
- Work with my classmates to solve mathematics problems

(Continued)

Social Learning Intentions

We are learning to:

- Listen to each other's explanations and provide feedback
- Ask questions about other students' thinking
- Politely challenge or disagree with explanations
- Apply my reasoning about multiplication of fractions to other situations
- Communicate with others to solve mathematics problems
- Create and use a representation to explain my thinking to others

Purpose:

☑ Conceptual Understanding   ☐ Procedural Fluency   ☐ Transfer

Task:

Who Ate the Most Brownies?

Twin sisters, Satthiya and Priya, each made a pan of brownies for the fifth-grade school picnic. Satthiya made chocolate chunk brownies and Priya made caramel swirl brownies. The sisters set their brownie pans on the table to cool and when they got back they noticed that someone had been eating their brownies! Satthiya's pan had only $\frac{3}{4}$ of the brownies left in the pan! Priya had $\frac{2}{3}$ of the brownies left in the pan! They had no choice but to take the brownies to the picnic and explain what happened to their teachers. After the picnic, Satthiya saw that her class had eaten $\frac{2}{3}$ of the $\frac{3}{4}$ brownies that were in the pan. Priya saw that her class had eaten $\frac{2}{4}$ of the $\frac{2}{3}$ brownies left in her pan. Now the sisters are arguing about the class that ate the most brownies! Help the sisters find out. Show a representation to prove your idea.

Materials (representations, manipulatives, other):

Color tiles, one-inch graph paper, markers, chart paper

Misconceptions or Common Errors:

- Believing that multiplication always makes things bigger, and therefore the same will be true for fraction multiplication
- Believing that procedural fluency (multiplying numerators and multiplying denominators) is the same as conceptual understanding
- Believing that multiplication is the same as addition by creating common denominators

Format:

☑ Four-Part Lesson   ☐ Game Format   ☐ Small-Group Instruction

☐ Pairs   ☐ Other_____

Formative Assessment:

Individual and paired interviews: Ask students, "How does your representation show multiplication of fractions?"

Launch:

Reveal this picture to the students and conduct a Notice and Wonder:

1. Record the students' Notices and Wonders. (Students might notice that the brownie pans are not full. Students might also notice that the brownie pans have different kinds of brownies and the brownie pans show different amounts.)

2. Introduce the first part of the problem to the students and ask them to add to the Notice and Wonder. They might notice that $\frac{3}{4}$ is greater than $\frac{2}{3}$.

   Twin sisters, Satthiya and Priya, each made a pan of brownies for the fifth-grade school picnic. Satthiya made chocolate chunk brownies and Priya made caramel swirl brownies. The sisters set their brownie pans on the table to cool and when they got back they noticed that someone had been eating their brownies! Satthiya's pan had only $\frac{3}{4}$ of the brownies left in the pan! Priya had $\frac{2}{3}$ of the brownies left in the pan! They had no choice but to take the brownies to the picnic and explain what happened to their teachers.

3. Reveal the last part of the problem:

   After the picnic, Satthiya saw that her class had eaten $\frac{2}{3}$ of the $\frac{3}{4}$ brownies that were in the pan. Priya saw that her class had eaten $\frac{2}{4}$ of the $\frac{2}{3}$ brownies left in her pan. Now the sisters are arguing about the class that ate the most brownies! Help the sisters find out. Show a representation to prove your idea.

4. Share and discuss the language and social learning intentions. Do not reveal the mathematical intentions because this is an inquiry lesson.

(Continued)

Facilitate:

1. Ask the students to turn and talk to a partner about the brownie problem. Then have the students make a prediction about whose class ate the most brownies. Record their predictions.

2. Arrange the students into groups of four and distribute chart paper to the students.

3. Tell the students that they must decide which of the sister's classes ate the most brownies. They will need to find out how much of Satthiya's and Priya's brownie pans is left over after the picnic. Tell the students that they must represent their thinking using manipulatives and/or drawings. Offer graph paper, color tiles, and markers for the students to use.

4. As the students are working, monitor the groups as they solve. Ask questions and encourage the students to talk to each other and show their thinking. If students struggle, encourage them to show the amount of brownies in each pan first by creating an array.

   Satthiya started with $\frac{2}{3}$ of the brownie pan. Priya started with $\frac{3}{4}$ of the brownie pan.

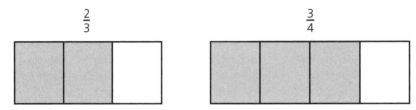

5. Then ask, "How can you show how much of the brownie pan was eaten by the class?" Encourage the students to share their ideas and represent their thinking using representations. Students might also use color tiles to represent the amount of the brownie pan eaten.

6. Continue to monitor the students as they work. Ask:
   - How could an array model help you?
   - How can you represent each pan's value?
   - How can you represent $\frac{2}{4}$ of $\frac{2}{3}$? What does that look like?
   - How can you represent $\frac{2}{3}$ of $\frac{3}{4}$? What does that look like?
   - How can you explain your reasoning to each other?
   - How can drawing a math picture help you solve this problem?
   - Convince a classmate about your thinking and reasoning.

7. After the students have completed the posters, ask the students to hang their posters for a gallery walk.

8. Give each student two sticky notes and tell them to examine the posters and give two pieces of feedback to two different groups. Explain to the students that the feedback must be specific and constructive. While the students are giving feedback, select two to three groups' posters and ask those groups to share during the whole-group closure.

Closure:

1. Ask the students to look at their original predictions. Ask:

    - What do you notice about our predictions?

    - If you were to make a new prediction, what might you think about?

2. Ask the groups to share their solutions with the whole class. Sequence the groups' sharing from least sophisticated solution to most sophisticated solution. The prior gallery walk should have provided the students with an opportunity to give feedback and familiarize the students with their classmates' thinking. As the groups share, provide the following prompts:

    - What representation did you use to show multiplication of fractions?

    - What did you notice about fraction multiplication?

    - How is fraction multiplication same as/different from whole-number multiplication?

    - How did the array model help you figure out which sister's class ate the most brownies?

3. Connect the students' work to the learning intentions and success criteria by asking the students to look at the learning intentions and success criteria:

    I know I am successful when I:

    - Use a model to show multiplication of fractions

    - Use a model to multiply fractional side lengths to find the area

    Ask the students to turn and talk with each other to answer the prompts:

    - How did you use a model to show multiplication of fractions?

    - What is one thing you can do to improve your success?

 Download the complete fifth-grade lesson plan from resources.corwin.com/mathlessonplanning/3-5

Appendix B

Lesson-Planning Template

Big Idea(s):

Essential Question(s):

Content Standard(s):

Mathematical Practice or Process Standards:

Learning Intention(s):
(mathematical/language/social)

Success Criteria:
(written in student voice)

Purpose:

☐ Conceptual Understanding   ☐ Procedural Fluency   ☐ Transfer

Task:

Materials (representations, manipulatives, other):

Misconceptions or Common Errors:

Format:

☐ Four-Part Lesson   ☐ Game Format   ☐ Small-Group Instruction

☐ Pairs   ☐ Other_____

Formative Assessment:

Launch:

Facilitate:

Closure:

Appendix C

Further Reading/Resources

Online

Mathematics Content, Standards, and Virtual Manipulatives

http://www.achievethecore.org

A nonprofit organization dedicated to helping teachers and school leaders implement high-quality, college- and career-ready standards. The site includes planning materials, professional development resources, assessment information, and implementation support.

http://illustrativemathematics.org

A variety of videos, tasks, and suggestions for professional development accessible to all teachers.

http://ime.math.arizona.edu/progressions

The series of progressions documents written by leading researchers in the field summarizing the standards progressions for specific mathematical content domains.

http://nlvm.usu.edu

The National Library of Virtual Manipulatives offers a library of uniquely interactive, web-based virtual manipulatives or concept tutorials for mathematics instruction.

Sources for Problems, Tasks, and Lesson Protocols

https://bstockus.wordpress.com/numberless-word-problem

Numberless word problems designed to provide scaffolding that allows students the opportunity to develop a better understanding of the underlying structure of word problems.

https://gfletchy.com

3-Act Lessons and Mathematical Progressions videos for Grades K–7.

http://www.pz.harvard.edu/projects/visible-thinking

Harvard Zero Project describes thinking routines that can be applied to K–12 mathematics classrooms.

http://illuminations.nctm.org

A collection of high-quality tasks, lessons, and activities that align with the Common Core standards and include the standards for mathematical practice.

http://mathforum.org

The Math Forum at NCTM provides a plethora of online resources, including Problem of the Week and the Notice and Wonder protocol.

http://mathpickle.com

A free online resource of original mathematical puzzles, games, and unsolved problems for K–12 teachers. It is supported by the American Institute of Mathematics.

http://nrich.maths.org

Free enrichment materials, curriculum maps, and professional development for mathematics teachers.

http://www.openmiddle.com

A crowd-sourced collection of challenging problems for Grades K–12. Open middle problems all begin with the same initial problem and end with the same answer, but they include multiple paths for problem solving and require a higher depth of knowledge than most problems that assess procedural and conceptual understanding.

http://robertkaplinsky.com/lessons

A collection of free real-world, problem-based lessons for Grades K–12.

http://www.stevewyborney.com

A collection of ideas and activities for K–8 teachers.

Books

Fennell, F., Kobett, B. M., & Wray, J. A. (2017). *The formative 5: Everyday assessment techniques for every math classroom.* Thousand Oaks, CA: Corwin.

Gojak, L., & Harbin Miles, R. (2015). *The common core mathematics companion: The standards decoded, grades 3–5.* Thousand Oaks, CA: Corwin. [For Common Core states]

Gojak, L., & Harbin Miles, R. (2017). *Your mathematics standards companion: What they mean and how to teach them, grades 3–5.* Thousand Oaks, CA: Corwin. [For Non–Common Core states]

Hattie, J., Fisher, D., Frey, N., Gojak, L. M., Moore, S. D., & Mellman, W. (2016). *Visible learning for mathematics, grades K–12. What works best to optimize student learning.* Thousand Oaks, CA: Corwin.

Hull, T., Harbin Miles, R., & Balka, D. S. (2014). *Realizing rigor in the mathematics classroom.* Thousand Oaks, CA: Corwin.

Huinker, D., & Bill, V. (2017). *Taking action: Implementing effective mathematics teaching practices in K– Grade 5.* Reston, VA: NCTM.

National Council of Teachers of Mathematics. (2014). *Principles to actions: Ensuring mathematical success for all.* Reston, VA: NCTM.

O'Connell, S., & SanGiovanni, J. (2013). *Putting the practices into action: Implementing the common core standards for mathematical practice, K–8.* Portsmouth, NH: Heinemann.

Otto, A., Hancock, S. W., Caldwell, J., & Zbiek, R. M. (2011). *Developing essential understanding of multiplication and division for teaching mathematics in grades 3–5.* Reston, VA: NCTM.

Ray-Reik, M. (2013). *Powerful problem solving: Activities for sense making with the mathematical practices.* Portsmouth, NH: Heinemann.

Schrock, C., Norris, K., Pugalee, D., Seitz, R., & Hollingshead, F. (2013). *NCSM great tasks for mathematics K–5.* Reston, VA: NCTM.

Smith, M. S., & Stein, M. K. (2011). *Five practices for orchestrating productive mathematics discussions.* Reston, VA: National Council of Teachers of Mathematics and Corwin.

Van de Walle, J. A., Karp, K. S., & Bay Williams, J. M. (2016). *Elementary and middle school mathematics: Teaching developmentally* (9th ed.). Upper Saddle River, NJ: Pearson Education.

Van de Walle, J. A., Lovin, L. A. H., Karp, K. S., & Bay-Williams, J. M. (2017). *Teaching student-centered mathematics: Developmentally appropriate instruction for grades 3–5* (3rd ed.). Upper Saddle River, NJ: Pearson Education.

Appendix D

Glossary

academic language. The vocabulary used in schools, textbooks, and other school resources.

access to high-quality mathematics instruction. Phrase refers to the National Council of Teachers of Mathematics (NCTM) position statement on equal opportunity to a quality K–12 education for all students. Related to the NCTM position on equitable learning opportunities.

agency. The power to act. Students exercise agency in mathematics when they initiate discussions and actively engage in high-level thinking tasks. When students exercise agency, they reason, critique the reasoning of others, and engage in productive struggle.

algorithm. In mathematics, it is a series of steps or procedures that, when followed accurately, will produce a correct answer.

big ideas. Statements that encompass main concepts in mathematics that cross grade levels, such as place value.

classroom discourse. Conversation that occurs in a classroom. Can be teacher to student(s), student(s) to teacher, or student(s) to student(s).

close-ended questions. Questions with only one correct answer.

closure. The final activity in a lesson with two purposes: (1) helps the teacher determine what students have learned and gives direction to next steps; (2) provides students the opportunity to reorganize and summarize the information from a lesson in a meaningful way.

coherence. Logical sequencing of mathematical ideas. Can be vertical, as in across the grades (e.g., K–2), or horizontal, as in across a grade level (e.g., first-grade lessons from September through December).

common errors. Mistakes made by students that occur frequently; usually these mistakes are anticipated by the teacher due to their frequency.

computation. Using an operation such as addition, subtraction, multiplication, or division to find an answer.

conceptual understanding. Comprehension of mathematical concepts, operations, and relationships.

content standards. See *standards.*

decompose. To break a number down into addends. A number may be decomposed in more than one way (e.g., 12 can be decomposed as 10 + 2, 9 + 3, and 5 + 5 + 2).

discourse. See *classroom discourse.*

district-wide curriculum. A K–12 document outlining the curriculum for a school system.

drill. Repetitive exercises on a specific math skill or procedure.

English Language Learner (ELL). A person whose first language is not English but who is learning to speak English.

essential question. A question that unifies all of the lessons on a given topic to bring the coherence and purpose to a unit. Essential questions are purposefully linked to the big idea to frame student inquiry, promote critical thinking, and assist in learning transfer.

exit task. A task given at the end of a lesson or group of lessons that provides a sampling of student performance. An exit task is more in depth than an *exit slip.*

exit ticket/exit slip. A form of lesson closure where students answer a question related to the main idea of the lesson on a slip of paper. Teachers collect these slips of paper.

formative assessment. Also called *formative evaluation.* The ongoing collection of information about student learning as it is happening and the process of responding to that information by adapting instruction to improve learning.

formative evaluation. See *formative assessment.*

habits of mind. Ways of thinking about mathematics as mathematicians do (e.g., always choosing solution methods, asking questions, and having productive attitudes). These habits help us understand mathematics and solve problems, and they are linked to process standards. Habits of mind include (but are not limited to) perseverance in problem solving, comparing, finding patterns, and asking "what if …" questions.

hands-on learning. Learning that takes place while students are using manipulatives.

high cognitive demand. Characteristic of a problem or task that requires using higher-order thinking skills as defined by Bloom's Taxonomy. Also see *higher-order thinking skills.*

higher-order thinking skills. The more complex thinking skills as defined by Bloom's Taxonomy. Examples include predicting, creating, synthesizing, and analyzing.

hinge questions. A classroom-based assessment technique where the teacher delivers a question at a pivotal point in a lesson. Student responses to the question determine the path the teacher takes on the next part of the lesson.

horizontal coherence. See *coherence.*

identity. How individuals know and see themselves such as student, teacher, good at sports, and how others know and see us such as short, smart, or shy. Defined broadly, it is a concept that brings together all the interrelated elements that teachers and students bring to the classroom, including beliefs, attitudes, and emotions.

Individualized Education Plan (IEP). A road map for a particular student's learning. Usually written for students in a special education program, it includes goals and accommodations needed for the child to be successful.

instructional decisions. Decisions made that affect classroom teaching and learning.

interleaving. The practice of cycling back to a previous skill, concept, or big idea to help children build their understanding of that topic.

interview. A classroom-based assessment technique where the teacher has a brief talk with a student to collect more information on the student's thinking.

learning community. A group of teachers (usually at the same grade level)—and sometimes other professionals—who work together to plan lessons, discuss student concerns, and support one another's teaching.

learning intention. Statement of what a student is expected to learn from a lesson. Also known as the lesson goal. There are three types: mathematical, social, and language goals.

learning progressions. Specific sequence of mathematical knowledge and skills that students are expected to learn as they progress from kindergarten through high school and beyond.

lesson format. The manner in which students are organized for a lesson. Whole-group lessons and small-group lessons are two examples.

lesson launch. How the teacher introduces a lesson.

manipulative. Any concrete material that can be used by students to further their mathematical understanding. Examples include counters, blocks, coins, and fraction circles.

math anxiety. A feeling of stress, fear, or worry about one's ability to do mathematics, which may interfere with one's mathematical performance.

math talk. See *number talk.*

mathematical discourse. See *classroom discourse.*

metacognitive. Adjective for *metacognition,* the process of thinking about one's thinking. One type of metacognition includes knowing about using certain strategies for problem solving.

misconception. An incorrect understanding or belief about a mathematical topic or concept.

multiple entry points. The many different methods one can use to attack a problem. Methods can range from simple approaches to more complex approaches.

number routine. A mathematics activity that takes place on a regular basis (e.g., daily, every Friday, etc.).

number sense routine. A number routine that focuses on building students' reasoning about numbers.

number talk. Also known as *math talk.* A number routine that focuses on building student number sense through scaffolded problem-solving experiences where students verbalize and justify their solutions to one another and the teacher.

numberless word problem. A word problem with the numbers blocked out, encouraging students to make sense of the problem before they work with the numbers.

observation. A classroom-based formative assessment technique where the teacher informally watches students and documents what is seen in order to inform instruction.

open-ended questions. Description for mathematical problems that have more than one acceptable answer and multiple solution strategies.

pacing guide. Grade-level document for district-wide implementation that determines the order of the standards to be taught and the amount of time to be spent on each topic. The level of specificity of these documents varies.

practice. Brief, engaging, and purposeful exercises, tasks, or experiences on the same idea spread out over time.

precise use of vocabulary. Using exact mathematical language as a strategy to build a shared understanding of important mathematical terms. Some common mathematics terms have nonmathematical meanings. Precise use of vocabulary refers to using the mathematical definition.

prior knowledge. Mathematical knowledge students know before they begin a topic or task.

problem solving. The process of finding a solution to a situation for which no immediate answer is available. What may be a problem for one student may not be a problem for another.

procedural fluency. The ability to carry out procedures/algorithms flexibly, accurately, efficiently, and appropriately.

process standards. See *standards.*

productive struggle. Students wrestle with ideas to make sense of mathematics; this phrase describes the effort involved in solving a problem when an immediate solution is not available.

reflecting in action. See *reflection.*

reflecting on action. See *reflection.*

reflection. The process of thinking about one's learning. For teachers, there is *reflecting in action,* which occurs during teaching so that the teacher can monitor and adjust instruction as it occurs. *Reflecting on action* occurs when the teacher looks back on a lesson and the students after instruction takes place.

representations. Any concrete, pictorial, or symbolic model that can stand for a mathematical idea.

resources. For a primary mathematics teacher, anything that can be used to assist in the design and implementation of lessons (e.g., textbooks, curriculum guides, manipulatives, and supplemental materials).

rigor. Results from active participation in rich mathematical problem-solving tasks. The two types of rigor are *content* and *instructional. Content rigor* results from a deep connection among the concepts and the breadth of supporting skills that students are expected to master. *Instructional rigor* is the continuous interaction between the instruction and students' reasoning about concepts, skills, and challenging tasks.

scaffold. Name for a variety of teaching strategies that support student learning; techniques that help students bridge from what they know to something new.

Show Me. A classroom-based assessment technique where the teacher asks students to demonstrate what they have learned. Students may use any materials such as manipulatives or drawings.

spaced practice. Also called *distributed practice.* A learning strategy where practice is broken up into a number of short sessions over a period of time.

standards. Concise, written descriptions of what students are expected to know and be able to do at a specific grade level, age, or stage of development. In mathematics, there are *content standards* (what students are expected to know) and *process standards* (how students are expected to do the mathematics). Process standards are closely linked to mathematical habits of mind. The *Standards for Mathematical Practice* define the processes for the Common Core State Standards for Mathematics (CCSS-M).

Standards for Mathematical Practice. See *standards.*

strategy. A plan for solving a problem. Some common problem-solving strategies in primary mathematics are counting down, drawing a picture, and using a model.

subitizing. The ability to immediately identify a quantity without counting.

success criteria. Defines what learning looks like when achieved.

summative assessment. Testing used to determine students' achievement levels at specific points in time, such as at the end of teaching units, semesters, and grade level.

task. A mathematical problem. Rich tasks or worthwhile tasks are problems with several characteristics, such as accessibility, authenticity, and being active with a focus on significant mathematics for the grade level.

teaching experiments. Research in education conducted through three components: modeling, teaching episodes, and individual or group interviews where student thinking is the focus of the experiment.

textbook. In mathematics, textbooks are one of the many types of resources teachers use; contents follow a logical teaching order and usually match the curriculum being taught.

timed tests. In mathematics, assessments to be completed within a specific period of time; often associated with basic fact practice.

transfer. One of the three main types of math lessons that prompt students to demonstrate their ability to use content knowledge and skill in a problem situation.

unintended consequences. Unforeseen outcomes from a purposeful action.

unit plan. Several coherent lessons on a given topic that flow logically from one another.

unpack. Using one's knowledge to extract the main ideas and knowledge embedded in the standard; to break down a standard into its main ideas.

vertical coherence. See *coherence.*

whole group. A type of classroom grouping where the entire class is instructed as one large group. This contrasts with small groups, where the whole class is divided into small groups of students for instruction.

word problem. Any mathematical exercise where significant background information on the problem is presented as text rather than in mathematical notation.

References

Annenberg Learner Foundation. (2003). *Teaching math, Grades 3–5*. Retrieved from https://learner.org/courses/teachingmath/grades3_5/session_05/index.html

Aguirre, J. M., Mayfield-Ingram, K., & Martin, D. B. (2013). *The impact of identity in K–8 mathematics learning and teaching: Rethinking equity-based practices*. Reston, VA: NCTM.

Bamberger, H. J., Oberdorf, C., Schultz-Ferrell, K., & Leinwand, S. (2011). *Math misconceptions, preK–Grade 5: From misunderstanding to deep understanding*. Portsmouth, NH: Heinemann.

Banse, H. W., Palacios, N. A. G., Merritt, E. G., & Rimm-Kaufman, S. (2016). 5 strategies for scaffolding math discourse with ELLs. *Teaching Children Mathematics, 23*(2), 100–108.

Barousa, M. (2017). *Which one doesn't belong?* Retrieved from http://wodb.ca

Boaler, J. (1997). *Experiencing school mathematics: Teaching styles, sex, and setting*. Buckingham, UK: Open University Press.

Boaler, J. (2012, July). Timed tests and the development of math anxiety. *Education Week*. Retrieved from www.edweek.org/ew/articles/2012/07/03/36boaler.h31.html

Boaler, J. (2015). *Mathematical mindsets: Unleashing students' potential through creative math, inspiring messages and innovative teaching*. San Francisco, CA: Jossey-Bass.

Boaler, J. (2017). *Brains grow and change*. Retrieved from www.youcubed.org/resources/many-ways-see-mathematics-video/

Boaler, J., & Staples, M. (2008). Creating mathematical futures through an equitable teaching approach: The case of Railside School. *Teachers College Record, 110*(3), 608–645.

Bransford, J. D., Brown, A., & Cocking, R. (1999). *How people learn: Mind, brain, experience, and school*. Washington, DC: National Research Council.

Braswell, J. S., Dion, G. S., Daane, M. C., & Jin, Y. (2005). *The nation's report card: Mathematics 2003* (NCES 2005–451). U.S. Department of Education, Institute of Education Sciences, National Center for Education Statistics. Washington, DC: Government Printing Office.

Bushart, B. (2017). *Numberless word problems*. Retrieved from https://bstockus.wordpress.com/numberless-word-problems/

Calmenson, S. (1991). *The principal's new clothes*. New York, NY: Scholastic.

Cavanaugh, R. A., Heward, W. L., & Donelson, F. (1996). Effects of response cards during lesson closure on the academic performance of secondary students in an earth science course. *Journal of Applied Behavior Analysis, 29*(3), 403–406.

Committee on Early Childhood Mathematics National Research Council. (2009). *Mathematics learning in early childhood: Paths toward excellence and equity*. Washington, DC: National Academies Press.

Constantino, P. M., & De Lorenzo, M. N. (2001). *Developing a professional teaching portfolio: A guide for success*. Boston, MA: Allyn & Bacon.

Cooperrider, D. L., & Whitney, D. (2005). Appreciative inquiry: A positive revolution in change. In P. Holman & T. Devane (Eds.), *The change handbook* (pp. 245–263). Oakland, CA: Berrett-Koehler.

Crayton, C. (2017). *Robert Q. Berry: Think of math as a social endeavor*. Retrieved from https://ced.ncsu.edu/news/2017/08/05/robert-q-berry-think-of-math-as-a-social-endeavor/

Danielson, C. (2016). *Which one doesn't belong?* Retrieved from http://wodb.ca

Danielson, L. M. (2008). Making reflective practice more concrete through reflective decision making. *The Educational Forum, 72*, 129–137.

Day, C. (1999). Researching teaching through reflective practice. In J. J. Loughran (Ed.), *Researching teaching: Methodologies and practices for understanding pedagogy*. London: Falmer.

Dewey, J. (1933). *How we think: A restatement of the relation of reflective thinking to the educative process.* New York, NY: D.C. Heath.

Dewey, J. (1944). *Democracy in education.* New York, NY: Free Press. (Original work published 1916)

Dolezal, S. E., Welsh, L. M., Pressley, M., & Vincent, M. M. (2003). How nine third-grade teachers motivate student academic engagement. *The Elementary School Journal, 103*(3), 239–267.

Dougherty, B. J., Karp, K., Caldwell, J., & Kobett, B. (2014). *Putting essential understanding of addition and subtraction into practice pre-K–2.* Reston, VA: NCTM.

Erickson, K., Drevets, W., & Schulkin, J. (2003). Glucocorticoid regulation of diverse cognitive functions in normal and pathological emotional states. *Neuroscience & Biobehavioral Reviews, 27*(3), 233–246.

Farah, M. J., Shera, D. M., Savage, J. H., Betancourt, L., Giannetta, J. M., Brodsky, N. L., Malmud, & Hurt, H. (2006). Childhood poverty: Specific associations with neurocognitive development. *Brain Research, 1110*(1), 166–174.

Fennell, F. (2006, December). Go ahead! Teach to the test! *NCTM News Bulletin.* Retrieved from www.nctm.org/News-and-Calendar/Messages-from-the-President/Archive/Skip-Fennell/Go-Ahead,-Teach-to-the-Test!/

Fennell, F., Kobett, B. M., & Wray, J. A. (2017). *The formative 5: Everyday assessment techniques for every math classroom.* Thousand Oaks, CA: Corwin.

Fletcher, G. (2017). *3-Acts lessons.* Retrieved from https://gfletchy.com/3-act-lessons/

Ganske, K. (2017). Lesson closure: An important piece of the student learning puzzle. *The Reading Teacher, 71*(1), 95–100.

Gelman, R., & Lucariello, J. (2002). Role of learning in cognitive development. In H. Pashler (Series Ed.) & C. R. Gallistel (Vol. Ed.), *Stevens' handbook of experimental psychology: Vol. 3. Learning, motivation, and emotion* (3rd ed., pp. 395–443). New York, NY: John Wiley.

Grootenboer, P. (2000). Appraisal for quality learning. *Waikato Journal of Education, 6*(1), 121–132.

Hammond, S. (1998). *The thin book of appreciative inquiry.* Plano, TX: Thin Book Publishing.

Harris, A. S., Bruster, B., Peterson, B., & Shutt, T. (2010). *Examining and facilitating reflection to improve professional practice.* Lanham, MD: Rowman & Littlefield.

Harvard Center for the Developing Child. (2007). *The impact of poverty on early development.* Retrieved from http://46y5eh11fhgw3ve3ytpwxt9r.wpengine.netdna-cdn.com/wp-content/uploads/2015/05/inbrief-adversity-1.pdf

Hattie, J. (2009). *Visible learning: A synthesis of over 800 meta-analyses relating to achievement.* New York, NY: Routledge.

Hattie, J., & Yates, G. C. (2013). *Visible learning and the science of how we learn.* New York, NY: Routledge.

Hattie, J., Fisher, D., Frey, N., Gojak, L. M., Moore, S. D., & Mellman, W. (2016). *Visible learning for mathematics, Grades K–12: What works best to optimize student learning.* Thousand Oaks, CA: Corwin.

Herbel-Eisenmann, B. (2010). Beyond tacit language choice to purposeful discourse practices. In L. Knott (Ed.), *The role of mathematics discourse in producing leaders of discourse* (pp. 451–485). Charlotte, NC: Information Age Publishing.

Herbel-Eisenmann, B., & Breyfogle, M. (2005). Questioning our patterns of questioning. *Mathematics Teaching in the Middle School, 10*(9), 484–489.

Hiebert, J. (1999). Relationships between research and the NCTM standards. *Journal for Research in Mathematics Education, 30*(1), 3–19.

Hiebert, J., & Morris, A. (2012). Teaching, rather than teachers, as a path toward improving classroom instruction. *Journal of Teacher Education, 63*(2), 92–102.

Hogan, M. P. (2008). The tale of two Noras: How a Yup'ik middle schooler was differently constructed as a math learner. *Diaspora, Indigenous, and Minority Education, 2*(2), 90–114.

Huinker, D., & Bill, V. (2017). *Taking action: Implementing effective mathematics teaching practices in K–Grade 5.* Reston, VA: NCTM.

Hull, T., Harbin Miles, R., & Balka, D. S. (2014). *Realizing rigor in the mathematics classroom.* Thousand Oaks, CA: Corwin.

Illustrative Mathematics. (2017). *Content standards*. Retrieved from www.illustrativemathematics.org/content-standards

Inside Mathematics. (2017). *Problem of the month*. Retrieved from www.insidemathematics.org/problems-of-the-month/download-problems-of-the-month

Institute of Educational Sciences (IES). (2009). *Assisting students struggling with mathematics: Response to intervention (RtI) for elementary and middle schools*. Retrieved from https://ies.ed.gov/ncee/wwc/PracticeGuide/2

Isaacs, A. C., & Carroll, W. M. (1999). Strategies for basic-facts instruction. *Teaching Children Mathematics*, 5(9), 508–515.

Jensen, L. (2001). Planning lessons. In M. Celce-Murcia (Ed.), *Teaching English as a second or foreign language* (pp. 403–408). Boston, MA: Heinle & Heinle.

Kaplinsky, R. (2017). *Lessons*. Retrieved from http://robertkaplinsky.com/lessons/

Kapur, M. (2010). Productive failure in mathematical problem solving. *Instructional Science*, 38(6), 523–550.

Karp, K. S., Bush, S. B., & Dougherty, B. J. (2014). 13 rules that expire. *Teaching Children Mathematics*, 21(1), 18–25.

Kazemi, E., & Hintz, A. (2014). *Intentional talk: How to structure and lead productive mathematical discussions*. Portland, ME: Stenhouse Publishers.

Lager, C. A. (2006). Types of mathematics-language reading interactions that unnecessarily hinder algebra learning and assessment. *Reading Psychology*, 27(2–3), 165–204.

Lappan, L., & Briars, D. (1995). How should mathematics be taught? In I. M. Carl (Ed.), *75 years of progress: Prospects for school mathematics* (pp. 131–156). Reston, VA: NCTM.

Larson, J. (2002). Packaging process: Consequences of commodified pedagogy on students' participation in literacy events. *Journal of Early Childhood Literacy*, 2(1), 65–95.

Leinwand, S. (2009). *Accessible mathematics: 10 instructional shifts that raise student achievement*. Portsmouth, NH: Heinemann.

Leinwand, S. (2014, July). *Math misconceptions*. Paper presented at the Summer Utah Academy, Salt Lake, UT.

Lucariello, J. (2012). *How my students think: Diagnosing student thinking*. Retrieved from www.apa.org/education/k12/student-thinking.aspx

Lupien, S. J., King, S., Meaney, M. J., & McEwen, B. S. (2001). Can poverty get under your skin? Basal cortisol levels and cognitive function in children from low and high socioeconomic status. *Development and Psychopathology*, 13(3), 653–676.

Markworth, K., McCool, J., & Kosiak, J. (2015). *Problem solving in all seasons*. Reston, VA: NCTM.

Math Forum. (2015). *Beginning to problem solve with "I notice, I wonder."* Retrieved from http://mathforum.org/pow/noticewonder/intro.pdf

Math Forum. (2017). *Primary problems of the week*. Retrieved from http://mathforum.org/library/problems/primary.html

Math Learning Center. (2017). *Free math apps*. Retrieved from www.mathlearningcenter.org/resources/apps

Math Pickle. (2017). *Puzzles, games and mini-competitions organized by grade*. Retrieved from http://mathpickle.com/organized-by-grade/

Middleton, J. A., & Jansen, A. (2011) *Motivation matters and interest counts: Fostering engagement in mathematics*. Reston, VA: NCTM.

Mohyuddin, R. G., & Khalil, U. (2016). Misconceptions of students in learning mathematics at primary level. *Bulletin of Education and Research*, 38(1), 133–162.

Morris, A., & Hiebert, J. (2017). Effects of teacher preparation courses: Do graduates use what they learned to plan mathematics lessons? *American Educational Research Journal*, 54(3), 524–567.

Moyer, P. S., Bolyard, J. J., & Spikell, M. A. (2002). What are virtual manipulatives? *Teaching Children Mathematics*, 8(6), 372–377.

Moyer-Packenham, P. S., & Milewicz, E. (2002). Learning to question: Categories of questioning used by preservice teachers during diagnostic mathematics interviews. *Journal of Mathematics Teacher Education*, 5(4), 293–315.

National Center for Children in Poverty. (2017). *Child poverty*. Retrieved from www.nccp.org/topics/childpoverty.html

National Council of Supervisors of Mathematics. (2009). Improving student achievement in mathematics by addressing the needs of English language learners. *NCSM Student Achievement Series*, 6, 1–4.

National Council of Teachers of English (NCTE). (2008). *English language learners: A policy research brief produced by the National Council of Teachers of English*. Retrieved from www.ncte.org/library/NCTEFiles/Resources/PolicyResearch/ELLResearchBrief.pdf

National Council of Teachers of Mathematics. (1991). *Professional standards for teaching mathematics*. Reston, VA: Author.

National Council of Teachers of Mathematics. (2000). *Professional standards for teaching mathematics*. Reston, VA: Author.

National Council of Teachers of Mathematics (NCTM). (2014a). *Access and equity in mathematics education*. Retrieved from www.nctm.org/uploadedFiles/Standards_and_Positions/Position_Statements/Access_and_Equity.pdf

National Council of Teachers of Mathematics (NCTM). (2014b). *Principles to actions: Ensuring mathematical success for all*. Reston, VA: Author.

National Council of Teachers of Mathematics (NCTM). (2017). *Taking action: Implementing effective teaching practices*. Reston, VA: Author.

National Governors Association Center for Best Practices & Council of Chief State School Officers. (2010). *Common core state standards for mathematics*. Washington, DC: National Governors Association Center for Best Practices & Council of Chief State School Officers. Retrieved from www.corestandards.org/Math/

National Institute of Child Health and Human Development Early Child Care Research Network. (2005). Duration and developmental timing of poverty and children's cognitive and social development from birth through third grade. *Child Development*, 4(76), 795–810.

National Library of Virtual Manipulatives. (2017). *All topics, Grades PreK–2*. Retrieved from http://nlvm.usu.edu/en/nav/grade_g_1.html

National Research Council. (2001). *Adding it up: Helping children learn mathematics* (J. Kilpatrick, J. Swafford, & B. Findell, Eds.). Washington, DC: National Academies Press.

NRICH. (2017). *Primary curriculum*. Retrieved from http://nrich.maths.org/12632

Open Middle. (2017). *Open middle: Challenging problems worth solving* [Kindergarten, Grade 1, Grade 2]. Retrieved from http://www.openmiddle.com

Panasuk, R., Stone, W., & Todd, J. (2002). Lesson planning strategy for effective mathematics teaching. *Education*, 122(4), 808–829.

Parrish, S. (2011). Number talks build numerical reasoning. *Teaching Children Mathematics*, 18(3), 198–206.

Piaget, J. (1964). Part I: Cognitive development in children: Piaget development and learning. *Journal of Research in Science Teaching*, 2(3), 176–186.

Piaget, J., & Inhelder, B. (1969). *The psychology of the child*. New York, NY: Basic Books.

Pollock, J. E. (2007). *Improving student learning one teacher at a time*. Alexandria, VA: Association for Supervision and Curriculum Development.

Powell, A. B. (2004). The diversity backlash and the mathematical agency of students of color. In M. J. Høines & A. B. Fuglestad (Eds.), *Proceedings of the twenty-eighth conference of the International Group for the Psychology of Mathematics Education* (Vol. 1, pp. 37–54). Bergen, Norway: International Group for the Psychology of Mathematics Education.

Protheroe, N. (2007). What does good math instruction look like? *Principal*, 87(1), 51–54.

Raposo, J., & Stone, J. (1972). *One of these things is not like the other* [Song lyrics]. Retrieved from www.metrolyrics.com/one-of-these-things-is-not-like-the-others-lyrics-sesame-street.html

Rasmussen, C., Yackel, E., & King, K. (2003). Social and sociomathematical norms in the mathematics classroom. In R. Charles (Ed.), *Teaching mathematics through problem solving: It's about learning mathematics* (pp. 143–154). Reston, VA: National Council of Teachers of Mathematics.

Ray-Reik, M. (2013). *Powerful problem solving: Activities for sense making with the mathematical practices*. Portsmouth, NH: Heinemann.

Reimer, K., & Moyer, P. S. (2005). Third-graders learn about fractions using virtual manipulatives: A classroom study. *The Journal of Computers in Mathematics and Science Teaching, 24*(1), 5–10.

Resnick, L. B. (1982). Syntax and semantics in learning to subtract. In T. Carpenter, J. Moser, & T. A. Romberg (Eds.), *Addition and subtraction: A cognitive perspective* (pp. 136–156). Hillsdale, NJ: Lawrence Erlbaum.

Resnick, L. B. (1983). A developmental theory of number understanding. In H. P. Ginsburg (Ed.), *The development of mathematical thinking* (pp. 109–151). New York, NY: Academic Press.

Resnick, L. B., & Omanson, S. F. (1987). Learning to understand arithmetic. In R. Glaser (Ed.), *Advances in instructional psychology* (Vol. 3, pp. 41–95). Hillsdale, NJ: Lawrence Erlbaum.

Ritchhart, R., Church, M., & Morrison, K. (2011). *Making thinking visible: How to promote engagement, understanding, and independence for all learners.* New York, NY: John Wiley.

Rodgers, C. (2002). Defining reflection: Another look at John Dewey and reflective thinking. *Teachers College Record, 104*(4), 842–866.

Rohrer, D. (2012). Interleaving helps students distinguish among similar concepts. *Educational Psychology Review, 24,* 355–367.

Schmidt, W. H., Wang, H. C., & McKnight, C. (2005). Curriculum coherence: An examination of US mathematics and science content standards from an international perspective. *Journal of Curriculum Studies, 37*(5), 525–559.

Schön, D. A. (1983). *The reflective practitioner: How professionals think in action.* New York, NY: Basic Books.

Schrock, C., Norris, K., Pugalee, D., Seitz, R., & Hollingshead, F. (2013). *NCSM great tasks for mathematics, K–5.* Denver, CO: National Council of Supervisors of Mathematics.

Sealander, K. A., Johnson, G. R., Lockwood, A. B., & Medina, C. M. (2012). Concrete-semiconcrete-abstract (CSA) instruction: A decision rule for improving instructional efficacy. *Assessment for Effective Intervention, 30,* 53–65.

Smith, M. S., & Stein, M. K. (2011). *Five practices for orchestrating productive mathematics discussions.* Reston, VA: National Council of Teachers of Mathematics.

Smyth, J. (1992). Teachers' work and the politics of reflection. *American Educational Research Journal, 29*(2), 267–300.

Sousa, D. (2014). *How the brain learns mathematics.* Thousand Oaks, CA: Corwin.

Steen, K., Brooks, D., & Lyon, T. (2006). The impact of virtual manipulatives on first grade geometry instruction and learning. *Journal of Computers in Mathematics and Science Teaching, 25*(4), 373–391.

Stein, M. K., Engle, R. A., Smith, M. S., & Hughes, E. K. (2008). Orchestrating productive mathematical discussions: Five practices for helping teachers move beyond show and tell. *Mathematical Thinking and Learning, 10*(4), 313–340.

Stein, M. K., & Smith, M. S. (1998). Mathematical tasks as a framework for reflection: From research to practice. *Mathematics Teaching in the Middle School, 3*(4), 268–275.

Trocki, A., Taylor, C., Starling, T., Sztajn, P., & Heck, D. (2015). Launching a discourse-rich mathematics lesson. *Teaching Children Mathematics, 21*(5), 276–281.

Troiano, J. (2001). *Spookley the square pumpkin.* Wilton, CT: Holiday Hill Enterprises, LLC.

Tschannen-Moran, B., & Tschannen-Moran, M. (2010). *Evocative coaching: Transforming schools one conversation at a time.* Hoboken, NJ: John Wiley.

Van de Walle, J., Karp, K., & Bay-Williams, J. (2016). *Elementary and middle school mathematics: Teaching developmentally.* New York, NY: Pearson.

Vogler, K. E. (2008, Summer). Asking good questions. *Educational Leadership, 65* (9). Retrieved from www.ascd.org/publications/educational-leadership/summer08/vol65/num09/Asking-Good- Questions.aspx

Vygotsky, L. S. (1964). Thought and language. *Annals of Dyslexia, 14*(1), 97–98.

Vygotsky, L. S. (1978). *Mind in society: The development of higher mental processes* (M. Cole, V. John-Steiner, S. Scribner, & E. Souberman, Eds. & Trans.). Cambridge, MA: Harvard University Press.

Waddell, L. R. (2010). How do we learn? African American elementary students learning reform mathematics in urban classrooms. *Journal of Urban Mathematics Education, 3*(2), 116–154.

Wagganer, E. L. (2015). Creating math talk communities. *Teaching Children Mathematics*, 22(4), 248–254.

Walsh, J. A., & Sattes, B. D. (2005). *Quality questioning: Research-based practice to engage every learner.* Thousand Oaks, CA: Corwin.

Walshaw, M., & Anthony, G. (2008). The role of pedagogy in classroom discourse: A review of recent research into mathematics. *Review of Educational Research*, 78, 516–551.

Wenmoth, D. (2014). *Ten trends 2014: Agency* [Video file]. Retrieved from https://vimeo.com/85218303

Wiliam, D. (2011). *Embedded formative assessment.* Bloomington, IN: Solution Tree Press.

Wiliam, D., & Thompson, M. (2008). Integrating assessment with instruction: What will it take to make it work? In C. A. Dwyer (Ed.), *The future of assessment: Shaping teaching and learning* (pp. 53–82). Mahwah, NJ: Lawrence Erlbaum.

Wood, T., Williams, G., & McNeal, B. (2006). Children's mathematical thinking in different classroom cultures. *Journal for Research in Mathematics Education*, 37, 222–255.

Yackcl, E., & Cobb, P. (1996). Sociomathematical norms, argumentation, and autonomy in mathematics. *Journal for Research in Mathematics Education*, 27, 458–477.

Young, C. B., Wu, S. S., & Menon, V. (2012). The neurodevelopmental basis of math anxiety. *Psychological Science*, 23(5), 492–501.

Index

About the Authors

Ruth Harbin Miles coaches rural, suburban, and inner-city school mathematics teachers. Her professional experience includes coordinating the K–12 Mathematics Teaching and Learning Program for the Olathe, Kansas, public schools for more than 25 years, teaching mathematics methods courses at Virginia's Mary Baldwin University, and serving on the Board of Directors for the National Council of Supervisors of Mathematics, The National Council of Teachers of Mathematics, and the Kansas Association of Teachers of Mathematics. Ruth is a coauthor of 37 books, including 11 Corwin publications. As an International Fellow with the Charles A. Dana Center, Ruth works with classroom teachers in Department of Defense Schools, helping them implement College and Career Ready Standards. Developing teachers' content knowledge and strategies for engaging students to achieve high standards in mathematics is Ruth's specialty.

Beth McCord Kobett, EdD, is an associate professor in the School of Education at Stevenson University, where she works with preservice teachers and leads professional learning efforts in mathematics education both regionally and nationally. She is also the lead consultant for the Elementary Mathematics and Specialist and Teacher Leadership Project. She is a former classroom teacher, elementary mathematics specialist, adjunct professor, and university supervisor. She is the current president of the Association of Maryland Mathematics Teacher Educators (AMMTE) and former chair of the Professional Development Services Committee of the National Council of Teachers of Mathematics (NCTM). Dr. Kobett is a recipient of the Mathematics Educator of the Year Award from the Maryland Council of Teachers of Mathematics (MCTM). She has also received Stevenson University's Excellence in Teaching Award as both an adjunct and full-time member of the Stevenson faculty.

Lois A. Williams, EdD, has worked in mathematics education (K–Algebra I) teaching, supervising, coaching, and doing international consulting for more than 35 years. She is a retired mathematics specialist for the Virginia Department of Education. Currently, Lois is an adjunct professor at Mary Baldwin University and The College of William and Mary. She is an International Fellow with the Charles A. Dana Center helping teachers in Department of Defense Schools implement College and Career Ready Standards. She is a recipient of a Fulbright Teacher Exchange and honored as a Virginia Middle School Mathematics Teacher of the Year.

ALL students should have the opportunity to be successful in math!

Trusted experts in math education offer clear and practical guidance to help students move from surface to deep mathematical understanding, from procedural to conceptual learning, and from rote memorization to true comprehension. Through books, videos, consulting, and online tools, we offer a truly blended learning experience that helps you demystify math for students.

Get the series!
Also available for Grades K–2, and Grades 6–8 coming in 2019.

Your blueprint to planning K–2 math lessons for maximum impact and understanding

Beth McCord Kobett, Ruth Harbin Miles, and Lois A. Williams

Grades K–2

The what, when, and how of teaching practices that evidence shows work best for student learning in mathematics

John Hattie, Douglas Fisher, Nancy Frey, Linda M. Gojak, Sara Delano Moore, and William Mellman

Grades K–12

Everything you need to promote mathematical thinking and learning

Page Keeley and Cheryl Rose Tobey

Grades K–12

Move the needle on math instruction with these 5 assessment techniques

Francis (Skip) Fennell, Beth McCord Kobett, and Jonathan A. Wray

Grades K–8

eCourse and PD Resource Center now available!

Corwin educator discount
★★★
20% OFF EVERY DAY!
★★★

Supporting Teachers, Empowering Learners

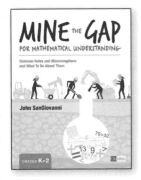 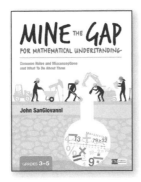 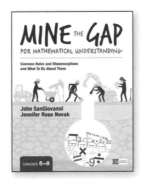

See what's going on in your students' minds, plus get access to hundreds of rich tasks to use in instruction or assessment

John SanGiovanni and Jennifer Rose Novak

Your whole-school solution to mathematics standards

When it comes to math, standards-aligned is achievement-aligned...

Linda M. Gojak and Ruth Harbin Miles
Grades K–2

Linda M. Gojak and Ruth Harbin Miles
Grades 3–5

Ruth Harbin Miles and Lois A. Williams
Grades 6–8

Frederick L. Dillon, W. Gary Martin, Basil M. Conway IV, and Marilyn E. Strutchens
High School

New series for states with state-specific mathematics standards

Grades K–2, Grades 3–5, Grades 6–8, High School

N185H0

CORWIN
A SAGE Publishing

CORWIN
A SAGE Publishing Company

Helping educators make the greatest impact

CORWIN HAS ONE MISSION: to enhance education through intentional professional learning.

We build long-term relationships with our authors, educators, clients, and associations who partner with us to develop and continuously improve the best evidence-based practices that establish and support lifelong learning.

NATIONAL COUNCIL OF
TEACHERS OF MATHEMATICS

The National Council of Teachers of Mathematics supports and advocates for the highest-quality mathematics teaching and learning for each and every student.